"This may just be the finest treatment of biblical-theological perspectives on the nature, significance, and purpose of suffering that I have ever read. The exegetical roots of Talbot's work run deep, his theological reflections are profound, his grasp of wide-ranging secondary literature is extraordinary, and his pastoral passion is transparent. We pray that this book will challenge, comfort, and inspire many whose experiences have landed them in the swamp of confusion and despair, and that it will be a helpful resource for those whom God calls to walk—or swim—with those in this state."

Daniel I. Block, Gunther H. Knoedler Professor Emeritus of Old Testament, Wheaton College; author, *The Triumph of Grace* and *For the Glory of God*

"Suffering is the greatest mystery of life, and God's people have struggled with it since the days of Job. There is much about it that we shall never be able to understand, but Christians can know that whatever happens to us, we are children of God, and he will not allow us to fall away from his loving care. That is where we must begin, and the Scriptures offer us a rich resource for establishing our faith on a firm foundation. Mark Talbot takes us where we need to be."

Gerald Bray, Research Professor of Divinity, History, and Doctrine, Beeson Divinity School; author, *God Is Love* and *God Has Spoken*

"Mark Talbot operates like a calm, rational medic checking his patients. His careful, clear accounts of the Bible's teaching of suffering, his case that human suffering arises from the race's fallenness—its rebellion—looks forward to the redemption and consummation that await those who repent and put their faith in Christ. Mark shows himself sensitive to the Bible's details, its modes and idioms, and to how we humans bear our suffering, cataloging the perplexity, frustration, and futility of human life, the litany of human sin and woe, that comes from our sin. The book forms an armory for the Christian and for his family and friends, outfitting us to endure our suffering through childbearing and motherhood, through the duty and drudgery of daily work, through lives cut short and old age, and through wealth and its loss. The careful reader will want more and more of Mark's unique books."

Paul Helm, former Professor of the History and Philosophy of Religion, King's College London

T0335157

"None of us make it through this life without seeking to make sense of its inherent suffering. To help us in this pursuit, Mark Talbot takes us to the central story that helps us make sense of the suffering in our individual stories, the story of creation impacted by the curse because of sin. With insight and analysis of the original goal, original order, and original goodness of creation, he helps us to see not only how the impact of the curse has disrupted that order and goodness, but also what God is doing through Christ to redeem, restore, and bring us into the life of goodness and glory he intends to share with us forever."

Nancy Guthrie, author, *Even Better than Eden*

"Mark Talbot joins together what can be easy to separate when thinking about suffering: consistently insightful investigation of the Bible (especially Genesis 1–3), clear-headed reflection on the human condition, and a deep tenderness toward actual sufferers. The way in which he folds together the stories we tell about our own lives with Scripture's story was especially gratifying to read. Mark also manages to write about difficult subjects without ever being difficult to understand—he carries the reader along beautifully. I learned a lot from this book, and I recommend it highly."

Eric Ortlund, Lecturer in Old Testament and Biblical Hebrew, Oak Hill College; author, *Suffering Wisely and Well*

"We need to avoid two mistakes: seeing our lives as pointless or thinking we'll win an Oscar for best director. Wheelchair-bound Mark Talbot shows with soaring spirit that we have important roles as supporting actors in a majestic drama of creation, rebellion, suffering, and redemption plotted out by God."

Marvin Olasky, Senior Fellow, Discovery Institute; author, *The Tragedy of American Compassion* and *Lament for a Father*

"With this volume, Mark Talbot continues what looks set to be a tour de force on Christianity and the suffering Christian. In his first book, he pressed the existential power and importance of individual narratives of pain and anguish. Here he steps back and sets those stories within the larger framework of the great narrative of God's dealings with his people. If it is true that every story of human suffering has its unique pain for those involved, Talbot demonstrates with characteristic conviction and authority that all redemption from suffering must be understood in terms of the unique revelation of God in Christ."

Carl Trueman, Professor of Biblical and Religious Studies, Grove City College

"This second volume in Mark Talbot's tetralogy on suffering is a masterful handling of the vexing and deeply personal problem of suffering in the life of the Christian. Talbot the philosopher shows his skill as a biblical theologian by situating suffering within the grand sweep of the Bible's fourfold storyline: creation, fall, redemption, and consummation. Both elegant and wise, as well as judicious and kind, this is biblical and theological reflection at its very best—the kind of thoughtful, mature analysis that feeds the people of God. There are treasures to be found on every page—and, as a bonus, in many of the endnotes! Christian, here you have a sure and steady guide. Take and read—and learn from someone who has thought more deeply and scripturally about suffering than anyone I know. Highly recommended!"

Todd Wilson, President, Center for Pastor Theologians; author, *Real Christian*; coauthor, *The Pastor Theologian*

"One of the greatest difficulties about enduring a time of suffering or sorrow is that it so often seems purposeless. It hurts so much and appears to accomplish so little. The path to peace is to set our suffering in the context of a wider story that God is telling in and through us—a story that Mark Talbot describes so well in the pages of this precious book."

Tim Challies, author, *Seasons of Sorrow*

Books in the Suffering in the Christian Life series:

Give Me Understanding That I May Live: Situating Our Suffering within God's Redemptive Plan (2022)

When the Stars Disappear: Help and Hope from Stories of Suffering in Scripture (2020)

GIVE ME UNDERSTANDING THAT I MAY LIVE

*Situating Our
Suffering within God's
Redemptive Plan*

Suffering and the Christian Life
VOLUME 2

Mark Talbot

WHEATON, ILLINOIS

Give Me Understanding That I May Live: Situating Our Suffering within God's Redemptive Plan

Copyright © 2022 by Mark Talbot

Published by Crossway
   1300 Crescent Street
   Wheaton, Illinois 60187

Cover design: Jordan Singer

Cover image: Bridgeman Images

First printing 2022

Printed in the United States of America

Trade paperback ISBN: 978-1-4335-6746-9
ePub ISBN: 978-1-4335-6749-0
PDF ISBN: 978-1-4335-6747-6
Mobipocket ISBN: 978-1-4335-6748-3

Library of Congress Cataloging-in-Publication Data

Names: Talbot, Mark R., author.
Title: Give me understanding that I may live : situating our suffering within God's redemptive plan / Mark Talbot.
Description: Wheaton, Illinois : Crossway, 2022. | Series: Suffering and the Christian life ; volume 2 | Includes bibliographical references and index.
Identifiers: LCCN 2021055039 (print) | LCCN 2021055040 (ebook) | ISBN 9781433567469 (trade paperback) | ISBN 9781433567476 (pdf) | ISBN 9781433567483 (mobipocket) | ISBN 9781433567490 (epub)
Subjects: LCSH: Suffering in the Bible. | Suffering—Religious aspects—Christianity. | Bible—Theology.
Classification: LCC BS680.S854 T348 2022 (print) | LCC BS680.S854 (ebook) DDC 231/.8—dc23/eng/20220120
LC record available at https://lccn.loc.gov/2021055039
LC ebook record available at https://lccn.loc.gov/2021055040

Crossway is a publishing ministry of Good News Publishers.

VP		31	30	29	28	27	26	25	24	23	22
15	14	13	12	11	10	9	8	7	6	5	4	3	2	1

For Cindy

The abyss and the light of the world,
Time's need and the craving for eternity,
Vision, event, and poetry:
Was and is dialogue with you.[a]

a. Martin Buber's dedication to his wife of his book *Zwiesprache* in 1932.

CONTENTS

PROLOGUE

Picking Up the Thread

Therefore, since we have been justified by faith,
we have peace with God through our Lord Jesus Christ.
Through him we have also obtained access by
faith into this grace in which we stand,
and we rejoice in hope of the glory of God.
Not only that, but we rejoice in our sufferings,
knowing that suffering produces endurance,
and endurance produces character,
and character produces hope,
and hope does not put us to shame,
because God's love has been poured into our hearts
through the Holy Spirit who has been given to us.

Romans 5:1–5

A central claim of *When the Stars Disappear: Help and Hope from Stories of Suffering in Scripture*, the first volume in this series, is that we understand our lives as stories. Stories help us orient ourselves in life by placing us somewhere on a trajectory that has a beginning, middle, and end. Moreover, we need two different kinds of stories to give our lives their full meaning: a particular (or personal) story and a general one. The particular story is about what our individual lives mean. Each of us needs to be able to tell a story that orients us to the particular people, places, and things around us, describing where we have come from, where we are, and where we think we can go so that we can project ourselves into hopeful futures where we can get what we want and need. The general story answers questions about what human life as such means. For instance, are we just chance products of blind, meaningless cosmic forces, or have we been created by God to fulfill some specific purpose? Is human life about nothing but making money and pursuing our own personal happiness, or is it about believing and obeying God and caring for others? Metaphorically, these two kinds of stories set the stars that must guide us in place, enabling us to navigate life's otherwise uncharted seas. These "stars" are the deep and firm convictions we rely on to tell us who we are and what sort of world we live in. They include convictions about who our parents are, what we take to be deeply meaningful, what we take to be worth doing, whether there is a God, and whether Jesus Christ is God's Son who redeems us from our slavery to sin.[a]

Suffering tends to challenge our stories, prompting us to question whether the stories we accept are true. Even a mild headache can make me doubt a small part of my personal story—the part that assumes that in a few hours I will be relatively pain-free. Profound suffering may threaten to blot out completely the light of the stars that are guiding us by making us doubt the general story we have accepted about what human life means.

When the Stars Disappear examined the personal stories of Naomi, Job, Jeremiah, and some of the psalmists in order to help those of us who are suffering not lose hope that God is with us and working in and through our suffering for our good. *Give Me Understanding That I May Live: Situating Our Suffering within God's Redemptive Plan* steps back to look at the general Christian story that explains why there is any suffering, why there is so much of it, and what will finally, gloriously, be true

---

a. For more on the need for such metaphorical stars, see Mark Talbot, *When the Stars Disappear: Help and Hope from Stories of Suffering in Scripture* (Wheaton, IL: Crossway, 2020), 20–23.

for those who confess with their mouths that Jesus is Lord and believe in their hearts that God raised him from the dead (see Rom. 10:9).

When suffering overwhelms us, it is hard to focus on anything else. Yet often our focus needs to shift. As we saw in *When the Stars Disappear*, when God finally spoke to Job, he did not commiserate with him. He didn't answer Job's questions or address his complaints. Instead, he shifted Job's focus to the world's creation, accusing Job of obscuring his plans "by words without knowledge" (Job 38:2). He then battered Job with questions, exposing Job's ignorance and impotence while celebrating his own knowledge, power, and dominion over all things, including his dominion over wicked human beings and the world's most terrifying creatures.[b]

By shifting Job's focus, God enabled Job to gain some perspective on his suffering. What had seemed to Job in his suffering to be life's full story was not in fact the full story. Job came to see that the full story involved much more than his suffering. This led him to confess that he had spoken of things that were, in fact, too wonderful for him to understand (see Job 40:1–5; 42:1–6).

This volume tells the full Christian story, "the true story of the whole world."[1] That story has four parts: creation, rebellion, redemption, and consummation. Scripture considers each part, and our coming to understand the main features of each is crucial if we are to live the lives for which God has made us and to which he calls us.

Just as our high schooler in *When the Stars Disappear* made sense of her life by embracing a storyline that aimed at her becoming a primary-care physician,[c] so all of us make sense of our lives by the stories we tell. And none of us cook up these stories by ourselves. We learn to tell stories by others telling us stories that help us make sense of our lives.[2]

Even very young children understand that their personal stories are anchored in the past. They ask questions like, "Who made me?" "Who was your daddy, Grandma?" and "What did you do when you

---

b. See Talbot, *When the Stars Disappear*, 75–76.
c. See Talbot, *When the Stars Disappear*, 65, 91–92, 96–97.

were a little girl, Mommy?" The answers they are given set some of the metaphorical stars that guide them in place. It is the same for us all. In particular, having an answer to the question, "How have human beings come to be?" is essential to answering other questions like, "Why are we here?" and "What does life mean?"

Whether we believe that God has created us to fulfill a specific role in creation or that we have evolved entirely by chance should make all the difference in how we think about ourselves now. A little girl's "Who made me?" expanded to "How have we"—meaning all of us—"come to be?" is one of life's most crucial questions. Moreover, knowing whether our ancestors made good or bad choices and whether their lives went well or poorly can be crucial for understanding ourselves. Learning that my grandfather was an alcoholic who left my grandmother very early in my father's life tells me something important about my father's history that inevitably has shaped his relationship with me.

In Scripture, God answers life's most fundamental questions, helping us get our stories straight. As Luther recognized, the opening chapters of Genesis are "certainly the foundation of the whole of Scripture," providing a true account of our beginnings.[3] He found nothing more fascinating than the Bible's first book. Of course, "curiosity about our beginnings," as Henri Blocher notes, "continues to haunt the human race."[4] It accounts for the current flood of books about human beginnings, especially from those who deny divine creation.[5]

The question, "How have we come to be?" is answered by the story of creation in Genesis 1–2. The question, "Did our first parents make good or bad choices?" is answered in Genesis 3 where we are told that they chose to rebel against God's command not to eat from the tree of the knowledge of good and evil. The consequences of that most disastrous of all choices started to become clear immediately. They became horrifyingly apparent in Genesis 4.

Even Christians may find themselves doubting God's goodness or power when they become aware of some kinds or degrees of suffering. They can find themselves asking, How is suffering like this possible if there is a perfectly good, all-powerful God? Wouldn't such a God prevent such suffering?[d] Those doubts require us to consider the first two parts of the Christian story. We have to understand creation and rebellion in order to understand that while nothing that happens falls out of God's hands, he is at the same time not to be blamed for the world's suffering, either for its first appearance or for its persistence.

My first chapter considers *creation*, emphasizing the world's perfection as God created it. Chapter 2 considers *rebellion*, telling how suffering entered the world. Chapter 3 explains what suffering is and how it affects us. And then chapter 4 begins considering *redemption* and *consummation*, the story's third and fourth parts. Our redemption and creation's ultimately complete restoration at the consummation of all things are the great gifts that suffering should lead us to seek. The epilogue returns to stressing how crucial it is for us to keep in mind all four parts of "the true story of the whole world"—and especially its first and final parts. If in your reading of my first two chapters you find yourself wondering why I am not immediately engaging the topic of suffering, reading the epilogue may help you see that we need to be concerned about much more than our suffering if we are to live the lives to which God is calling us.

Sometimes when we are perplexed about what should be our next step in life, we seek wisdom. In Scripture, the basic meaning of *chokhmah*, the Hebrew word for *wisdom*, is "skill"—as Allen Ross puts it, its various grammatical forms "can be applied to commonplace things in life that require skill,[e] or to the religious life that may also be described as living life skillfully."[6] Two Hebrew words for *understanding* are often paired with its word for *wisdom* (see, e.g., Prov. 3:13–15, 18). *Bin* involves gaining the *insight* necessary to live wisely or skillfully, and *tebunah* the *know-how* necessary actually to live such a life.[7] In the final analysis, we will have lived our lives wisely and skillfully to the degree that we have gained the insight and know-how to align the trajectories

---

d. See, for instance, the series of insistent, unanswered questions that Graham's parents kept asking after he committed suicide in Talbot, *When the Stars Disappear*, 15. An adequate answer to their questions can only come at the end of surveying the full Christian story. I attempt to give part of that answer in this volume's fourth chapter.

e. Such as having the skill to discern what would be a good career for me, given my interests and talents.

of our individual life stories with the trajectory of the world's true general story, which has been revealed to us by God, who alone is truly wise (see Rom. 16:25–27).

If the price to be paid for our coming to understand the need for that alignment is that we must suffer, then ultimately we may see such suffering to be, as the apostle Paul claimed, a very small price to pay (see 2 Cor. 4:16–18). That was also the testimony of the psalmist who prayed, "Give me understanding that I may live" (Ps. 119:144), when he wrote:

> You have dealt well with your servant,
>> O Lord, according to your word. . . .
> Before I was afflicted I went astray,
>> but now I keep your word.
> You are good and do good. . . .
> It is good for me that I was afflicted,
>> that I might learn your statutes. . . .
> *I know, O Lord, that . . . in faithfulness you have afflicted me.* (Ps.
>> 119:65, 67–68, 71, 75)[f]

---

f. For advice on how to read my books, please see the appendix "More Advice for My Readers" in this volume as well as the appendix "A Reader's Guide" at the end of *When the Stars Disappear*.

CREATION

When Everything Was "Very Good"

In the beginning, God created the heavens and the earth.
The earth was without form and [empty],
and darkness was over the face of the deep.
And the Spirit of God was hovering over the face of the waters.
And God said, "Let there be light," and there was light.
And God saw that the light was good.
And God separated the light from the darkness.
God called the light Day, and the darkness he called Night.
And there was evening and there was morning, the first day.

Genesis 1:1–5

This is the account of the heavens and the
earth when they were created,
when the LORD God made the earth and the heavens. . . .
Then the LORD God formed a man from the dust of the ground
and breathed into his nostrils the breath of life,
and the man became a living [person].
Now the LORD God had planted a garden in the east, in Eden;
and there he put the man he had formed.
The LORD God made all kinds of trees grow out of the ground
—trees that were pleasing to the eye and good for food.

In the middle of the garden were the tree of life
and the tree of the knowledge of good and evil. . . .
The Lord God took the man and put him in the Garden of Eden
to work it and [keep] it.
And the Lord God commanded the man,
"You are free to eat from any tree in the garden;
but you must not eat from the tree of the
knowledge of good and evil,
for when you eat from it you will certainly die."

Genesis 2:4, 7–9, 15–17 NIV

What is mankind that you make so much of them,
that you give them so much attention,
that you examine them every morning
and test them every moment?

Job 7:17–18 NIV

In *When the Stars Disappear*, I tried to administer a kind of spiritual first aid to Christians who have felt ambushed by their suffering. That is why I recounted Naomi's, Job's, and Jeremiah's stories. They suffered terribly, yet God rescued them in the end. And no matter how hard it may be for us to believe when we are suffering, as long as we don't deny him our Lord will rescue us too.[a]

In fact, Paul declares that not even death can separate us from the love of the God we have come to know through Christ (see Rom. 8:38–39). Ultimately, God can and will redeem all of our suffering. He may not rescue us during our earthly lifetimes. Here we may fall by sickness or sword.[1] Yet someday, Scripture attests, whether in this life

---

a. See Mark Talbot, *When the Stars Disappear: Help and Hope from Stories of Suffering in Scripture* (Wheaton, IL: Crossway, 2020), 82–83.

or the next, the clouds will break, and we will realize that our suffering has been only a "light momentary affliction" that has prepared us for "an eternal weight of glory beyond all comparison" (2 Cor. 4:17). It will then be clear that our loving heavenly Father has been with us all along our way.

Of course, our suffering may not seem light and momentary. It may seem interminable and too heavy to bear. And even when it is bearable, we may wonder why life includes any suffering or why it includes so much. This book explains why we Christians suffer, showing how God works in and through our suffering for our good, and thus how our suffering is in fact an aspect of God's mercy.

FROM CREATION TO CONSUMMATION

Scripture's first two chapters recount the world's origin, and its last two chapters foretell this world's end. *Creation* and *consummation* are thus the Christian story's bookends. Consummation will involve God's *re*-creation of all things. The symmetries between Genesis's first two chapters and Revelation's last two chapters show God wrapping up "the true story of the whole world" in profoundly satisfying ways. Creation and consummation are the full Christian story's outermost coordinates. They are still points—fixed stars—that help to hold the rest of the story in place.

They tell us that once there was no human sin, suffering, or death, and that God's people will be delivered from sin, suffering, and death once again in the end. In between, from Genesis 3 through Revelation 20, we have the panorama of human rebellion and redemption. Human suffering began *after* our first parents ate the forbidden fruit. So the portion of the Christian story that focuses on creation doesn't directly address our suffering. Yet our suffering can't be understood without considering it. We need to know who God created us to be *before* there was any sin or suffering. And then we need to know how our first parents' rebellion altered everything because this will enable us to understand the part suffering plays in prompting us to embrace the redemption that God offers us in Christ.

In telling the story of creation in this chapter, I haven't attempted to show the relevance of that story to our suffering by making a comment to that end every few pages. The awe that we should feel in learning what God was doing in making our world should be allowed to stand independently of what comes later in the full Christian story. In fact, in the end our suffering is not going to be the focus of the full story. The apostle Paul, who the New Testament suggests suffered more than anyone other than our Lord (see 2 Cor., especially 11:21–29; 12:7–10), put it like this: "I consider that our present sufferings cannot even be compared to the coming glory that will be revealed to us" (Rom. 8:18 NET; cf. Ps. 30:5; 2 Cor. 1:3–11; 4:17; 1 Pet. 1:3–7). Our suffering is meant to prompt us, as we have already seen that it prompted the psalmist, to turn to God's word for understanding—and for understanding a great deal more than simply why we are suffering (see Ps. 119:65–75).

So human suffering plays no part in the first part of the full Christian story. In the second part—rebellion—we learn about the choice that our first parents made that brought human suffering into the world, but even then, in my second chapter, suffering isn't the primary topic. Suffering arose as a consequence of our first parents' rebellion, so what it is and how it affects us get the third chapter. Then, finally, the role of suffering in our redemption and our anticipation of the world's consummation will occupy us in this volume's fourth chapter.

The story of creation helps us counter false assumptions about God, the world, and ourselves that we easily make. It helps us grasp what human life in God's world was to look like so that we, as God's redeemed people, can begin living closer to what God intends. It also helps us understand creation's proper patterns and rhythms—patterns and rhythms that, once we are aware of them and try to live by them, can alleviate some suffering.

At first glance, Genesis 1 and 2 appear to give two different creation accounts. But in fact they are one account, told from two perspectives.[2] Genesis 1:1–2:3 tells the story from God's cosmic perspective. It places our creation at the story's peak, as God's final creative act. Genesis 2:4–25 retells the story from our local perspective, where we are at the center of God's creative acts. Chapter 1:1–2:3 situates us in the rest of creation, and especially in relation to God as our Creator. It emphasizes our unique *role* in creation. Chapter 2:4–25 emphasizes the uniqueness of our *nature*.[3] Together these two perspectives enable us to understand who God has made us to be.

We can glean what we need from these two chapters by considering three topics: our creation, our composition, and our calling.

OUR CREATION

In Genesis 1:1–2:3 we were created after God created everything else and before he judged everything to be "very good" (Gen. 1:31). While Genesis 1:1 is properly interpreted as creation *ex nihilo*—in other words, as God's creation of everything from nothing, simply by speaking[4]—many of God's subsequent creative acts involved his *separating* and *differentiating between* various things. For instance, after he said, "Let there be light," he "separated the light from the darkness," calling the light Day and the darkness Night, and thus created the first day (1:3–5). On the second day, he separated the atmospheric waters from the surface waters—the clouds from the seas—and on the third day, he separated the land from the seas (see 1:6–9).

God began filling some of these separated spaces on the third day. He commanded the earth to produce all sorts of plants to cover the land, *differentiating* the various plants and trees he created from each other by means of their seeds (see 1:11–12). On the fourth day, he filled the heavenly expanse with lights "to give light upon the earth" and "to separate the day from the night." They were also to be "for signs and for seasons, and for days and years" (1:14–15), enabling Israel to know when to celebrate her appointed feasts (see, e.g., Lev. 23). On the fifth and sixth days God filled the waters, the skies, and the land with living creatures, each "according to their kinds" (vv. 21, 24–25).

In all of this God was preparing a place for us. He "formed [the earth] to be inhabited" (Isa. 45:18). From the earth's formlessness in 1:2, he was fashioning an ordered cosmos where we can understand, name, and classify things. As C. John Collins writes, Genesis 1:1–2:3 informs us that "the things [we] are familiar with work the way they do because God intended them to work that way: there are edible plants and domesticable animals—every farmer knows this, and Genesis explains why."[5]

"Let Us Make"

Into this ordered, inhabitable world God prepared to introduce human beings. All of the story's earlier elements point toward our creation, including its increasingly detailed focus on those elements that affect us most directly.[6] The progression from plants through the aquatic and winged creatures to the land animals involved creating a biological hierarchy to which we were now to be added as the highest living beings. As Paul Beauchamp observes, "The living creatures converge towards the man."[7] But our creation involved another difference. For the first time, God paused to announce what he was about to do, making an unexpected first-person-plural statement: "Let *us* make mankind in *our* image, in *our* likeness" (Gen. 1:26 NIV). As Gerhard von Rad has written, "Nothing [in this account] is here by chance; everything must be considered carefully, deliberately, and precisely. . . . What is said here is intended to hold true entirely and exactly as it stands."[8] *Us* and *our* are here for good reason.

They alert us that something momentous was about to happen, something of a different order than all that had happened before.[9] These pronouns are probably what Derek Kidner calls "the plural of fullness,"[10] which suggests "there is within the divine Being the distinction of personalities, a plurality within the deity."[11] They match the fact that the word for *God* in Genesis 1 is the plural noun *elōhîm*, which in Scripture unexpectedly takes singular verbs.[12] These pronouns may echo the possible distinction of personalities that Genesis 1:2 may have been hinting at with its observation that "the Spirit of God was hovering over the face of the waters." Verse 26 merely suggests such a distinction. It doesn't refer explicitly to the members of the Trinity, since the fact that God is three-in-one became clear only in later biblical writings. Yet "this fullness," Kidner writes, was indeed eventually "to be unfolded as tri-unity, in the further 'we' and 'our' of John 14:23 (with 14:17)."[13] So these pronouns represent "the first glimmerings of a Trinitarian revelation," which "illumine all the more brightly the announcement of the creation of mankind" as imaging God.[14] Our lives as human beings—as persons in relation—are patterned on the fact that the Christian Godhead involves persons in relation. And thus these pronouns illumine why God declared, "It is not good that the man should be alone; I will make him a helper fit for him" (Gen. 2:18), as we shall see later in this chapter.

"Human Beings in Our Image, after Our Likeness"
The "Let us *make*" in God's announcement emphasizes that we are only creatures,[15] while the "in our *image*, after our *likeness*" stresses our difference from all other living beings. Because these are God's first words concerning human being,[b] we must understand ourselves primarily in their terms. As Blocher says, "An image *is only an image. It exists only by derivation. It is not the original, nor is it anything without the original. Mankind's being an image stresses the radical nature of his dependence.*"[16] Ultimately, we must understand who we are in terms of the relationship that defines us.[17] We will never adequately understand ourselves if we think of ourselves merely as the most highly developed animal species or if we try to calculate our worth against the vastness of the stars. We must think of ourselves primarily as God's earthly images. This divine word is one of the most crucial of the metaphorical stars that Scripture puts in place.[18]

David understood this. In Psalm 8 he cast his eyes upward toward the starry heavens and felt "the staggering contrast between a human and the great bodies, processes, and powers in the world and the cosmos," which, "when noticed, [can bring] with it an overwhelming sense of insignificance and displacement."[19] This led him to ask, "What are mere mortals that you"—that is, God—"should think about them,

---

b. *Being* here is the present participle of the verb *to be*, thus emphasizing that we exist only as images, as Blocher states.

human beings that you should care for them?" (Ps. 8:4 NLT). But then with the ears of faith he heard God say that he has situated us just a little below himself and thus crowned us with glory and honor.[20] David cured the vertigo induced by looking up at the heavens by accepting a truth he could know only by faith (see Heb. 11:3). As one wise commentator has put it, Psalm 8's main point is that "we can say 'human being' only after we have learned to say 'God.' . . . Humankind recognizes itself fully only in the recognition of the Being from whom all reality arises."[21]

"And Let Them Have Dominion over All the Earth"

After declaring that he would make us in his image, God said: "Let them have dominion over the fish of the sea and over the birds of the heavens and over the livestock and over all the earth and over every creeping thing that creeps on the earth" (Gen. 1:26). As the sovereign Creator's images, we are creation's sovereigns, meant to reign benevolently over the rest of creation.

David reiterated this. For right after he declared that God made us only a little lower than himself, crowning us with glory and honor, he went on to say:

> You gave them charge of everything you made,
>   putting all things under their authority—
> the flocks and the herds
>   and all the wild animals,
> the birds in the sky, the fish in the sea,
>   and everything that swims the ocean currents. (Ps.
>   8:6–8 NLT)

David glanced downward after he glanced upward, surveying the rest of creation. Perhaps he had been wondering whether we are just another animal species (cf. Eccles. 3:18–21). Yet by hearing God's word he had steadied himself, coming to understand that our being made in God's image makes us unique. He then understood our situation for what it actually is: as God's images, we stand between him and the rest of the creation, where we are to fulfill the office of ruling all the rest of it wisely and well.

"So God Created Man in His Own Image"

Then God did what he had declared he was about to do:

> So God created human beings in his own image,
>   in the image of God he created them;
>   male and female he created them. (Gen. 1:27 NLT)

Here the singular pronouns referring to God imply that whatever sort of plurality of persons the *us* and *our* in the previous verse may suggest, it involves a "unanimity of intention and plan."[22]

In declaring in verse 26 what he was about to do regarding human beings, God used the word *make*—*'asah* in Hebrew. Here in verse 27 the Hebrew word for *created* is *bara'*, as it is in verses 1, 21, and 2:4. Collins says Genesis 1 and 2 uses *bara'* more narrowly than it uses *'asah*, using *bara'* when it "wants especially to stress that [what God is producing involves] some kind of fresh start."[23] At 1:1 and 2:4 God is creating the cosmos from nothing, bringing into being the visible creation. At 1:21 God creates animate life. Passages like Job 34:14–15 and Psalm 104:29 suggest that animate life did not just spring out of what existed before.[24] God imparts to all living creatures their life and breath. The appearance of something from nothing and of animate life are, then, fresh starts that reveal the world's dependence on God in a way that the separation of light from darkness and the gathering of the seas so that dry land may appear do not.

Since nothing in this account is accidental, the threefold repetition of *bara'* in our verse must be significant. Scripture's other threefold repetition occurs when the seraphim attending God on his throne call out to each other, "Holy, holy, holy is the LORD of hosts; the whole earth is full of his glory!" (Isa. 6:3). "Hebrew uses repetition," Alec Motyer writes, "to express superlatives or to indicate totality. . . . Holiness is supremely the truth about God," and being created in his image is supremely the truth about us.[25] The threefold repetition of *bara'* in verse 27 confirms how significant our creation in God's image is. We have been made in his image as the special objects of his love.

The alternation of the words *created* and *image* in verse 27's first two lines reiterates that we must understand who we are in terms of who God is. As Blocher said, who we are is radically dependent on who God is.[26] This is another orienting star that Scripture sets in place.

Everything about us images God. As Kidner says:

> The Bible makes man a unity: acting, thinking and feeling with his whole being. This living creature, then, and not some distillation from him, is an expression or transcription of the eternal, incorporeal creator in terms of temporal, bodily, creaturely existence— as one might attempt a transcription of, say, an epic into a sculpture, or a symphony into a sonnet.[27]

Understanding ourselves as God's image, Kidner goes on to say, "excludes the idea that our Maker is the 'wholly Other'" and "requires us to take all human beings infinitely seriously (cf. Gn. 9:6; Jas. 3:9). And our Lord implies, further, that God's stamp on us constitutes a declaration of ownership (Mt. 22:20, 21)."

What Does It Mean to Be Made in God's Image?

What does it mean to be made, as it is usually translated, *in God's image*? Ordinarily, we take being-made-in-the-image-of something to mean being made to copy its visible form. Yet Moses reminded the Israelites that when God made his covenant with them, they heard him speak but saw no form: "There was only a voice" (Deut. 4:12; see 4:9–20). So our being made in God's image is not primarily a matter of our possessing some visible form but, rather, of our imaging the sovereign Creator God in more profound ways.[28] God created us to *be* his image, caring for the creation as he himself would. He created us *as*—and not (as most translations have it) *in*—his earthly image, as his earthly representatives.[29]

In the ancient Near East around the time when Genesis was written, kings erected images of themselves throughout their realms to assert their sovereignty where they weren't physically present.[30] And thus the incorporeal Creator has made us as his corporeal images so that we may assert his sovereignty. We do so by acting as kings and queens reigning benevolently for him over the rest of the creation.[31]

Our role as God's images is a *structural* feature of our place and role in creation. It is thus something we cannot lose, although we can obscure, mar, tarnish, diminish, or abuse our place and our role by our disobedience. We were made to obey God, and we truly fulfill our calling only when we wholeheartedly obey the words of the God whose form we do not see. God's words are to resound through every aspect of our lives. They should shape all that we are and do.[32]

"Then God Blessed Them and Said, 'Be Fruitful and Multiply'"

> Then God blessed them and said, "Be fruitful and multiply. Fill the earth and govern it. Reign over the fish in the sea, the birds in the sky, and all the animals that scurry along the ground." (Gen. 1:28 NLT)

These words, along with God's declaration that he gave our first parents the seed-bearing plants and trees for food (see v. 29), heighten the contrast between the biblical story and other ancient Near Eastern creation accounts. Biblically, as David summarized it, God has made us just a little lower than himself, crowning us with glory and honor (see Ps. 8:5). He has made us rulers over the works of his hands, putting everything under our feet (see Ps. 8:6–8). But in the ancient Near Eastern creation myths, we were not the gods' focus, and when we were finally created as a kind of afterthought, we were "created to be [their] servant . . . and to relieve them of their toil."[33] For example, in the Babylonian Atrahasis Epic, we were created to relieve the lesser gods of the grunt work assigned to them by the greater gods. This task "took the form of digging the beds of the waterways, the corvée work later considered a menial occupation."[34] As A. R. Millard states, "The underlying idea of the Atrahasis Epic and the other Babylonian Creation stories . . . is that man was made to free the gods from the toil of ordering the earth to produce their food." In these myths, we labor so the gods can rest. But in Genesis, God works so he can bless us.

To bless, Kidner tells us, "is to bestow not only a gift but a function . . . and to do so with warm concern. *At its highest, it is God turning full-face to the recipient . . . in self-giving.*"[35] The greatest gift we can receive is unhindered and full fellowship with God himself. On the earthly level, God bestowed a twofold function on us: to have children and reign over the rest of creation. In Scripture, Gordon Wenham writes, God's blessing

> is always regarded as the result of a divine promise of blessing. *The word of blessing, [when] pronounced by God . . . , guarantees and effects the hoped-for success.* So . . . the words . . . "be fruitful and multiply" carry with them the divine promise that they can be carried out. Once uttered, the word carries its own life-giving power. . . . Genesis may be described as the story of the fulfillment of the divine promises of blessing.[36]

In blessing the water and air creatures in verse 22, God simply issued a command—"Be fruitful and multiply"—while in verse 28 it is added, "'and God said to them,' thus drawing attention to the personal relationship between God and man."[37] The fact the land creatures didn't receive their own blessing may mean they are blessed along with or through us. Blessings are to flow down to them from us.

"God Saw Everything That He Had Made, and Behold, It Was Very Good"

After making and blessing us, "God saw everything that he had made, and behold, it was very good" (1:31). Then we are told, "Thus the heavens and the earth were finished, and all the host of them" (2:1). The word the ESV translates as "host of them" can refer in Scripture to an army, the countless stars, or the myriads of angels as "models"—or patterns—"of perfect obedience and of regular motion."[38] "In all its usages," Blocher observes, "the word translated 'army' or 'host' designates a diverse totality that is properly arranged, organized and differentiated." He comments that it "is not for nothing that the throng of creatures is . . . called literally an *army"*—although this army "does not fight, it parades." "When they were created, earth's living creatures followed as perfect an order as the order of the heavens" and thus "the heavens and the earth and their inhabitants constitute a *cosmos*." Wenham adds, "The harmony and perfection of the completed heavens and earth express more adequately the character of their creator than any of the separate components can."[39] No wonder that on seeing it, God pronounced the finished creation "very good"![40]

OUR COMPOSITION

The creation account in Genesis 1 portrays us as living within a framework involving three kinds of relationships, each shaping and sustaining us in its own way. Our primary relationship is with God, then there is our relationship with other human beings, and finally there is our relationship with the rest of creation. Living within the space created by these three kinds of relationships constitutes our specifically human way of being.

Once we know our place in creation, it helps to know how our nature makes us capable of occupying it. Genesis 1:1–2:3 identifies our *position* relative to God and other creatures. Genesis 2:4–25 specifies our *composition*.

Here we have two crucial questions. First, what did the creation of the first human person entail both naturally and supernaturally? And, second, what are the implications of God's declaration, "It is not good for the man to be alone"?

The First Human Person

> *When* no bush of the field was yet in the land and no small plant of the field had yet sprung up . . . , *then* the LORD God formed the man of dust from the ground and breathed into his nostrils the breath of life, and the man became a living [person]. (Gen. 2:5, 7)[41]

This sentence signals Genesis 2:4–25's changed perspective in at least three ways. First, no local plant life appears until after the creation of the first man. He is the center around which all else clusters, including the planting of a garden (see vv. 8–9),[42] the appearance of the animals (see v. 19), and the making of the woman (see v. 22). Second, God is no longer just *elōhîm*, the world's creator and sustainer. He is also "the Lord"—that is, *Yahweh*, God's "real" or personal name[43]—who makes and keeps covenant with his people.[44] Third, Yahweh's personal—dare we say *hands-on?*—involvement with our first parents is shown by a shift in the kinds of verbs describing his creative activities. "The word of God (1:26ff.) is now augmented by the work of God (2:7)."[45] God no longer creates or makes just by speaking; he now *forms* (vv. 7, 19) and *breathes* (v. 7), *plants* and *places* (v. 8 NLT), *builds* a woman (see v. 22 ESV margin note[46]), and *brings* the animals and her to the man (vv. 19, 22).[47]

Formed from the Ground

> Then the Lord God formed the man of dust from the ground. (Gen. 2:7a)

Here God is portrayed as a potter "who forms [the] man from moistened dust."[48] The Hebrew has a definite article affixed to the word *adam*,[c] implying that this verse is focusing on the creation of the first human being as a real individual who is also a prototype for future human beings. The fact that he was formed from the ground means we are earthly beings, like the animals in verse 19. The fact that we share the sixth day with other creatures (see 1:24–31), are made of dust as they are (2:7, 19), feed as they feed (1:29, 30), and reproduce with a blessing similar to theirs (1:22, 28a) means that we, as Kidner writes, "can . . . be studied partly through the study of them; they are half [our] context."[49]

Breathed into Life

> . . . and breathed into his nostrils the breath of life, and the man became a living [person]. (Gen. 2:7b)

In spite of the fact that we can be studied partly through a study of the earth's other creatures, the stress throughout Genesis's first two chapters, Kidner emphasizes, "falls on [humanity's] distinctness." Here at Genesis

---

c. He isn't named *Adam* until v. 20, although sometimes I'll call him Adam now.

2:7 we are told that the Lord God breathed into the first human being's nostrils the breath—the Hebrew word is *neshamah*—of life, something he didn't do with any other creature.[50]

This made him an earthly *person*, with capacities that distinguished him from all of the earth's other living creatures. As Elihu declared in attempting to get Job to listen to him in spite of his youth,

> it is the spirit in man,
>> the breath [*neshamah*] of the Almighty, that makes him
>> understand.
> It is not the old who are wise,
>> nor the aged who understand what is right. (Job 32:8–9)

In other words, wisdom and understanding—traits we may attribute to persons but never in the same way to any other living being[d]—are not endowments that arise naturally in the ordinary course of biological development or that we inevitably acquire as we grow older. They are attributes that ultimately depend on supernaturally bestowed capacities from God.[51]

What capacities? Here the parallelism in Job 32:8 proves crucial: "It is the spirit [*ruach*] in man, the breath [*neshamah*] of the Almighty, that makes him understand." When Elihu applied Genesis 2:7 to himself a few verses later, he paired spirit and breath again: "The Spirit [*ruach*] of God has made me, and the breath [*neshamah*] of the Almighty gives me life" (Job 33:4).[52] Isaiah similarly declared that God,[e] the Lord (*Yahweh*), who created the heavens and the earth, "gives breath [*neshamah*] to the people on it and spirit [*ruach*] to those who walk in it" (Isa. 42:5). *Neshamah* and *ruach*, then, often (although not invariably) refer to the same, divinely conferred aspect of our being[53]—the aspect that makes us unique among the earth's creatures.[54] In other words, it was by the Lord God breathing this breath into Adam that he became God's earthly image.

When we read that the Lord's Spirit will rest on the future Messiah— "the Spirit [*ruach*] of wisdom and understanding, the Spirit of counsel

---

d. See, for instance, Ps. 32:8–9 (quoted in note f, below), and Ps. 49:20, which says, "People who have wealth *but lack understanding are like the beasts that perish*" (NIV). When the word *wise* is applied to animals at places like Prov. 30:24–28 and Matt. 10:16 it is being used analogically.

e. *El*, a short, singular, often poetic form of the plural *elōhim*.

and might, the Spirit of knowledge and the fear of the LORD" (Isa. 11:2)—we begin to see what the Lord God's breathing the breath of life into the first man implies. It means that God has endowed us with the created equivalents of those aspects of himself that enable us to be his earthly images. We alone, of all earthly creatures, possess understanding. God can then instruct, teach, and counsel us.[f] For instance, when the Lord filled Bezalel with his Spirit, "with wisdom, with understanding, with knowledge and with all kinds of skills," he and the others to whom God gave these skills knew "how to carry out all the work of constructing the sanctuary," enabling them to do it "just as the LORD [had] commanded" (Ex. 31:3 and 36:1 NIV).[55] God also inspired them to teach others (see Ex. 35:34).

To be made as God's image, to have him breathe into us the breath of life, means then that we possess the supernaturally bestowed gift of personhood that enables us to think, learn, speak, teach, and make free decisions.[56] We thereby become living, *spiritual* creatures, *in* the natural world yet not entirely *of* it. As biological *persons*, we are to live, so to speak, on the edge of the natural world where we are not to be dominated by entirely biological processes.[57]

Recognizing that God has endowed us with breath and spirit protects us against the pseudo-scientific claptrap of our day that seeks to subvert our sense of human uniqueness by submerging us entirely in the natural biological world. Human societies, Roger Scruton writes, are

> not just groups of cooperating primates: they are communities of persons, who live in mutual judgment, organizing their world in terms of moral concepts that arguably have no place in the thoughts of chimpanzees.[58]

We belong "to another order of explanation than that explored by biology." We are not just highly evolved animals. As living, *spiritual*

---

f. See Ps. 32:8–9 NIV: "I will instruct you and teach you in the way you should go; I will counsel you with my loving eye on you. Do not be like the horse or the mule, *which have no understanding* but must be controlled by bit and bridle or they will not come to you."

creatures we transcend the standard scientific taxonomy of living organisms with its differentiation between the kingdom of plants and the kingdom of animals. We belong to another kingdom, the kingdom of persons, which includes not only us but also the angels and God.[59] In that way we are, so to speak, "amphibians"[60]—complex creatures who were created by God to be a bridge between two worlds, the earthly and what the New Testament calls the heavenly (see, e.g., 1 Cor. 15:35–49; Heb. 3:1).

Recognizing our amphibian nature helps us to avoid succumbing to thoughts like those found in Ecclesiastes 3:19–21, where the Preacher seems to wonder whether we are, after all, just animals[g] and whether there could possibly be any explanation for our suffering.

Put in the Garden

> And the Lord God planted a garden in Eden, in the east, and there he put the man whom he had formed. And out of the ground the Lord God made to spring up every tree that is pleasant to the sight and good for food. . . . The Lord God took the man and put him in the garden of Eden to work it and keep it. (Gen. 2:8–9a, 15)

As we have noted, a crucial difference between the ancient Near Eastern creation myths and the Genesis account is that in those myths human beings are created to serve the gods, while God serves us. God's care for us becomes even clearer in these verses. The Hebrew word for *Eden* suggests "delight."[61] It was a place of luxurious abundance, a "tree park" with fruit trees where the man's food "was ever ready at hand."[62] Adam would experience pleasure in God's garden (see Ezek. 31:9) as long as he obeyed God's commands (cf. Ps. 16:11).

---

g. "Surely the fate of human beings is like that of the animals; the same fate awaits them both: As one dies, so dies the other. All have the same breath [*ruach*]; humans have no advantage over animals. . . . All go to the same place; all come from dust, and to dust all return. Who knows if the human spirit [*ruach*] rises upward and if the spirit [*ruach*] of the animal goes down into the earth?" (NIV). The Preacher decisively rejected this possibility in his final chapter: "Remember your Creator in the days of your youth, before the days of trouble come and the years approach when you will say, 'I find no pleasure in them'—before . . . the dust returns to the ground it came from, and the spirit [*ruach*] returns to God who gave it" (12:1–2, 7 NIV). Much more on Ecclesiastes's assessment of our lives "under the sun" in chap. 4, below.

This included the pleasure of work. Cultivating the garden was part of the blessing God bestowed on our first parents. It supplied the kind of work that is essential to a satisfying human life.[h]

Properly keeping the garden would have included repulsing any suggestion to disobey God's command not to eat from the forbidden tree.[63]

Commanded to Eat and Not Eat

In the middle of the garden were the tree of life and the tree of the knowledge of good and evil. . . . And the LORD God commanded the man, "You are free to eat from any tree in the garden; but you must not eat from the tree of the knowledge of good and evil, for when you eat from it you will certainly die." (Gen. 2:9b, 16–17 NIV)

God's command presupposes that to be made in his image normally includes the ability to hear and to speak. In saying to the man, "You are free to eat from any tree in the garden," the Lord was encouraging him to know the pleasure of eating from each. These words are in the imperative and thus were in fact part of God's command: God was *commanding* Adam to roam through the garden and experience the pleasure of tasting the fruit of each kind of tree.

But then God said, "You must not eat from the tree of the knowledge of good and evil." This was the crux of the Lord's first word to his newly created human being. In Hebrew, it is a very strong command with the same grammatical construction as the Ten Commandments' *You shall nots*.[64] The Lord's prohibition about eating from this tree was decisive, meaning, "You must *never* eat from it!" And then to this categorical you-must-never prohibition he appended a dire warning: "for when you eat from it you will certainly die."

From the time we first hear them as toddlers, we tend to resent life's prohibitions, taking them as rules that are intended to quench our fun. But in fact we need to hear strong *You shall nots* to counterbalance our inclinations and impulses. "Don't *ever* do that to your

---

h. See chap. 2, pp. 47–49.

baby brother again!" By having breathed into Adam the *neshamah* of life, God had given him the capacity to hear and obey. Now, by pronouncing this severely sanctioned *You shall not*, he was, so to speak, establishing something psychologically firm enough that Adam could "push off" it in order to keep himself from going astray.

By speaking this severe word that was to be obeyed no matter the cost, God was commanding Adam to rule over himself. In doing so, Adam would have begun living a truly human life. This command was calling Adam into full human personhood, opening the way for him to mature from merely possessing the capacity to obey God to actual life-sustaining obedience. By this severe word God was calling him into the glorious state of freely choosing to be his obedient child.

God's breathing into Adam the *neshamah* of life made him accountable. To be accountable means to be capable of giving an account of—in other words, of *answering for*—who we are and what we do. Proverbs 20:27 declares, "The human spirit [*neshamah*] is the lamp of the Lord that sheds light on one's inmost being" (NIV). By breathing into Adam the breath of life, God made him self-conscious and thus capable of knowing himself as "I."[65] Adam became capable of knowing at least some of his own motives. And so God could address him as a person answerable for them. He could consequently speak to our first parents person to person, commanding them to act in some ways:

> Be fruitful and multiply and fill the earth and subdue it, and have dominion over the fish of the sea and over the birds of the heavens and over every living thing that moves on the earth. (Gen. 1:28)

But not in others:

> And the Lord God commanded the man, "You are free to eat from any tree in the garden; but you must not eat from the tree of the knowledge of good and evil, for when you eat from it you will certainly die." (Gen. 2:16–17 NIV)

He could then hold them accountable for their responses, calling out to them after they disobeyed to ask where they were and what they had done (see Gen. 3:9–13).

As a biological creature with a body formed from the ground like the animals and a spirit formed by the Lord, there was, as Blocher says, a *duality* to Adam's constitution, a duality that we still possess and that makes us unique—and uniquely accountable—among the earth's creatures. And so even after Adam and Eve disobeyed, we find God addressing their son Cain and asking, "Why are you angry? Why is your face downcast? If you do what is right, will you not be accepted? But if you do not do what is right, sin is crouching at your door; it desires to have you, *but you must rule over it*" (Gen. 4:6–7 NIV).[66]

Our first parents' disobedience doesn't cancel our accountability (see, e.g., Rom. 2:1–16 with 3:19–20). We are still to rule over ourselves and the rest of creation (see Rom. 6:12–14).[67] We still need categorical prohibitions, along with severe warnings about violating them, to counterbalance our strong and often sinful impulses and inclinations and thus help us rule over ourselves. By resounding in our consciousness, these prohibitions promote self-consciously accountable personhood. They are an integral part of the word we must hear (see Prov. 13:24; 22:15; 29:15).

Human persons are, Blocher stresses, psychosomatic unities— each of us is one thing and not two—yet there is still a kind of "structural composition" to our unity.[68] With one foot (so to speak) in the natural world and one foot in the spiritual world, we are accountable to God for all we think and do. "From this point of view," he says, "Scripture places mankind firmly alongside the world, before the LORD."

CREATION'S ONLY "NOT GOOD"

So far we have seen that God has made us as earthly, biological persons. Both our biology and our personhood depend on our being socially related to other human beings. God's declaration at Genesis 2:18 recognizes this: "It is not good for the man to be alone. I will make a helper suitable for him" (NIV)[69]—a helper "who is just right for him" (NLT). The ensuing short story is a literary marvel.

Naming the Beasts and the Birds

> Now the LORD God had formed out of the ground all the wild animals and all the birds in the sky. He brought them to the man to see what he would name them; and whatever the man called each living creature, that was its name. So the man gave names to all the livestock, the birds in the sky and all the wild animals. But for Adam no suitable helper was found. (Gen. 2:19–20 NIV)

"Physically," Collins says, "God made these animals *before* man, but conceptually, he made the animals anticipating man's dominion over them—that is, in God's mind the animals were a logical consequence of the man," and so it makes sense that from Genesis 2's perspective within the confines of the garden they don't appear until after the man was made.[70] In taxonomizing them, the man realized that not one of them could be his true companion. None was "just right for him."

At this point, the Hebrew word *adam* lacks the definite article for the first time, making it a proper name. Naming the first man "Adam" at this point in the story shows the Lord's concern for the individual person who was still companionless.

Building a Woman

> So the LORD God caused a deep sleep to fall upon the man, and while he slept took one of his ribs and closed up its place with flesh. And the rib that the LORD God had taken from the man he built into a woman. (Gen. 2:21–22a)[i]

With Adam himself now acutely aware of his predicament, God knocked him out, taking some flesh and bone from his side to build a woman.[71]

---

i. The ESV margin notes that the word *made*, which it has as its translation, is actually the Hebrew word for *built*, so I have modified the translation accordingly.

Build may seem inappropriate for describing the woman's creation, but it's the best English can do. The Hebrew word is *banah*, which has quite different connotations than the word *yatsar* used to describe Adam's and the animals' creation in verses 7 and 19. *Yatsar* suggests shaping something from some preexisting material. In Genesis 2:7 and 19 it emphasizes the way the man and the animals were formed from earth. *Banah*, on the other hand, involves the thoughtful architectural construction of something like a city, a house, an altar, a wall, or a gate.[72] So as Samuel Terrien says, "While the man was 'molded' out of the finest clay . . . , the woman is compared to a work of the architectural arts." He goes on to observe:

> in the ancient Near East . . . [where] architecture necessitated, as much as today, a whole concentration of scientific, technological, and aesthetic faculties[,] . . . the use of the verb "to build" for the woman implies an intellectual and aesthetic appreciation of her body, the equilibrium of her forms, and the volumes and proportions of her figure.[73]

The fact that the woman was built from stuff taken from the man's side links her to him in much the same way as the fact that Adam and the animals were formed from earth links them to the soil from which they came. The use of *banah* instead of *yatsar* stresses God's artistry in suiting the woman to the man. Terrien says *banah* "implies beauty, stability, and durability," and Christoph Uehlinger has argued that this means the woman was "a living work of art."

This is certainly how Adam saw her when God brought her to him. The story takes its time getting from God's observation that "it is not good for the man to be alone" to God's remedy of presenting Adam with a helper who suited him. It lingers over the Lord's presentation of the earth's animals to Adam in order to make sure we feel the drama: it is not good for the man to be alone, but will a suitable helper be found for him? Adam pondered and then named all the livestock, birds, and wild animals, "but for Adam no suitable helper was found." Thus the drama increases: it is not good for the man to be alone, but in all of creation no suitable helper can be found for him. And none will be unless God does something unprecedented. The Lord has to turn away from the earth, the source from which he had formed all other life, and turn to the man himself in order to find material suitable to provide this remedy. He has to build this remedy from human stuff. The woman has to be like the man to a unique degree. "The special creation of Eve," Kidner says, "clinched the fact that *there is no natural bridge from animal to man.*"[74] Yet in building Eve, God didn't just clone Adam. The compound Hebrew prepositional phrase translated by the New Living Translation at Genesis 2:18 and 20 as "just right for him" means that the woman was the man's "like opposite." She was *like* him because she was created out of him. But she was unlike—or *opposite*[75]—him because she didn't simply mirror him. She matched him. As his complement, she completed him. She fit him like hand and glove.

The man God had created required the company of another human being. Our completion through human companionship images God's fullness as a Trinity of distinct persons. In naming the animals, Adam realized that none of them could fully complement him. None could help him as he needed. The Lord would always be his ultimate help and shield (see, e.g., Ps. 115:9), yet he had no companion who could look him lovingly in the eye, share his bread and his bed,[j] and speak with him face-to-face. Before the woman was made, he could look up or down but not straight across at someone who could relate to him as possessing the same dignity and accountability before God as he did. After she was made, he had just such a person, and yet someone distinct enough—genetically, hormonally, physically, emotionally, socially, morally, and spiritually—to be his true counterpart and thus help him as a partner and full companion.[k]

"At Last!"

   . . . and brought [the woman] to the man. (Gen. 2:22b)

When Adam awoke, God brought the woman to him,[76] in effect challenging him, "Now name this!" And Adam saw someone who could

---

j. The English word *companion* comes from a Latin word meaning "to share bread with."

k. The complementarity of highly similar but somewhat different perspectives means that all sorts of human companionship, when we take them sufficiently seriously, help us not to miss what others see.

be his full companion, one who was indeed "just right for him," which prompted him to exclaim:

> At last! . . . This one is bone from my bone,
>   and flesh from my flesh!
> She will be called "woman" [*ishsha*]
>   because she was taken [out of] "man" [*ish*]. (Gen. 2:23 NLT)[1]

This poem shows Adam to be "an artist as well as a taxonomist in his speech."[77] It reiterates the centrality of language to normal human personhood. *At last* expresses "the idea of a wait, 'finally after numerous tries.'" As his wordplay on *ish* and *ishsha* suggests, Adam saw the woman he would name Eve as completing what God meant human life to be. Kidner notes that while Adam's naming of the animals portrayed him as a monarch of all he surveyed, it also poignantly revealed him "as a social being, *made for fellowship, not power; he will not live until he loves, giving himself away . . . to another on his own level.*" So the woman is first "presented wholly as his partner and counterpart; nothing is yet said of her as childbearer. *She is valued for herself alone.*"[78]

Here, in contrast to everything else he could see in God's creation, Adam saw someone who matched him and thus remedied the one aspect of creation that had previously been "not good."

Yet Adam's response to God's gift to him of Eve was probably much more than just a "jubilant welcome." It was probably a *verba solemnia*—a solemn, binding vow—that declared his relation to her to be a covenant that fulfilled the conditions for verse 24's declaration, "Therefore a man shall leave his father and his mother and [cling] to his wife,[m] and they shall become one flesh."[79]

---

l. These, the first words recorded from any human being, are poetry because Adam could not otherwise express the depth of his appreciation for the gift God had just given him. Poetry is thus essential to express and experience human life's full meaning. For a short yet incisive defense of this truth, see the editor's introduction to Leland Ryken's *The Soul in Paraphrase: A Treasury of Classic Devotional Poems* (Wheaton, IL: Crossway, 2018).

m. See Ruth 1:14; 1 Kings 11:2; and Ps. 63:8, which translate the Hebrew word used here in Gen. 2:24 as "cling." Gen. 34:3 would pack more of a punch if it were translated as "And his soul clung to Dinah the daughter of Jacob."

Unashamed

The Lord's having remedied creation's only "not good" by creating Adam's human counterpart explains why an *ish* should leave his parents and cling to his *ishsha* so that the two become one flesh. The reference to *one flesh* is not, Collins notes, "primarily a reference to sexual union." It refers to "the complete identification of one personality with the other in a community of interests and pursuits." This union is then consummated in intercourse.[80] The nuances of the Hebrew term meaning "opposite" in verses 18 and 20 suggest that each spouse's presence *in front of* or *before*—in other words, *opposite*—the other helps reveal them to themselves.[81] Becoming one flesh should enhance rather than diminish each spouse's individuality: "It is as *others* that the man and the woman are made for each other, and the man must accept this otherness in order for the emptiness of his solitude to be filled."[82]

In blessing our first parents, God commanded them to be fruitful and multiply (see Gen. 1:28). Their sexual duality required their mutual obedience. "The duality of the sexes implies the plurality of the persons."[83] It circumscribes how each of us has come to be (see 1 Cor. 11:11–12). It inclines us toward person-to-person relationships.[84] It enables full communion through the covenantal sexual-union-in-duality that marriage establishes between two free, embodied persons.

"And the man and his wife were both naked and were not ashamed" (v. 25). "'They were unabashed' or 'they were not disconcerted,'" untroubled by their nakedness.[85] Appearing before each other completely uncovered, they lacked nothing, finding God's provision perfect for them. Indeed, they would have rejoiced in the display of their physical differences (see the Song of Solomon).

When the Hebrew word for *Eden* was translated into Greek, it became the Greek word meaning "paradise" (see Rev. 2:7).[86] This, for an all-too-fleeting moment, was what life in Eden was. Life in paradise was almost everything that human life was meant to be. Yet to make it absolutely everything, our first parents had to affirm their calling.

OUR CALLING

Job was forgetting himself when he asked, "What is mankind that you make so much of them, that you give them so much attention, that you examine them every morning and test them every moment?" (Job 7:17–18 NIV). He knew the answer. He knew that God has created us to be fully accountable to him and calls us to live accordingly (see, e.g., Job 1:1, 4–5, 8; 2:3; 28:28; and 31).

We can state our calling both generally and specifically.

Generally, we are called to be accountable persons who rule ourselves appropriately.[87] As Scruton put it, we are not just groups of cooperating primates but communities of persons who hold each other to account by organizing our world in terms of moral concepts that have no place in the lives of chimpanzees.[n] Even those who refuse to acknowledge their accountability before God and who deny that there are any objective moral standards inevitably hold other human beings to be morally accountable.[88] Our nature as socially interdependent persons entails our accountability. This is the inexpungible residue of God's having breathed into us the *neshamah* of life, to which our consciences inevitably bear witness (see Rom. 2:1–16).

But we are not called to be just generally accountable persons. More specifically, God as our Creator calls us to be his people who obey his commands and fulfill his specific purposes by resolving to be his chosen people.

Since our thoughts are not God's thoughts (see Isa. 55:8–9), God must reveal his thoughts to us (see 1 Cor. 2:11), which he does primarily through the Spirit-inspired Scriptures (see Rom. 15:4; 2 Tim. 3:14–17; 2 Pet. 1:19–21). We understand God's intentions for us only by knowing the Scriptures. This is emphasized in the Old Testament (see, e.g., Deut. 17:14–15, 18–20; Josh. 1:7–8; Neh. 8:1–3) and driven home in the New (see 2 Tim. 3:14–17). God's inscripturated word can transform us as persons by changing how we think (see Rom. 12:2), feel (see Deut. 6:5; Ps. 97:10; Prov. 1:7; 1 Pet. 1:8), speak (see Col. 4:6; 1 Pet. 3:15), and

---

n. See above, 32.

act (see Rom. 12:1; 1 Cor. 6:20; Eph. 4:1). Indeed, God calls us to be renewed in knowledge according to his image as our Creator (see Col. 3:5–10), which is seen in the face of Christ, who *is* the perfect image of God (see 2 Cor. 4:4–6; Col. 1:15; Heb. 1:3). More on this later.

As we have already seen, in Psalm 119 the psalmist confessed that suffering prompted him to attend to God's written word.[o] This potential fruit of suffering, we shall see, is one of the primary reasons why the world contains so much of it.

---

o. See above, 16.

REBELLION

The Cause of All Our Suffering

And God saw everything that he had made,
and behold, it was very good.

Genesis 1:31

Now the serpent was more crafty
than any of the wild animals the Lord God had made.
He said to the woman, "Did God really say,
'You must not eat from any tree in the garden'?"
The woman said to the serpent,
"We may eat fruit from the trees in the garden,
but God did say,
'You must not eat fruit from the tree that
is in the middle of the garden,
and you must not touch it, or you will die.'"
"You will not certainly die," the serpent said to the woman.
"For God knows that when you eat from
it your eyes will be opened,
and you will be like God, knowing good and evil."
When the woman saw that the fruit of the tree was good for food
and pleasing to the eye, and also desirable for gaining wisdom,
she took some and ate it.

> She also gave some to her husband, who
> was with her, and he ate it.
> Then the eyes of both of them were opened,
> and they realized they were naked.
>
> *Genesis 3:1–7 NIV*

> Sin entered the world through one man, and death through sin,
> and in this way death came to all people.
>
> *Romans 5:12 NIV*

Life in Eden was very different from life now. Our first parents knew no suffering or unhappiness. This chapter opens by clarifying what their life was like.

Yet the more we hear about their life before they disobeyed God's command not to eat from the forbidden tree, the more we may be tempted to think the biblical story of creation is a fairy tale. After all, doesn't science show that nature has always been red in tooth and claw? Hasn't life always been a matter of the survival of the fittest, with suffering and death always part of human existence? This chapter lays out why Scripture doesn't take suffering and death to be an inevitable part of human life. It takes Genesis 1–3 as truth rather than myth.[1] C. John Collins notes that if we believe this, then we will "recognize the yawning gap between our present experience and life in the garden," and we will "ache as we recognize [it], and insist on an explanation."[2] Genesis 3 explains it by showing how our first parents' rebellion brought us suffering and death.

LIFE IN THE GARDEN

As Genesis 3 opens, creation is complete, with everything in place for Adam and Eve to embrace the blessed life the Lord God was offering them.

Genesis 1 placed them at the summit of God's creative acts, emphasizing their unique role in creation. As God's earthly images, they were to represent him by ruling over creation wisely and benevolently (see Gen. 1:26–28).[3]

Genesis 2 focused on the God-breathed capacities that equipped them for their task. It tells us that after the Lord created Adam, he placed him in a garden of magnificent fruit trees. The garden's "lush fecundity was a sign of God's presence in and blessing on Eden."[4] The gold, gemstones, and aromatic resins found nearby (see Gen. 2:10–14) indicate that "there [was] more than primitive simplicity in store for the race."[5] Genesis 2 also records God's command not to eat the forbidden fruit. After Eve's creation,[a] Adam and Eve could expect a fully satisfying future as long as they resolved to obey their Lord's command—a future of meaningful work, abundant life in communion with God, and rich human relationships.

We won't grasp the full significance of our first parents' choice to disobey that command unless we understand what human life was supposed to be, given these three aspects of life in Eden.

Meaningful Work

When God declared that he would make us, he specified our task: "Let us make mankind in our image, in our likeness, *so that* they may rule over the fish in the sea and the birds in the sky, over the livestock and all the wild animals, and over all the creatures that move along the ground" (Gen. 1:26 NIV). This is the work we were made for. In Genesis 2, work appears "as the only definition of man's proper significance."[6] Henri Blocher comments that although the Lord "bestows gifts on those he wishes to love as his sons, he takes good care not to turn them into spoilt children" by giving them responsibilities. So Eden was "'no fairyland, no Utopia'; *[Adam re-ceived] a charge to fulfil in that place.*" As soon as God made Adam, and even before issuing his decisive prohibition, the Lord God "took

---

a. The first woman is not named *Eve* until 3:20, but I will sometimes call her Eve now for convenience.

the man and put him in the garden of Eden *to work it and keep it*" (Gen. 2:15).

Work is thus central to earthly life. Yet we may confuse the stress, difficulties, and failures of work in our fallen world with work itself, which may lead us to think that work is at best a necessary evil. Genesis 2, however, implies that a human life without work "could not be a complete life; it would be an existence quite unworthy" of human beings.[7] God "put [the] man into a garden," Claus Westermann remarks; "the garden and the land there [needed] to be worked; the land [was] entrusted to [the] man, who [was] both capable and industrious." God's task gave purpose and meaning to Adam's life—divine purpose and meaning. Whether we acknowledge it or not, our lives get their real meaning from God.[8] And so believing the biblical account of creation means believing that work is integral to the meaning and fulfillment of human life "because the living space which [God] has assigned to his people demands [their] work." Our specifically human existence "follows a pattern of duty." The world, even before the fall, required human labor. And so the work that God assigned to Adam and Eve fundamentally informs who God has created us to be.[9]

The Hebrew word for *work* at Genesis 2:5 and 15 means "to work or serve or honor or worship." Adam's "labor in the garden," Gordon Wenham comments, was "indeed a kind of divine service, for it [was] done for God and in his presence."[10] Most occurrences of the Hebrew word for *work* in Scripture are religiously significant. *Laborare est orare*—"work is prayer." Work in the garden involved the pleasure of performing useful service *for* and *to* the Lord, as acts of worship and honor.

At the end of a day's work our first parents would probably have been weary. Yet as C. S. Lewis observes, some very minor aches are actually pleasurable. They only become painful when increased.[11] Only spoiled children expect everything to be effortless.

Even after the fall, meaningful work done well brings pleasure (see Eccles. 2:24; 3:13). This is especially true when the work is important—and the work that God has assigned to us, as those who find our day-to-day meaning in imaging God by working, is as important as can be. After naming the earth and the seas (see Gen. 1:10), God named nothing in creation, tasking us with naming the animals as well as making other crucial classifications and distinctions (see Gen. 2:19–20, 23). Solomon continued this work (see 1 Kings 4:29–30, 33). We have the work of building and planting (see Prov. 24:30–34; Eccles. 2:4–5), of nurturing and educating (see, e.g., Deut. 6:4–7; Ps. 78:1–8; Prov. 31:26), of making and arranging proverbs (see 1 Kings 4:32; Eccles. 12:9), the work of writing and performing music (see Deut. 31:19–22; 1 Kings 4:32; 2 Chron. 5:13), and of worshiping and celebrating (see Ps. 95:1–2, 6–7; 100:1; 149:2). There are works of mercy (Job 29:11–17; Prov. 31:20; Matt. 25:31–46) as well as, in New Testament times, the work of evangelizing (Matt. 28:19–20; 2 Tim. 4:1–5) and preaching and teaching (see 1 Tim. 5:17–18).

Now, postfall and outside the garden, our work can be unpleasant, sometimes painful, and at times frustrating or futile. It can be like the hard, bitter work that Israel experienced as Egypt's slaves (see Ex. 1:13–14). Now we must pray that the Lord will look favorably on our work and thus "establish the work of our hands" (Ps. 90:17). Our reliance on God's favor to reward our work is, we shall see in chapter 4, part of what the Lord's having cursed the ground in Genesis 3:17–19 was meant to produce. The travails that now often accompany our daily tasks should keep us always mindful of him.

For creatures made in God's image and as his image, work is part of life itself (see John 5:17). The fact that God created Adam to fulfill a task and then told him what it was implies that Adam was to live his life in response to God's initiatives. His life was to consist in his hearing and obeying God.[12]

Personal and Potentially Abundant Life

As long as Adam heard and obeyed, he enjoyed life with God. By addressing Adam, God began to nourish him with a kind of life unknown to any other earthly creature (cf. Deut. 32:44–47; John 6:63). From the moment God breathed into him the breath of life and put him in the garden with instructions to work and keep it, Adam's life as *personal* life was "just there, as a given life, indeed life before God."[13] That life was capable of becoming a truly abundant life of deep communion with

God.[14] We shall see later in this chapter how, by addressing Adam and giving him a command, God was offering him that life.

As we shall see, God's command to Adam in Genesis 2 invited both him and Eve to respond to their Maker in a deliberate, covenant-like way. If they had, they would have basked in God's smile. We have already seen that God's blessing at its fullest involves "God turning full-face to the recipient . . . in self-giving."[b] His turning full-face to us is the acme and essence of abundant, fully personal life. As God the Father lives in the equivalent of triune face-to-face relationships with his Son and Spirit, so for those of us who accept his invitation (see Isa. 55:1 with John 7:37–39 and Rev. 22:17), our reflection of his image will one day be perfected in Christ's face-to-face presence with us as his bride (see Rev. 21:1–3; 22:4, and 1 Cor. 13:12 with 2 Cor. 4:4–6).

Yet Adam still had one great need.

Rich Human Relationships

"From the very beginning," Blocher observes, God did not intend for Adam to be alone, for "the human being is a *Mitsein*, a being-with; human life attains its full realization only in community."[15] Unrelieved solitude "contradicts the calling of humanity." Community requires communication—that is, two or more persons addressing each other—and commitment. Members of a community are mutually committed to sharing their way of life.[16]

Yet when God said, "It is not good that the man should be alone; I will make him a helper fit for him" (Gen. 2:18), he intended the life that Adam was to share with Eve to involve much more than merely sharing a way of life. It was to be a life of communion—that is, a life of explicitly covenantal commitment binding them to each other in the closest of ways, a life of intimate attunement with each other that would inspire, guide, strengthen, and encourage them as they went along their way.[17]

Of course, ultimately nothing must be allowed to rival our desire for life with God. As Asaph affirms:

---

b. See chap. 1, 28.

Whom have I in heaven but you?
    And there is nothing on earth that I desire besides you.
My flesh and my heart may fail,
    but God is . . . my portion forever. (Ps. 73:25–26; cf. 16:2)

Yet God himself declared that Adam's life without Eve was "not good." Until Eve was created, Adam lacked the pleasure of hearing, obeying, and serving the Lord in concrete acts of worship and honor *with another human being*—and, indeed, with one whom he had vowed to be one flesh.[18] His exclamation, "At last! . . . This one is bone from my bone, and flesh from my flesh!" (Gen. 2:23 NLT), was his pledge that he would be with Eve "a common body, a 'fellowship for life'"—a fellowship designed for sharing an abundant life with God *together*.[19]

Yet there is still more here. The good that Adam and Eve were to know as husband and wife was to be just the first instance of a much fuller good. God's command that Adam and Eve be fruitful, multiply, and fill the earth meant that their life was to blossom with children, siblings, cousins, neighbors, and friends.

"The fact that the first company given by God to man in order to break his solitude was of the other sex," Blocher notes, "reminds us that God does not institute an abstract otherness." In presenting Eve to Adam, God gave him "a *neighbour* and not merely an 'other'"—that is, he gave him "a concretely qualified presence" in a unique human being.[20]

The place of sexual duality in human reproduction summons us to human community. In fact, it is only among real, flesh-and-blood human beings that we grow into fully addressable persons. The details are significant. Unborn babies recognize their mother's voice.[21] At birth, our mothers tend to greet us as they greet other persons: "Why, hello there! How are you?" Newborns require their parents to take the initiative not just to feed and protect them but also to engage them as persons. By treating their infants as persons, they draw them into the kingdom of persons.[c]

---

c. See chap. 1, 33

By the second month, babies are more than just passive perceivers. They are starting to ponder and assess those around them. "This," Philippe Rochat states, "is unmistakable to any observer of young infants."[22] Life begins to involve reciprocal overtures to personal interaction. An infant's engagement with those around her, Rochat notes, is "reliably observed in relation to one particular, and very significant event: the emergence of the first socially elicited smile." Parents "observing for the first time their infant smiling while gazing at them or in response to their own smiles discover a person in their child: a person among other persons." Babies begin to "perceive other persons as differentiated from themselves." They begin responding as persons to other persons. They begin knowing their lives for what their lives essentially are: personal lives lived in the presence of—that is, face-to-face with—other persons.

God made us for this. "The socially elicited smiles that begin to be expressed in the second month," Rochat continues,

> are unambiguously correlated to events external to the infant, *in particular the perception of other people's faces* engaged in play games and other social exchanges. In addition to smiling, other behaviors emerge . . . that all confirm a new stance taken by the infant: *a conversational and contemplative stance whereby infants start deliberately to reciprocate with others as well as to explore and think about the environment.*

In other words, babies begin acting in ways that are in fact the first steps on the way to their becoming free and fully responsible persons who can assume their unique place in creation.

Our awareness of others, as Blocher stresses, is integral to our awareness of ourselves:

> Just as the most natural mirror we have is the eye that beholds us, so it is our encounter with another which allows our inner life to become aware of itself. The Genesis narrative says this in its own way. . . . *The self does not establish its identity over against the non-self*

of the impersonal universe. The self, the "I," discovers itself in greeting another. . . . The individual finds himself only beyond himself, in salutation.[23]

These greetings begin with the "intimate, [face-to-face], one-on-one reciprocal exchanges between infants and their caregivers [that] allow infants to develop an understanding of what they feel and experience from within." Faces are thus "the public theater of the mind."[24] Still or sad faces distress infants.[25] They bask in their parents' smiles.

Immediate, face-to-face human interaction is integral to our humanity. As earthly persons, we are accountable not only to God but also to other human beings. This web of interpersonal relationships draws us into fully responsible, free personhood and holds us in it. We need the help, comfort, encouragement, camaraderie, correction, and counsel of family, neighbors, and friends. "The sweetness of a friend comes from his earnest counsel" (Prov. 27:9).

Our social needs are never fully met in marriage—think of Naomi and Ruth, David and Jonathan, Jeremiah and Baruch, Mary and Elizabeth, Paul and Timothy, and our Lord and his beloved disciple (see John 13:23; 20:2; 21:20). We need the presence of a variety of other persons. We need regular, caring human companionship.[26] We need it when we are too young, too old, or whenever we are unable to make sense of life for ourselves. We need it to stay on track as others help us pursue good and also address us when we need correction. You must contradict me when need be. "Let the godly strike me! It will be a kindness! If they correct me, it is soothing medicine. Don't let me refuse it" (Ps. 141:5 NLT). "Faithful are the wounds of a friend" (Prov. 27:6).

The New Testament insists that we are complete only in human community (see 1 Cor. 12:4–30; 1 John 4:20–21). Human fellowship is essential to full Christian life (see Eph. 4:1–7, 11–16). At the consummation we will be among "a great multitude that no one [can] number" (Rev. 7:9). As Blocher observes, "No man is an island, and everyone"— like the good Samaritan (see Luke 10:29–37)—"must discover himself to be his neighbour's neighbour. At the final completion of the operations of the grace of God, the multitude in the City of God multiplies the victory of the first couple over human solitude (Rev. 21–22). In the final paradise, as in the first, mankind will never be completely alone."[27]

Whenever an individual in ancient Israel was "set apart or isolated," Hans Walter Wolff writes, "something unusual, if not something threatening, [was] happening."[28] "A solitary existence," Wenham observes, "was viewed as a calamity. . . . Biblical man knew he was meant to live in society, to be a member of God's people."[29] The notion of loneliness "as a longed-for benefit that gives active pleasure," Wolff insists, "is alien to the Old Testament." In the Old Testament, loneliness "always means misery."

Unrelieved isolation threatens a person's very humanity, exposing us to grave moral and spiritual dangers.[30] Insofar as truly abundant life comes from listening to and obeying God, his words need to reverberate through our lives, which they often do through the words of other human beings (see Deut. 6:4–9; 18:15–19; Jer. 29:19; Luke 9:35). Isolation from them can foster isolation from God.

As embodied persons, we are to treasure the physical presence of others. For our first parents, the physical details of the other person would have reminded them that they were God's highest earthly gifts to each other. Like the lovers in the Song of Solomon, they would have delighted in each other's beauty, taking it as coming directly from God's hand.[31] They would have felt all the passion of that song. Yet in their life together before God, they would not only have been lovers and friends but also have known the closeness of being like the best of siblings (see Song 4:9–10; 5:16; 8:1).

If our first parents had obeyed God's commands to be fruitful and multiply and not to eat from the forbidden tree, then they could have anticipated a fully satisfying future serving their Lord. Their work, God's presence, and their companionship with each other, with business associates, and with family and friends, would have been "very good"!

"If the calling of mankind is to be with his God," Blocher concludes, "it is fitting that his earthly existence should already be characterized by being-with; otherwise the relationship with God would be, as it were, laminated on to his nature, and he would risk becoming lost instead of fulfilled in it."[32] The capacities that enable us to be addressed by God echo in our human relationships, supplying depth to the Bible's claims.

TEMPTATION

Blocher urges us to pause before considering Genesis 3 in order to delight in the garden's peace and harmony. "There was no covetousness! There was no anxiety!"[33] Perhaps most tellingly, as they began life together "the man and his wife were both naked, but they felt no shame" (Gen. 2:25 NLT).

Adam and Eve were perfectly at ease with each other, with no barrier of any kind driving a wedge between them.[34] The Hebrew verb for "felt no shame" suggests that "the couples' reaction to each other . . . refers to a state they shared from the moment of their creation," an ongoing state of not feeling any sort of inhibition or embarrassment in each other's presence. In their innocence, they lived in perfect, open harmony, regarding each other with all the love and affectionate respect that those made in and as God's image deserve.

Following hard on that wonderful state, Genesis 3 wastes no time portraying the event that has led to our suffering.

The Serpent's Strategy

An unexpected, wily character opens the fateful scene, making an odd claim. Hebrew grammar suggests the serpent's craftiness was not merely a matter of his asking about what God had said: "Did God really say, 'You must not eat from any tree in the garden'?" (Gen. 3:1 NIV).[35] He was probably feigning surprise: "Indeed! To think that God said you are not to eat of any tree in the garden!"[36] This prompted from Eve a quick reply: "We may eat fruit from the trees in the garden, but God did say, 'You must not eat fruit from the tree that is in the middle of the garden, and you must not touch it, or you will die'" (vv. 2–3 NIV).

The serpent's retort shows he knew exactly what the Lord God's command had been. Eve left out the *certainly* in the Lord's warning to Adam that if he ate of the tree of the knowledge of good and evil, then he would certainly die (see 2:17). In disputing God's warning, the serpent put it back in: "'You will not certainly die,' the serpent said to the woman" (3:4 NIV), thus directly contradicting God's word in an attempt "to undermine the relationship of trust that is the engine of obedience" between God and human beings.[37] How was he attempting to do so? First, he omitted the reference to God's personal, covenantal name—that is, LORD (in Hebrew, Yahweh)—that runs throughout Genesis 2 and 3 to emphasize God's personal relationship with Adam and Eve. As Victor Hamilton notes, "The Bible's first conversation about God is about [*elōhîm*, which is God's generic name], not Yahweh."[38] As we have seen, the psalmists avoided this kind of general talk *about* God because it undercuts the truth that those who know the Lord trust him and address him directly.[d] Second, the serpent diverted Eve's attention from God's actual words to God's supposed inner thoughts. "Implicit here," Hamilton observes, "is the suggestion that the serpent knows God better than the woman does, for he can penetrate [God's] mind and claim to know what God knows." Third, he falsely insinuated that this distant deity had selfish reasons for warning our first parents not to eat from the tree: "God knows that when you eat from it your eyes will be opened, and you will be like God, knowing good and evil" (v. 5 NIV). He was suggesting that if Adam and Eve ate from this tree, they would dim God's glory.

This lie was "big enough to reinterpret life . . . and dynamic enough to redirect the flow of affection and ambition."[39] We all encounter lies like this. If we believe them, they can warp our whole approach to life (see, e.g., Prov. 1:10–19; 16:29; 1 Tim. 6:10). If Eve were to believe this one, then she would begin to regard her kind Creator, sustainer, and benefactor as her rival and enemy. The serpent was tempting her to take what would be, in fact, "a suicidal plunge as a leap into life."

The Woman's Error

Eve fell by permitting herself to look at the tree from a misleading angle: she "saw that the fruit of the tree was good for food and pleasing to the

---

d. See Mark Talbot, *When the Stars Disappear: Help and Hope from Stories of Suffering in Scripture* (Wheaton, IL: Crossway, 2020), 44.

eye, and also desirable for gaining wisdom" (3:6a NIV).[40] As a person whose life depended on her maintaining her personal relationship with God, she had to trust him.[41] As toddlers glance toward their mothers in order to know how they should react in unfamiliar and potentially dangerous situations, so Eve should have looked to her Lord in this moment.[42] But she "listened to a creature instead of the Creator, followed her impressions against her instructions, and made self-fulfillment her goal." Once the serpent dislodged her from God's perspective, the considerations she shouldn't have entertained began to press. With the only crucial consideration eclipsed, the tree's appearing to offer food, beauty, and wisdom "seemed to add up to life itself." Yet as Derek Kidner reminds us, our true "lifeline is spiritual," and so to make that calculation instead of obeying God and believing his word would be death.[43]

REBELLION

So Eve "took some and ate it. She also gave some to her husband, who was with her, and he ate it" (3:6b NIV). "Then the eyes of both of them were opened, and they realized they were naked; so they sewed fig leaves together and made coverings for themselves" (3:7 NIV). This pair who had known the joyous freedom of unabashed nakedness—that is, an existence where "no barrier of any kind drove a wedge between" them[44]—could no longer bear such openness.

This was the first consequence of their rebelling against God's command, "You are free to eat from any tree in the garden; but you must not eat from the tree of the knowledge of good and evil, for when you eat from it you will certainly die" (Gen. 2:16–17 NIV). In Hebrew, the permission—"You are free to eat"—and the warning—"for when you eat from it you will certainly die"—have the same grammatically emphatic construction.[45] As Blocher writes, "In the first case the tone [was] of the fullness of the permission: you shall eat *freely*, eat your fill without lacking any of the good things that I have created. *All the trees of the garden represent all the riches of the earth, placed at mankind's disposal.*"[46] It revealed God as a God of superabundant generosity, "the opposite of the castrating father of our pitiful fantasies." He is instead "the bestowing

Father who rejoices in the happiness of mankind." "God *commands* this permission," Blocher stresses.[47] "It is an order for the man to benefit from the life God gives him, to explore the magnificent park and taste its fruits. By refusing to be content with a stunted existence, the man will show his gratitude and glorify his LORD." Everything about this part of the commandment was meant to benefit him.[48] It beckoned, nay, ordered and indeed *commanded* him, "to feed on the fruits of paradise."

The warning was equally emphatic. The prohibition, "You must not eat from the tree of the knowledge of good and evil," was, as we are about to see, "the basis and the safeguard of the happiness of the human race." Its dire warning—"for when you eat from it you will certainly die"—underlined that. Why would rebelling against this prohibition result in pain, suffering, sickness, unhappiness, and death? Answering this question requires us to know more about what it means for us to be persons.

The Covenantal or Covenant-Like Basis of Abundant Life

As we saw in chapter 1, as persons we can be required to *give an account* of who we are and what we do. Genesis 2 explains how we became accountable. The Lord God's breathing into the first man the breath of life bestowed on him the gift of personhood, enabling him to listen, learn, think, speak, teach, and make free decisions. With these abilities came accountability. As an earthly person, Adam could then be addressed and required to *answer for* who he was and what he did. By making his first words to Adam the command of Genesis 2:16–17, the Lord was addressing him person to person and prohibiting him from eating from a particular tree. He became accountable for his choices regarding that tree.

Behind that prohibition stood the prospect that Adam could have a truly satisfying, fully abundant life only by resolving never to eat from that tree. Both the prohibition and the prospect were part of the Lord's invitation to Adam to choose what is in fact the only way to life by entering into communion with him.[49]

Communion with other persons involves being drawn into intimate fellowship with them through sharing experiences, interests, projects, or pursuits. It involves becoming interpersonally attuned with another person. As Daniel Stern notes, the prevailing feature of interpersonal interaction between infants and their parents involves both the infants and their parents wanting to share the same emotional states. Desiring this kind of intimacy, he reports, is the "largest single reason that mothers gave . . . for performing [such] an attunement." They naturally wanted "'to be with' [their infants], 'to share,' 'to participate in,' 'to join in'" their babies' experiences. And their babies wanted the same. Stern and other developmental psychologists call this kind of intimacy between parents and infants "interpersonal communion."[50]

We can share a sort of special closeness with different persons for longer or shorter periods of time and to different degrees. Perhaps you and I feel it when we are in the wilderness fly-fishing together. I may feel it with someone else whenever we engage in a project that is central to each of our lives and mutually engrossing. These moments of person-to-person communion enrich our lives in important ways.

Yet there is a deeper, fuller, and more extensive communion that we can share with just a few other persons when we identify with them in a way that involves the merging of our lives. Marriage is Scripture's prime example of the way that two people can enter into such communion. It involves two persons identifying with each other in a way that is meant to involve the full and exclusive merging of their lives. It is not, like the parent/infant relationship, a natural relationship. It must be explicitly chosen, thus creating and formalizing what otherwise would not exist. This makes marriage, in biblical language, a *covenant*—that is, "a formally confirmed agreement between two or more parties that creates, formalizes, or governs a relationship that does not naturally exist or a natural relationship that may have been broken or disintegrated."[51] Covenants, as the *Oxford English Dictionary* clarifies, always involve "a mutual agreement between two or more persons to do or refrain from doing certain acts."[52] Covenants, in other words, circumscribe our freedom.

The interpersonal attunement naturally sought by parents and infants can also blossom into a fuller communion if their commitment to each other matures in a way that results in an informal, usually implicit choice by each to share each other's lives and fortunes.[53] That choice binds them to each other and thus is covenant-like in circumscribing their freedom.[54]

At first, Adam and Eve's relationship with God was natural. He was their Creator and they were his creatures, made in his image and thus enough like him that God could visit with them while walking in the garden in the cool of the day (see Gen. 3:8). They could communicate freely with him, which reflected the openness of their relationship, an openness not yet broken by disobedience or sin. But true and full communion with God requires much more than uninhibited communication. As John Murray observes, our creation in God's image "implies an inherent, native, inalienable obligation" for us "to love and serve God with all the heart, soul, strength, and mind." This "God could not but demand and [we] could not but owe."[55] So true communion with God required our first parents to acknowledge and honor that obligation by choosing to identify fully and completely with him by making a decisive choice not to eat from the forbidden tree. To eat from it would break the incipient but not yet "full-orbed communion" that could (and should) have developed naturally between God and human beings.

Should we call this incipient relationship between our first parents and God a "covenant," where the covenant stipulation was that Adam and Eve would never eat from the forbidden tree? Scripture doesn't do so—and so perhaps we shouldn't either.[56] All of the Old Testament's uses of *berit*, the Hebrew word for covenant, refer to God's redemptive dealings with humankind. They involve God restoring what should have been natural between him and us after the natural Creator/creature relationship was broken.[57] Yet even before the fall, our first parents' entering into true communion with God would have required them to choose to identify fully with God by binding themselves to unswerving obedience to his mandates and commands. Their choice, in other words, would have been covenant-like, similar to the sort of mature communion that can develop between parents and their children.

So true human life, that is, truly abundant human life, is life lived in communion with God and other human beings. It is always covenantal or covenant-like, for it always involves crucial choices that circumscribe our freedom.[58]

The Lord's Invitation to Adam to Enter into Communion with Him

By issuing his categorical prohibition with its dire warning, the Lord God was enabling Adam to step into mature personhood. Without something like it, Adam could not have become a fully accountable person. Accountability requires that we be aware of limits we ought not to transgress. Maturity acknowledges and respects those limits.

Yet, as we have now seen, the Lord was offering Adam much more. He was inviting Adam to pledge his wholehearted, lifelong commitment to their fellowship. By addressing him and stipulating what he must not do, the Lord was giving Adam the opportunity to choose not only what he would do but also who he would be. As Adam's Creator, God had the right to require his obedience. Yet in issuing his command he was not just asserting his right. The transcendent God of creation was revealing himself also to be the immanent, personal God, who desires to be in face-to-face communion with human beings.[59]

In issuing his prohibition, God was in effect stepping back from our first parents and bidding them to choose to live in committed fellowship with him.[e] He was in effect placing himself before them and saying: "Behold, I stand at the door and knock. If anyone hears my voice and opens the door, I will come in to him and eat with him, and he with me" (Rev. 3:20). But communion with God requires keeping his commandments, as our Lord stressed:

> If you love me, you will keep my commandments. . . . Whoever has my commandments and keeps them, he it is who loves me. And he who loves me will be loved by my Father, and I will love him and manifest myself to him. . . . If anyone loves me, he will keep my word, and my Father will love him, and we will come to him and make our home with him. Whoever does not love me does not keep

---

e. While the command was issued to Adam while he was still alone, God intended it to apply to Eve as well, once she was created.

my words. And the word that you hear is not mine but the Father's who sent me. . . . I do as the Father has commanded me, so that the world may know that I love the Father. (John 14:15, 21, 23–24, 31)

Abide in my love. If you keep my commandments, you will abide in my love, just as I have kept my Father's commandments and abide in his love. . . . No longer do I call you servants, for the servant does not know what his master is doing; but I have called you friends, for all that I have heard from my Father I have made known to you. (John 15:9–10, 15)

The person who would walk in the garden in the cool of the day (see Gen. 3:8) was offering our first parents his friendship.[60] He was inviting them to ratify their love for him, to affirm their joy in his steady presence. The tree's fruit, "not in its own right, but as appointed to a function and carrying a word from God," confronted them "with God's will, particular and explicit, and [gave them] a decisive Yes or No to say with [their] whole being."[61] Its part was in the opportunity it offered rather than in any qualities it possessed. Obeying would not have deprived them of any true good.[62] Indeed, by enabling them to decide what their relationship to their God would be, the prohibition gave them *more* freedom, not less.

Our first parents' decision was to be their RSVP. They could secure truly abundant life only by decisively committing themselves always to obey God's command. They needed to respond to God's "You must never eat from that tree!" with a decisive "Yes, we will never eat from that tree!" Would they do so? Would they choose to gain human life's greatest possible good—deep personal communion with the Lord as real spiritual life, the only kind of life that ultimately matters for us because otherwise we become like beasts?[63] Or would they choose to throw it all away by disobeying him?

In issuing his command the Lord lifted his relationship with Adam and Eve out of the realm of mere duty, transferring it into the realm of true love, freely given in a love match. Their honoring his command by vowing never to eat from the forbidden tree would have been like honoring a wedding vow to forsake all others and be faithful to one another for as long as both would live.[64]

He was bidding them to make a glad surrender.

Acting and Living Humanly

We describe especially horrific acts—such as some Nazi medical experiments and the acts of some serial killers—as *inhuman*. They horrify us because they violate what we know should be the most binding prohibitions. Even if we have never heard them being explicitly prohibited, we know that some things should never be done by any human being.

More common acts—such as lying, cheating, or committing adultery—don't strike us the same way, although they still cross the line of what should never be done. Abimelech took Abraham's lie that Sarah was just his sister like that: "What have you done to us? And how have I sinned against you, that you have brought on me and my kingdom a great sin? *You have done to me things that ought not to be done*" (Gen. 20:9).

By pronouncing his Genesis 2 command and then holding Adam and Eve responsible to keep it, God was affirming their freedom. This indicated, as Dietrich Bonhoeffer observed, that they were human— in other words, they could be held accountable because they were free. Yet, Bonhoeffer continued, it was also part of Adam's humanity that God was commanding him to honor a specific *limit*. Distinctively human life is life that is to be freely lived within circumscribed limits.[65] We are the only earthly creatures who are subject to specific *shoulds* and *should nots*.

> I will instruct you and teach you in the way you should go;
>> I will counsel you with my loving eye on you.
> Do not be like the horse or the mule,
>> which have no understanding
> but must be controlled by bit and bridle
>> or they will not come to you. (Ps. 32:8–9 NIV)

These prescriptions and proscriptions outline the proper shape of our humanity, a shape we are accountable to keep. As created persons, we are free to decide if we will give our lives their proper shape.

Agreeing to be bound by the proper limits is covenantal or at least covenant-like. Six-year-old Billy might never explicitly say to his little sister Sally, "I promise not to hit you," but Sally will feel safe around him only if she senses that hitting her is something he is solemnly (if only implicitly) committed not to do.

These commitments circumscribe the living space of human communities, making room for community and communion. My resolving to treat you as I myself want to be treated contributes to the stability and continuity of our community.[f] Billy's resolution not to hit Sally allows their natural sibling relationship to grow so that over time it may blossom into an intimate and nourishing sibling friendship. The "I do's" of marriage, taken with full seriousness, explicitly define a relationship that can, over a lifetime, become the most intimate kind of human communion.

Making such agreements enables us to live and act humanly.

Life Centered in God

After creating and blessing our first parents, God specified their diet (see Gen. 1:29). Yet what they were to eat was not to be their most essential fare. As Jesus declared when the devil tempted him after forty days of fasting: "It is written, 'Man shall not live by bread alone, but by every word that comes from the mouth of God'" (Matt. 4:4, quoting Deut. 8:3). As created persons, our primary diet must be to feed on God's will as revealed in his word.[g] As Jesus said: "My food is to do the will of him who sent me and to accomplish his work" (John 4:34).[66]

Montaigne declared, "It is the proper office of a rational creature to obey."[67] God created us to listen to him and obey. Our lives become inhuman to the degree that we refuse.

The two trees at Eden's center (see Gen. 2:9; 3:3) convey what true human life must be. The tree of life stands for God and his word.[68] "At

---

f. "So whatever you wish that others would do to you, do also to them, for this is the Law and the Prophets" (Matt. 7:12).

g. Our word *diet* comes from the Latin word *diaeta*, meaning someone's "prescribed dietary regimen, from Greek *diaita*, literally, manner of living, from *diaitan* to arbitrate, govern, lead one's life" (*Merriam-Webster*, s.v. "diet," accessed November 9, 2021, https://unabridged.merriam-webster .com). We are to lead our lives by feeding on God's word.

the center of the world that has been put at Adam's disposal and over which Adam has been given dominion is not Adam himself," Bonhoeffer writes, "but God." God and his word were the fixed point around which Adam's freedom was to turn.[h] He was to live *from* that center by being oriented *toward* it, placing nothing else—including Eve!—at the center. The distinctive characteristic of human life as God intends it involves "utterly unbroken and unified obedience" to him, from whom and before whom we receive our life, "not as animals but as human beings," by living in fellowship with him. Human life is not primarily a biological quality we possess but "something given to humankind only in terms of its whole human existence."[69]

The placement of the tree of the knowledge of good and evil at the garden's center conveys the same truth. It emphasizes that "the human being's limit is at the center of human existence, not on the margin." We must not ask: What are we free *from*? but What are we free *for*? What is the *core* of our freedom? God created us with the freedom to hear and obey him and thus conform to the norms that define true humanity. "Knowledge of the boundary at the center" of human life, Bonhoeffer writes, "means knowing that the whole of [human] existence, . . . in every possible way that it may comport itself, has its [proper] limit." Created persons are called to govern their thoughts, desires, feelings, and behavior in ways that welcome whatever God permits and spurn whatever he prohibits (see 2 Cor. 10:5; Gal. 5:16–17; Eph. 2:1–10).

So, as Bonhoeffer concluded, "the *prohibition* in paradise [was actually] the *grace* of the Creator toward the creature" because "it is the basis of creatureliness and freedom." This implies, Blocher states, that we "cannot, *without destroying [ourselves]*, be anything other than what [we are] by God's decree."[70]

The two trees stood together, for God and his word "is at once the boundary and the center of our existence." When our first parents ate

---

h. Until the consummation, when Christ as the true morning star appears, God's words in Scripture are to function as the lamp by which we get our proper bearings for life (see 2 Tim. 3:14–17; 2 Pet. 1:19–21).

from the forbidden tree, true humanity disappeared. Human life lost its true center and became inhuman in the deepest and most tragic sense.

"DYING YOU SHALL DIE"

"When the woman saw that the fruit of the tree was good for food and pleasing to the eye, and also desirable for gaining wisdom, she took some and ate it. She also gave some to her husband, who was with her, and he ate it. Then the eyes of both of them were opened" (Gen. 3:6–7 NIV).

At first, it seemed as if the serpent had told the truth. As he claimed, Adam and Eve's eyes were opened, and they didn't immediately die. Yet this is the seminal instance of things not being as they seem.

Ruptured Communion

For while their eyes were now opened, they saw nothing good. Seeing their nakedness, they scrambled to cover themselves.[71] Eve had thought eating would bring pleasure and wisdom. She had sought to become shrewd only to discover that she was nude.[72]

Nakedness had crowned Eden's perfection. Now it became an imperfection that later in Scripture is linked with exposure and shame (see Gen. 9:22–23; Rev. 3:18; 16:15). Sexual differences meant to unite now divided. What had prompted rejoicing now abashed. The serpent's claim that they would become godlike in their knowledge became instead "the knowledge that they were no longer even like each other."[73] A world that had once been beautiful to see was now spoiled in the seeing (see Titus 1:15).

How did Adam and Eve respond to this unexpected turn of events? They self-medicated by covering up (see Gen. 3:7). In other words, they sought to block each other's gaze.

Was this because their disobedience produced shame? Blocher's answer is typical: "The narrative does not take up the word 'shame,' but the deliberate contrast between 3:7 and 2:25 suggests it immediately, and it is confirmed by the couple's behaviour. For what is shame, other than a feeling of embarrassment which makes us hide?"[4] "Sin's proper fruit," Kidner states, "is shame." Yet what their shame consisted in is puzzling. Perhaps, as Gerhard von Rad suggests, Adam and Eve began to experience "the loss of an inner unity, an unsurmountable contradiction at the basis of [their] existence." Perhaps they felt "something like a rift that [could] be traced to the depths of their being[,] . . . a grievous disruption" that now "governs the whole being of [each of us] from the lowest level of [our] corporeality" to the highest levels of our spirits.[75] We as their descendants know this to be true (see, e.g., Rom. 7:7–25). But Genesis remains remarkably restrained.

In any case, our first parents hid their most intimate parts. Their disobedience divided them from each other. We feel shame when some fault, imperfection, or vulnerability of ours conflicts with what we think we should be. Finding this shameful, we attempt to hide. We become uneasy in others' presence. We avoid looking in each other's eyes. Shame is interpersonal in the way it disrupts the kind of intimate and sympathetic face-to-face communion with other human beings that creates and sustains the personal life for which we have been made.[i]

Yet the disruption ran much deeper. "Shame in the form of embarrassment and inhibition," Wolff notes, "only penetrates the duality of man and woman as the result of their mistrust towards God and their disobedience towards his word."[76] While their transgression made them feel uneasy in each other's presence, "they were much more ashamed vis-à-vis the One who had given them the commandment."[77] They became aware of their guilty accountability. "Before the fall," as Herman Bavinck writes, "*there was . . . no gap between what they were and what they knew they had to be.* Being and self-consciousness were in harmony. But the fall produced separation," driving them "away from God, not toward him." Hearing him walking in the garden in the cool of the day, they hid from his presence among the garden's trees (see Gen. 3:8). The Hebrew reads "the man and his wife hid themselves *from the LORD God's face.*" "Shame

---

i. See chap. 3, 77, for more on this.

over their nakedness and [an unhealthy] fear of God," Bavinck observes, "are both rooted in their violation of the divine [command] and are proof that both their communion with each other and with God has been broken by sin."

Emotions like shame and fear outlast mere beliefs. They are harder to ignore. They are "the incurable stigmata of the Fall."[78] Adam's first words after eating the forbidden fruit—"I heard the sound of you in the garden, *and I was afraid*" (3:10)—identify an emotion that even now stubbornly witnesses to the fact that in disobeying God we transgress the limits of true human being.

Living Deaths

"The first doctrine to be denied" in Scripture, Kidner notes, "is judgment."[79] The serpent denied it in telling Eve that if she ate from the forbidden tree she would not die.

Genesis 3:8–19 is primarily a judgment scene tempered by mercy.[80] Adam's and Eve's replies to God's questions emphasize how devious and accusatory their own relationship had already become. Open, caring communication was over. Blocher calls God's warning in 2:17 "the protective clause of the first covenant."[81] Ironically, in disregarding it our first parents became self-protective—protecting themselves from each other and God. Their lives as healthy and whole persons in communion with other persons had come to an end.

Yet face-to-face communion with God and other human beings is the very essence of abundant and fully personal life. Our first parents' flight from God's face showed that their spiritual lifeline was broken. From the moment they ate from the forbidden tree, they were dead in their transgression and sin (see Rom. 5:12–19; 1 Cor. 15:21–22; Eph. 2:1–3). Granted, they did not die immediately. Their lives as biological creatures were temporarily and imperfectly sustained by their continuing to eat their earthly fare. Nor did their accountability cease. Yet they could no longer do what God required. They could no longer conform to the God-given limits that constituted true personhood and true human life. "In the Bible," Blocher writes, "death is the reverse of life—

it is not the reverse of existence. To die does not mean to cease to be, but in biblical terms it means [to be] 'cut off from the land of the living.'"[82] And

> since dying is still existing, other changes in existence will, by extension, be able to bear the name of "death." *In all experiences of pain, discomfort, discord and separation, we can recognize a kind of funeral procession.* . . . The narrative [of Genesis 3] shows us that the threat "You shall die" is fulfilled in a multiplicity of ways, by a whole succession of disastrous changes.

So God had not lied when he had declared, "When you eat from [the tree of the knowledge of good and evil] you will certainly die" (Gen. 2:17 NIV). Things were not as they initially seemed.

The New Testament declares, "The wages of sin is death" (Rom 6:23). This "corresponds to the . . . biblical theme of retribution: 'For the LORD is a God of retribution; he will *repay* in full' (Jer. 51:56 NIV)." The grammatical construction of the phrase, "he will repay in full" is the same as both the permissive and the warning clauses in Genesis 2:16–17. It is known as the *infinitive absolute*, which strengthens and intensifies the action. In Jeremiah 51 it may be rendered as "PAYING he will repay." In Genesis 2:16–17, it can be rendered as "EATING you may eat" and "DYING you shall die" (NIV).[83]

The full implications of God's warning that in the day Adam would eat of the forbidden tree, "DYING he would die" only "slowly unfold," Kidner observes, "in the last pages of the New Testament."[84] There we learn what it has cost God to redeem human beings as well as how those who remain rebellious will finally be thrown in "the lake that burns with fire and sulfur, which is the second death" (Rev. 21:8). That will be the final death—the death that comes after the usually slow process of biological decay. It will exclude any hope of ever partaking of God's saving mercy, of ever regaining communion with him. It will complete the process that began when our first parents ate the forbidden fruit.

From that initial act of rebellion onward, all human beings have been born spiritually dead, estranged from God's life-giving presence (see, e.g., Eph. 2:1–10).[85] We are now like zombies. Unless we have been born again (see John 3:3), we are just "animated corpses"—even though we continue to move about, we are just the "walking dead," no matter how healthy we seem. We are no longer capable of fulfilling the purpose for which God created us.

So how is our suffering relevant to this? As we are about to see, it is often only as suffering strikes us at a deeper, more fundamental level than mere thinking and daily living that we realize how desperate our condition is. God intends our suffering to prompt us to embrace his saving and sanctifying grace. As the apostle Paul said in a somewhat different context, "The kind of sorrow God wants us to experience leads us away from sin and results in salvation" (2 Cor. 7:10 NLT; cf. Deut. 4:30–31). My next two chapters explain how and why this is.

3

SUFFERING

What It Is and How It Affects Us

The Lord God said to the serpent, "Because you have done this,
cursed are you above all livestock and
above all beasts of the field. . . .
I will put enmity between you and the woman,
and between your offspring and her offspring;
he shall bruise your head, and you shall bruise his heel."
To the woman he said, "I will surely multiply
your pain in childbearing;
in pain you shall bring forth children.
Your desire shall be contrary to your husband,
but he shall rule over you."
And to Adam he said, "Because you have
listened to the voice of your wife
and have eaten of the tree of which I commanded you,
'You shall not eat of it,'
cursed is the ground because of you;
in pain you shall eat of it all the days of your life. . . .

By the sweat of your face you shall eat bread,
till you return to the ground,

<blockquote>

for out of it you were taken;

for you are dust, and to dust you shall return."

Genesis 3:14–19

</blockquote>

<blockquote>

For the moment all discipline seems painful rather than pleasant,

but later it yields the peaceful fruit of righteousness

to those who have been trained by it.

Hebrews 12:11

</blockquote>

So far, we have surveyed the first two parts of the full Christian story. In the next chapter we will consider the third and fourth parts: *redemption* and *consummation*. As we will see, redemption began when God spoke a solemn word of promise—an explicitly covenantal word[a]—that led Adam and Eve to trust him again, leading them and some of their descendants to begin calling on his name (see Gen. 3:15 and 4:26). As God revealed more of his redemptive plan first to his Old and then to his New Testament people, their faith in him and his word gave them greater and more specific hopes. We now hope for the return of our Lord Jesus Christ, knowing that we will enjoy full communion with God only at the consummation.

Once Adam and Eve began to trust God again, they regained real spiritual life, although it was not the life they had known in Eden. The inauguration of redemption did not reinstate creation's pristine state. After they opened the door to human suffering by their disobedience, the way forward to the establishment of full communion with God became a pathway strewn with suffering and death, culminating in the

---

a. As Daniel Block makes clear, after Adam and Eve broke their natural relationship with God by eating from the forbidden tree, all of God's overtures "to create and maintain relationship with his fallen creation" are not just covenant-like but are and must be explicitly covenantal. Daniel I. Block, *Covenant: The Framework of God's Grand Plan of Redemption* (Grand Rapids, MI: Baker Academic, 2021), 4.

suffering and death of our Lord.[1] We too are on this path, for the inauguration of redemption extends from the end of Genesis 3 to the Christian story's final part portrayed in Revelation 21–22 as the consummation of all things. In the meantime, all of us will suffer in some degree (see, e.g., Job 14:1–2; John 16:33; Acts 14:19–22; Rom. 8:16–22).

Most of us recognize when music is dissonant or when it is being played in a minor key. It sounds jarring, sad, somber, mysterious, or ominous, evoking feelings such as fear, horror, grief, melancholy, perplexity, or foreboding.[2] Suffering is life's dissonances and minor keys. Encountering it—ranging from mild dissonances lasting only moments to prolonged excursions in a minor key that suggest that the world has gone radically awry—is unpleasant, to say the least. Yet such experiences are crucial to our grasping our true situation as sinful human beings living in a sin-damaged world.

TWO CRUCIAL INSIGHTS

Our survey of the first two parts of the full Christian story allows us to harvest two crucial insights that counter very common reactions to suffering.

1. God Is Not to Be Blamed for Our Suffering

As I wrote in *When the Stars Disappear*, we are needy, "wanty" creatures who are constantly seeking various goods—things like air, food, water, shelter, safety, health, love, and happiness. In order to secure these goods, we must learn how to lead our lives so we can navigate through life in ways that are likely to obtain them. Learning to lead our lives involves learning to orient ourselves in terms of two different kinds of stories: a *personal story* about what our individual lives mean and a *general story* about what human life means. These stories set the stars that must guide us in place so that we are not lost on what would otherwise be uncharted seas.

Significant suffering tends to affront or offend us, striking us as something that should not be. This can impact the sort of general story we are inclined to accept and thus obscure some of the stars that may have been guiding us, for it can prompt us to doubt whether God exists. We may find ourselves asking, Would a good and all-powerful God have created a world where *this*—whatever sort of suffering it is—exists?

Yet the first two parts of the full Christian story counter this question. They suggest that our reaction to suffering may in fact arise from a very deep and basic part of ourselves that recognizes that human suffering is inconsistent with our world as a good, all-powerful God would have created it to be.[3] They tell us that human suffering was not in fact part of our world as God made it. It isn't "natural" to our world, having only entered through Adam and Eve's disobedience. So God is not to be blamed for it.

2. Atheists' Outrage at Suffering Cannot Justify Their Atheism

Moreover, atheists can't properly be affronted or offended by the world's pain in a way that justifies their atheism. For being affronted or offended involves believing that some person has done something he or she shouldn't have done.[4] I may be *frustrated* by my TV's remote not working, but because it isn't a person it can't affront or offend me because it isn't *doing* anything. While my remote may malfunction, it can't misbehave.

The world's pain can't affront or offend atheists because they don't believe there is a personal God who can be blamed for its pain. They take pain as an inevitable part of the evolutionary rise of animate life, one of the "survival mechanisms" of our world's life forms. Yet since they deny God's existence, they can't be affronted or offended by the way pain came to be. Since only persons can affront or offend us, an atheist's being affronted or offended by the fact that the world is full of pain is inconsistent with what he or she *doesn't* believe![5]

How we regard the world's pain should be determined by the general story we accept. General stories ultimately explain the world either "top down" or "bottom up"—either in terms of a person (or, for Christians, three persons) who created the world for some reason or in terms of impersonal natural laws accidentally producing increasingly complex kinds of beings.[6] The impersonal bottom-up perspective got its biggest boost from Darwin's *On the Origin of Species*, which for the first time made plausible—if still unproven—suggestions about how we could have arisen from lower life forms naturally, how creatures like us could have been "thrown up out of the blindfolded thrashings of evolution."[7] Until then, there was not even a remotely plausible biological explanation of the proverbial phylogenetic tree.[b]

Christianity's top-down story traces the origin of all human suffering back to our first parents' disobedience, which cut them off from the sort of abundant life for which they had been made. Suffering was then inevitable, given what disobeying God brings.

Judging the Christian explanation of human suffering unsatisfying doesn't mean it actually is. As Samuel Johnson said: "Sir, I have found you an argument; but I am not obliged to find you an understanding!"[8] In fact, we should expect that the biblical explanation of the presence of suffering in our world will be unsatisfying to those who are still out of sync with God and his purposes.

MORE SUFFERING

In chapter 2 we saw that Adam and Eve's disobedience to God's command not to eat from the forbidden tree ruptured their relationship with God, resulting in spiritual death. This is the greatest catastrophe humans can suffer, since we were made for everlasting communion with him. Biological death followed ineluctably on the spiritual death that our first parents bequeathed to all human beings (see, e.g., Gen. 5:5, 8, 11, 14; Rom. 5:12; Heb. 9:27). Yet it didn't follow immediately. In fact, Adam and Eve's earthly lives would continue for many years (see Gen. 5:1–5).

The Root of Human Suffering

When our first parents disobeyed God's commandment, their eyes indeed were opened, just as the serpent had said, but not, as he claimed, so that they now saw themselves to be like God. They saw only their

---

b. A phylogenetic tree—or "tree of life"—purports to show the biological relationships among all of the various kinds and species of earthly life.

nakedness. This drove them to make garments to shield themselves from each other.

Their desperate action showed that God's well-ordered creation was now profoundly disordered. As we saw in chapters 1 and 2, God created us to crown his creation, to be the earthly creatures with whom he could communicate and thus be in personal communion, and who would then be his earthly representatives—his images and echoes on earth. All of God's creative acts in Genesis 1—from verse 3's "Let there be light" through verse 11's "Let the earth sprout vegetation" to verse 21's "So God created the great sea creatures and every living creature that moves, with which the waters swarm"—prepared the earth for our creation.

Once he created us, God saw the whole creation to be "very good" (1:31). Everything was now well ordered (2:1). From its commencement in the regular alternation of night and day (see 1:5) up to us as creation's crown, creation was now configured to manifest a pattern of structurally ordered obedience to God and his word. This made the creation a *cosmos*—a "universe conceived as an orderly and harmonious system."[c]

Our first parents' disobedience fractured creation's order and harmony at its most crucial point by destroying the integrity of our personal relations. This manifested itself immediately in Adam and Eve's horror at their nakedness. The Hebrew word for their nakedness before the fall differs from the word for their nakedness after, indicating how their eyes were opened. The word at 2:25 is *'arom*, which in context means simply to be uncovered. But the word for *naked* in Genesis 3 is *'erom*, which in Deuteronomy depicts "the state of Israel's exiles who have been punished for their failure to trust and obey God's word."[9] This suggests that the author's use of different words in Genesis 2 and 3 provides "a subtle yet perceptible clue to the

---

c. *Merriam-Webster*, s.v. "cosmos," accessed November 9, 2021, https://unabridged.merriam-webster.com. The entry continues by saying that the universe, so defined, is "contrasted with *chaos*," which is significant in the light of Isa. 45:18 (NLT): "The Lord is God, and he created the heavens and earth and put everything in place. *He made the world to be lived in, not to be a place of empty chaos.*" More on this contrast in chap. 4.

story's meaning. The effect of the Fall was not simply that the man and the woman came to know" that they were uncovered in the Genesis 2 sense. "Specifically, they came to know that they were ['naked'] in the sense of being 'under God's judgment.'"

Their nakedness in Genesis 2 had produced no shame because Adam and Eve had done nothing that could produce a sense of exposure and judgment. The Hebrew word for *shame* in Genesis 2 means to "be ashamed *before one another*."[10] Shame can produce intense suffering because it involves "the notion of an audience . . . [with] the thought that eyes are upon one,"[11] where our faults and flaws are in some sense "visible" and being judged "through the eyes of another." Before they disobeyed, there was nothing faulty or flawed about Adam and Eve that could produce shame.

Genesis 3:7 observes that when they realized they were *'erom*, "they sewed fig leaves together and made themselves loincloths." This act, Wenham comments, "though somewhat ineffective, . . . suggests urgency and desperation; the innocent serenity of 2:25 is shattered." It also explains why, when they heard the sound of the Lord God walking in the garden in the cool of the day, they hid from him among Eden's trees.

Yet the worst effects of their disobedience were not those that an eyewitness of the scene in Genesis 3 would have actually seen. The worst effects involved invisible disturbances within them that were no doubt experienced as piercing pangs of conscience. This would have included their guilt and regret for having rebelled against God's command, and perhaps the loss of a sense of inner unity due to their realizing that they could no longer rule over their desires as they should.[d] Their scramble to cover themselves suggests that they had become suspicious of each other. Adam's reply to God's question, "Who told you that you were naked? Have you eaten of the tree of which I commanded you not to eat?" was that "the woman whom you gave to be with me, she gave me fruit of the tree, and I ate," indicating that he blamed both God and Eve

---

d. See chap. 2, 67, and note 75.

for the disaster that had befallen him (Gen. 3:11–12). And Eve's reply to God's question in 3:13, "What is this that you have done?" that the serpent had deceived her betrays her awareness that she had been taken in. Perhaps they realized, when it was too late, that what they had done indeed deserved death (see Rom. 1:32; 6:20–23).[12]

Multiplied Pains

Adam and Eve's disobedience is thus the root of all human suffering. Yet then, perhaps surprisingly, God intervened and sentenced them to more suffering:

The LORD God said to the serpent,

> "Because you have done this,
>> cursed are you above all livestock
>> and above all beasts of the field;
> on your belly you shall go,
>> and dust you shall eat
>> all the days of your life.
> I *will put enmity* between you and the woman,
>> and between your offspring and her offspring;
> he shall bruise your head,
>> and you shall bruise his heel."

To the woman he said,

> "I *will surely multiply* your pain in childbearing;
>> in pain you shall bring forth children.
> Your desire shall be contrary to your husband,
>> but he shall rule over you."

And to Adam he said,

> "Because you have listened to the voice of your wife
>> and have eaten of the tree
> of which I commanded you,
>> 'You shall not eat of it,'

cursed is the ground because of you;
> in pain you shall eat of it all the days of your life;
thorns and thistles it shall bring forth for you;
> and you shall eat the plants of the field.
By the sweat of your face
> you shall eat bread,
till you return to the ground,
> for out of it you were taken;
for you are dust,
> and to dust you shall return." (Gen. 3:14–19)

Here three phrases reveal that God was deliberately increasing our first parents' suffering.[e] First, he said to the serpent, "*I will put enmity* between you and the woman, and between your offspring and her offspring." The New Living Translation reads, "*I will cause hostility* between you and the woman, and between your offspring and her offspring." There can be no stronger assertion of God's personal agency than for him to say, "I will put" or "I will cause."

Second, God said to the woman, "*I will surely multiply* your pain in childbearing." These words have the same grammatical construction as the words found in Genesis 2:16–17 that we have seen are best translated as "EATING you will eat" and "DYING you will die." So here we should translate, "MULTIPLYING I will multiply your pain in childbearing; in pain you will bring forth children."[13] The pain Eve would now experience in childbearing would be part of her lifelong process of dying. And once again this "I will" is as strong an assertion of God's personal agency as can be.

Whether God's next statement—"Your desire shall be contrary to your husband, but he shall rule over you"—involved God's deliberately increasing the woman's suffering by giving the man a new kind of authority over her or whether this conflict was a natural result of

---

e. God is, in fact, referred to throughout this passage as the "Lord God." Since the ESV's small-caps Lord stands for Yahweh, his covenant-making name, this implies that God was addressing Adam and Eve personally and thus taking steps to bring them back into a saving relationship with himself.

the woman's disobedience is debatable.[14] In either case, it indicates that there is always going to be some conflict—and thus suffering—in our homes.[15]

Third, the Lord God said to the man, "*Cursed is the ground* because of you."[16] So painful toil became necessary if Adam was to secure the food he and his family would need—or, as the New Living Translation renders it, "All your life you will struggle to scratch a living" from the earth.

So in addition to the suffering that followed inevitably from their disobedience, God sentenced our first parents—and, through them, us (see Rom. 5:12, 14–18; 1 Cor. 15:22)—to even more suffering. His sentences struck at the heart of who each was meant to be. The woman would suffer most acutely in childbearing and most constantly as helper and wife. The man would suffer as worker and as his family's provider.[17] The pangs of conscience that struck Adam and Eve as soon as they disobeyed would have faded over time, but these sorts of suffering are chronic and unavoidable.[18] Our first parents were doomed to suffer virtually every day of their lives—and ever since suffering and death dog us all.[19]

Why did God do this? Why did he increase human suffering and pain? To answer these questions requires us to understand what suffering is and how it affects us.

WHAT IS SUFFERING?

We suffer whenever we experience anything that is either unpleasant enough or harmful enough that we want it to end.

Why characterize suffering this way?

Suppose . . .

Suppose your life is proceeding normally and then you get a mild headache. Usually we want headaches to end because their unpleasantness unsettles us as we feel and anticipate continuing to feel the pain.

But now suppose that when you have previously gotten mild headaches, they occasionally have grown into full-blown migraines that landed you moaning on your stomach in bed. Then what would getting a mild headache do to you? You would find it unsettling in a way going beyond the disagreeableness arising directly from the pain. For now that pain might not be the whole story. Given what has sometimes happened before, it would no longer be merely a matter of your hurting in a particular way. Now your headache could possibly be heralding something worse to come—greater pain, and perhaps disabling pain. That would make your getting a mild headache now more than mildly unpleasant by adding the anxiety of wondering what the near future might bring.

Now vary the picture again. Suppose you (like one of my former students) had a brain tumor several years ago that first manifested itself in mild headaches that eventually became severe migraines. Surgery removed it, with radiation therapy following, but there was no guarantee it wouldn't regrow. If you were to get a headache now, especially if it seemed to be threatening to grow into a migraine, then how would that tend to affect you? Unless you were certain this headache was not being caused by the tumor's regrowth, it would be unpleasant in a new way. Now your primary concern would not be whether you might soon be feeling greater pain. You would want to know if your life was at risk. Your future would darken, seeming shorter and more ominous. You would become unsure about how your life's story might end. Distant pleasures, such as attending a toddler's college graduation, would no longer seem inevitable. Nearer ones, such as planning to buy something next week that you really want, would lose some appeal. In fact, some pleasures might not seem worth pursuing at all.

If you were to learn that this headache was in fact being caused by the tumor's regrowth, then you might start questioning some of your more significant beliefs. You might start doubting God's power or goodness. Knowing the tumor had regrown would threaten many of your hopes, plans, and dreams. And if you became convinced it was going to kill you, then you would probably start feeling grief.

The Nature of Suffering

We can mine some useful generalizations about suffering from these possibilities. For instance, we can rank having a mild headache and feeling deep grief on a vertical scale where the center represents experiences that are neither pleasant nor unpleasant and the termini represent what is extremely pleasant and extremely unpleasant. Then having a mild headache, being deeply depressed, and feeling inconsolable grief will all fall below the scale's center point, with feeling such grief ranging much closer to *extremely unpleasant* than having a mild headache, as portrayed on this scale:

Feeling great joy	↑ Extremely pleasant
Having a loving marriage	
Regularly doing rewarding work	
Rejoicing in a child's success	
Getting a promotion	
Feeling welcomed	
Having a really nice day	
Enjoying a good workout	
Tasting something delicious	
	Neither pleasant nor unpleasant
Having a couple of mosquito bites	
Having a mild headache	
Having an unpleasant day of work	
Feeling ostracized	
Having a migraine	
Being very worried for a child	
Being deeply depressed	
Being unsure you will live	
Feeling inconsolable grief	↓ Extremely unpleasant

We can also rank our lives' events as more or less beneficial or harmful, regardless of how they feel. Sometimes something may be happening to us that doesn't feel unpleasant, yet it is harmful. For instance, there are some kinds of dementia that aren't unpleasant to those suffering from them but which disrupt their lives so significantly that anyone aware of their condition would say they are suffering and want that suffering to end. Moreover, all of us have suffered the loss of unhindered communication with God, yet none of us feels that loss to be as harmful as it is.

We shouldn't ignore these kinds of suffering, but the kinds that are most relevant to us right now are those that feel unpleasant. What do they suggest about the nature of suffering?

First, suffering's unpleasantness usually unsettles us. Of course, we wouldn't describe the anxiety involved in learning that a brain tumor had regrown as merely unpleasant. *Unpleasant* would be too mild a term for that. But most suffering is unpleasant in the sense that we don't like it.

Yet an experience must be more than merely unpleasant for us to call it suffering. Most of us dislike having a few mosquito bites, yet they aren't unpleasant enough for us to say we are suffering. So, second, an experience involves suffering only if it exceeds a certain threshold of unpleasantness, one we can specify only roughly as our finding it unpleasant enough that we really want it to end.

Third, similar experiences are more or less unpleasant to different people at different times. What one person counts as suffering or as significant suffering may not strike someone else in the same way.[20] Young children usually suffer when they lose a puppy, while adult dog breeders probably find such losses merely unpleasant. Likewise, a secure adult may find being taunted on the Internet by teenagers to be insignificant, while a child may feel it to be so unpleasant that she would rather kill herself than face it again.[21]

Fourth, suffering may be physical or psychological. Mild headaches are physical pains that may not ruffle us psychologically. The anxiety felt when we are worried about a child or when we are struggling to complete a crucial task is primarily psychological. Some suffering is both psychological and physical. For example, the emotional horror parents feel upon hearing that a child has committed suicide is usually accompanied by something like a sick stomach, which (those parents tell me) sometimes develops into a kind of physical ache that lasts for months or years. Conversely, the physical pain caused by migraines may become increasingly more consequential psychologically as the dread of getting new ones grows.

Finally, we may take something to be real suffering and yet choose to endure it, even though, considered by itself, we definitely would want it to end. Athletes endure suffering, as the author of Hebrews reminded his readers when he was urging them to continue running the race God had set before them (see Heb. 12:1–12). His readers needed encouragement because their race included divinely ordained disciplinary suffering.[22] God's discipline was, of course, good (see Heb. 12:5–6, 10; cf. Deut. 8:16). It meant God was treating them as his children (see Heb. 12:7 with Deut. 8:5). Yet while it is happening, "all discipline seems *painful* rather than *pleasant*" (Heb. 12:11)[23]—and hence those experiencing it needed encouragement not to do whatever they could to make it end, even though to the degree that it was painful, they wanted it to end (see vv. 3, 12).

So suffering involves unpleasantness that comes in various degrees and kinds. Some of it is so negligible that we barely care if it ends, and some is so overwhelming that it feels as if we can't survive another moment of it.

HOW SUFFERING AFFECTS US

Suffering affects us in primarily two ways. Both lend themselves to the metaphor of the stars that orient our lives disappearing.

It Obscures Life's Stars by Tempering Our Happiness

Suffering affects us directly and immediately by tempering our happiness. As it does so, life's guiding stars can begin to disappear. A headache's disagreeableness can't be evaded. We feel badly and want it to end. This discourages us because our lives are usually pleasant, as Scripture suggests (see Acts 14:17).[24]

So suffering disturbs and unsettles us by obscuring the normal horizon of our lives—our sense of well-being. It throws us off course, forcing us to hear life's dissonances and minor keys.[25] Even a mild confrontation with a colleague makes us uneasy and perhaps a bit restless. More severe suffering can dominate our minds, making us miserable and driving awareness of anything else away.

Mild or severe, suffering casts clouds over life whenever it occurs. Newborns suffer in this sense. Animals do too.

It Disrupts Our Lives and Disorients Us

Suffering often affects us in a more distinctively human way. It can disrupt our lives and disorient us by challenging the stories we tell ourselves about what life means.

It can challenge our personal stories. Our personal stories orient us by setting in place the stars that chart our life trajectories. These trajectories start with our birth, progress through the present, and project outward into futures where we try to secure what we want and need.[f] Our personal stories may be more or less detailed, but no human being can lead a distinctively human life without one. Scripture has preserved some fairly detailed personal stories in books like Ruth, Job, and Jeremiah. It tells us about the lives of people like Joseph, David, Elijah, Elisha, and the apostle Paul, and it gives us the unique story of our Lord. All of these stories involve personal suffering.

Getting a headache shows how suffering can challenge our personal stories. Having a mild headache wouldn't affect your story much at all. By itself, it wouldn't be likely to alter your story's trajectory; you would probably just continue doing what you had planned even though you were a bit uncomfortable, so it wouldn't eclipse any of the stars that are guiding you. But getting a full-blown migraine that landed you moaning on your stomach in bed would disrupt your story's short-range trajectory concerning your plans for later today. It could also disorient you if it left you worrying that you might get another, and thus leave you uncertain about what a future including migraines would mean. Having a migraine that you learned was caused by a brain tumor would disrupt your long-range trajectory. It would almost certainly disorient you because you could no longer be sure of what the future might bring.

---

f. See Mark Talbot, *When the Stars Disappear: Help and Hope from Stories of Suffering in Scripture* (Wheaton, IL: Crossway, 2020), 20–21.

By eclipsing the stars by which we are guiding our personal lives, suffering shows us that our lives are not entirely in our own hands. Yet even the disappearance of those stars may not be deeply disorienting if we, like Paul, remain convinced that God is still providentially guiding us along our earthly way.[g]

But suffering can also challenge our faith in God's providence. Profound suffering can prompt us to reconsider the general story we have been telling ourselves regarding what human life means. It can blot out all the stars that we have been relying upon to guide us on life's way.

For instance, my student Graham's parents' perplexity and sorrow over his struggle and suicide have made life feel so catastrophic that they cannot imagine how his death could ever be part of any "overwhelming victory" that will one day be theirs through Christ (Rom. 8:37 NLT).[h] How could this turn of events involve God being good to him and them (see Rom. 8:28)? Their insistent, unanswered questions about God's apparent indifference to Graham's struggle and death have left them profoundly disoriented, disrupting their ability to find a way to move forward as Christians.

We all must subscribe to some general story about the ultimate meaning of human life that serves as the backdrop for our personal stories. As we have seen, these stories ultimately explain the world—and thus the ultimate meaning of human life—either top down or bottom up, either in terms of a person who created the world for some reason or in terms of impersonal natural laws that have accidentally produced us. Suffering shouldn't impact anyone's belief in a bottom-up story because it is just one more product of the ultimately meaningless interaction of

---

g. See Talbot, *When the Stars Disappear*, 19–23.

h. For Graham's story, see Talbot, *When the Stars Disappear*, chap. 1. Here is my characterization of *profound suffering* from that volume, pp. 14–15:

Profound suffering involves experiencing something so deep and disruptive that it dominates our consciousness and threatens to overwhelm us, often tempting us to lose hope that our lives can ever be good again. Both acute calamities (such as losing a child to suicide) and chronic conditions (such as the day-by-day care of a severely disabled child or Graham's seemingly never-ending struggle with depression) can produce profound suffering.

When suffering tempts Christians to lose hope that our lives can ever be good again, it challenges our faith in the general story about the meaning of human life that we have believed up until now and which has been the source of our hopes.

impersonal, purposeless natural laws. Yet belief in a bottom-up story can affect your personal story because you might decide that since nothing we do ultimately makes any difference, there is no good reason why, if you are suffering, you shouldn't just end it all now.

Only believers in top-down stories—and, more specifically, some monotheistic story that portrays God as intending human life to have some ultimate significance—are likely to find that profound suffering may threaten their general beliefs. For then they may ask, Would a good and all-powerful God create a world where *this*—whatever sort of profound suffering it is—takes place? When profound suffering threatens to destroy our belief in a top-down story that we have been relying upon to guide us on our earthly ways, all the stars of faith and hope can disappear.[i]

From Disorientation to Reorientation

As sinners living in a sinful world, even we Christians tend to believe general stories that distort the truth. For instance, even we may be prone to believe the false story that one important measure of human life is how much someone owns (see Luke 12:13–21; James 2:1–4). This may have been true for the writer of Psalm 119. The psalm's complex acrostic structure shows he was well educated, and the fact that he had the leisure to compose such a poem may suggest he was wealthy.[26] His life before he wrote his poem may have been very pleasant, tempting him to trust that his wealth would bring him life's best things.[j] As long as his life went smoothly, he didn't keep God's word and was inattentive to God's statutes. But then God afflicted him. Initially, this may have been deeply disorienting if he was trusting in his wealth. But ultimately it reoriented him by dimming his faith in the stars that his wealth had set in place. It led him to start seeing and loving God's word for what it actually is.

And so his suffering, which he knew came from God,[k] didn't ultimately tell against God's goodness. It was a sign of it.

---

i. See Talbot, *When the Stars Disappear*, 20–23.

j. This seems likely given how he ultimately views wealth in vv. 72, 127, and 162. Proverbs counsels us to value divinely revealed wisdom and understanding more than any degree of worldly wealth (see Prov. 3:13–15; 8:10, 11, 12–19).

k. "I know, O Lord, that . . . in faithfulness you have afflicted me" (Ps. 119:75).

We also often assume we control our lives in ways we do not (see James 4:13–16), crediting our power, our industriousness, our intelligence, our winsomeness, or whatever, for our good fortune, rather than acknowledging that all true blessings come from God (see 1 Chron. 29:14; Isa. 26:12; John 3:27; 1 Cor. 4:7).

From the moment our first parents rebelled, wanting to judge for themselves what is good and what is evil, we have been prone to distortions like these.[27] This led Moses to warn the Israelites that once they were settled in the promised land and had become prosperous with lives that were relatively trouble-free, they would tend to forget their Lord and begin crediting themselves for their prosperity:

> Take care lest you forget the LORD your God by not keeping his commandments and his rules and his statutes, which I command you today, lest, when you have eaten and are full and have built good houses and live in them, and when your herds and flocks multiply and your silver and gold is multiplied and all that you have is multiplied, then your heart be lifted up, and you forget the LORD your God. . . . *Beware lest you say in your heart, "My power and the might of my hand have gotten me this wealth."*

"You shall remember the LORD your God," Moses concluded, "for it is he who gives you power to get wealth, that he may confirm his covenant that he swore to your fathers, as it is this day" (Deut. 8:11–14a, 17–18).

When our lives are going well, life's fleeting goods can shine so brightly that they obscure the stars that should be guiding us. Almost two centuries ago, Søren Kierkegaard put it like this:

> When the prosperous man on a dark but starlit night drives comfortably in his carriage and has the lanterns lighted, aye, then he is safe, he fears no difficulty, he carries his light with him, and it is not dark close around him.
>
> But precisely because he has the lanterns lighted, and has a strong light close to him, precisely for this reason, he cannot see the stars. For his lights obscure the stars, which the poor peasant, driving without lights, can see gloriously in the dark but starry night.

So those deceived ones live in the temporal existence: either, occupied with the necessities of life, they are too busy to avail themselves of the view, or in their prosperity and good days they have, as it were, lanterns lighted, and close about them everything is so satisfactory, so pleasant, so comfortable—but the view is lacking, the prospect, the view of the stars.[28]

Suffering may temporarily eclipse the stars that should be guiding us, but by dimming our temporal happiness, it can ultimately make those stars shine more brightly.

In other words, when we are in danger of forgetting God and his ways, he may mercifully call us back to himself through suffering—"Before I was afflicted I went astray, but now I obey your word" (Ps. 119:67 NIV). As C. S. Lewis emphasized:

Pain insists upon being attended to. God whispers to us in our pleasures, speaks in our conscience, but shouts in our pain: it is His megaphone to rouse a deaf world. A bad man, happy, is a man without the least inkling that his actions do not "answer," that they are not in accord with the laws of the universe.[29]

In one psalm, David tells us that God kept a heavy hand on him when he wouldn't confess his sin, sapping his strength by making him suffer. Then, when he finally confessed, God forgave him and lifted his hand (see Ps. 32:1–5).

As we shall see in the next chapter, God often keeps his people close to himself by means of life's pains and toils. This may involve chronic suffering that keeps us living in some minor key. Or it may involve experiencing some great sorrow—some great dissonance—that blares out at us, jarring us into awareness that what we have been trusting can't be relied upon. Suffering can teach us to look to God for every good thing (see Ps. 90:13–17).

Lewis put it like this:

The Christian doctrine of suffering explains . . . a very curious fact about the world we live in. The settled happiness and security which we all desire, God withholds from us by the very nature of the world: but joy, pleasure, and merriment, He has scattered broadcast. We are never safe, but we have plenty of fun, and some ecstasy. It is not hard to see why. The security we crave would teach us to rest our hearts in this world and [act as] an obstacle to our return to God: a few moments of happy love, a landscape, a symphony, a merry meeting with our friends, a bath or a football match, have no such tendency. Our Father refreshes us on the journey with some pleasant inns, but will not encourage us to mistake them for home.

Late in his life when he and his loved ones were suffering in various ways, Lewis observed that we should live in "cheerful insecurity." This, he said, is one of "the simplest and earliest Christian lessons," but one we usually come to learn "late and surprised."[30]

We should also remember, as we shall see reiterated in the next chapter, that some of the suffering we experience is part of what God has added to our world as punishment for sin.[31] Yet seeing some of our suffering as punishment, Lewis noted, can actually make it more bearable:

Christ said it was difficult for "the rich" to enter the Kingdom of Heaven. . . . I think [this] covers riches in every sense—good fortune, health, popularity, and all the things one wants to have. All these things tend—just as money does—to make you feel independent of God, because if you have them you are happy already and contented in this life. You don't want to turn away to anything more, and so you try to rest in a shadowy happiness as if it could last for ever. But God wants to give you a real and eternal happiness. Consequently, he may have to take all these "riches" away from you: if He doesn't, you will go on relying on them. It sounds cruel, doesn't it? But I am beginning to find out that what people call the cruel doctrines are really the kindest ones in the long run. I used to think it was a "cruel" doctrine to say that troubles and sorrows were "punishments." But I find in practice that when you are in trouble, the moment you regard it as a "punishment," it becomes easier to bear. If you think of this world as a place intended simply for our happiness, you find it quite intolerable: think of it as a place of training and correction and it's not so bad.

Imagine a set of people all living in the same building. Half of them think it is a hotel, the other half think it is a prison. Those who think it a hotel might regard it as quite intolerable, and those who thought it was a prison might decide that it was really surprisingly comfortable. So that what seems the ugly doctrine is the one that comforts and strengthens you in the end. The people who try to hold an optimistic view of this world would become pessimists: the people who hold a pretty stern view of it become optimistic.[32]

Sin blinds. We never feel adequately life's greatest tragedy—our loss of communion with God. Yet suffering strikes near enough to our hearts to help us avoid being too contented with anything less. The suffering God added to human life in Genesis 3:14–19 prompts us to look up and reconsider what our lives are meant to be.

Scripture declares that the day of final judgment, when Jesus will judge everything we have done and left undone during our earthly lives, will come like a thief in the night (see Mark 13:32–37; Luke 21:34–36; 1 Thess. 5:1–2). It will be too late to repent then. Suffering prompts us to reconsider our lives now, before it is too late. It can burn the fat off our hearts, teaching us by God's grace to delight in his ways (see Ps. 119:69–70).[33] It can set us on a quest for understanding that leads us to love him, his commandments, and his word in a way that involves far more than our seeking simply to end our suffering (see Ps. 119:73–74). It can encourage us to set the right stars in place. Insofar as God uses our suffering to bring us back to himself and to hope in the glories that await those who love him, we can indeed affirm with the psalmist, "You *are* good and *do* good. . . . I know, O Lord, . . . that in faithfulness you have afflicted me" (Ps. 119:68, 75).

A STORY SHAKEN THOUGH NOT ABANDONED

The full Christian story sometimes affirms, sometimes supplements, sometimes enhances, and sometimes counters the stories we usually accept. It affirms our expectations about nature's regularities.[l] It supplements empirical psychology's story about life's usual pleasantness by telling us that God reveals himself and his goodness through life's ordinary pleasures (see Acts 14:8–18). It enhances our sense of our unique place in the world by telling a theological story about human personhood that distinguishes us from the rest of creation in ways that the standard evolutionary story cannot.[34] And it counters a story most of us are inclined to believe—namely, the story that if God is good, then he won't let us suffer too much—by telling a much larger, longer, and more subtle story. That story explains that God has planned from eternity past to defeat what is truly evil by making it an essential element in a much greater and everlasting good, a good won through the innocent suffering and death of our Lord.

Yet suffering may still disorient us. Indeed, profound suffering can shake even the most steadfast among us by making it hard for us to embrace the storyline that makes it part of a much greater good.

And so it was for the great Reformed theologian Robert Lewis Dabney after he lost his first two sons to diphtheria near the end of 1855.[35]

Robert Dabney's Story

Dabney's first great sorrow came when his five-year-old, Jimmy, died after a week of excruciating suffering that left him mute while still capable of "turning his beautiful liquid eyes to me and his weeping mother for help."[m] This prompted Dabney to write that he had "learned rapidly in the school of anguish this week, and am many years older than I was a few days ago." He felt "the mighty wings of the angel of death" hovering over his "heart's treasures," with "his black, noisome shadow" brooding over his home. Jimmy's death drove home the fate stalking us all. It became fearful "to live and love in such a world." Yet Dabney could still remind himself that, while these were

---

l. See Gen. 8:20–9:17, noting especially God's vow at 8:22: "While the earth remains, seedtime and harvest, cold and heat, summer and winter, day and night, shall not cease."

m. Diphtheria often produces a membrane in the throat that can lead to a high whistling or wailing in breathing and then to muteness and suffocation.

the feelings with which the natural heart regards these calamities[,] . . . to the Christian faith they wear a different aspect. Death is no longer a hellish minister and tyrant, but Christ's messenger. Our parting is not for long. [Jimmy's] despoiled and ruined body will be raised, and all its ravished beauties more than repaired. And as to the other beloved ones whom I see exposed to disease and death, I know that death cannot touch them, unless that Heavenly Father who orders everything for me in love and wisdom, sees it best. So . . . I can trust them, *though tremblingly*, to his keeping, and be at peace.

When his firstborn son, Bobby, died twenty-three days later, his feelings changed. "When my Jimmy died," he wrote,

grief was pungent, but the actings of faith, the embracing of consolation, the conception of all the cheering truths which ministered consolation were proportionably vivid; but when the stroke was repeated, and thereby doubled, I seem to be paralyzed and stunned. I know that my loss is doubled, and I know also that the same, cheering truths apply to the second as to the first, but I remain stupid, downcast, almost without hope and interest.

This blighted Dabney's feelings for Charles, his then-youngest son. When he turned away from Jimmy's corpse to his "lovely [five-month-old] infant," he wrote, his "affections and . . . fears seemed . . . to flow out towards [Charles] with a strength [both] delicious and agonizing. I never tired of folding him in my arms, as the sweet substitute for my loss, nor of trembling for him also, lest the loss should extend to him. But when Bobby was taken," he wrote,

and our little one [seemed to remain] our only hope, . . . I was both afraid and reluctant to centre my affections on him. I feel towards him a strange mixture of languor and pain, not having the heart to be happy in his caresses, and not daring.

"This," he observed, "is strange, perhaps inexplicable. Death has struck me with a dagger of ice. *He has not only wounded, but benumbed.*"

As one of Dabney's students later wrote to one of Dabney's surviving children:

> In the many burial scenes I have witnessed, your father was about the only heart-broken mourner, without visible tears, that I have ever seen. Before that, I had never realized the deep and well-nigh unearthly significance of a sorrow too deep for tears. At [Bobby's] burial, there was something in his features so pallid and deathly, as he took a parting look at his dead first-born child, that some of us [thought] he was not long to survive.

In fact, he was to live another forty years.

In losing Jimmy and Bobby, Dabney continued to hope they were "saved, renewed, and glorified by the grace of God" even though he lost his capacity to rejoice in that hope. Yet his griefs were not over. In 1862 his favorite sister, Betty, died in his arms, victim to a lung infection caught during her labors in the Civil War. The infection emaciated and then killed her, in part because "the effort of eating was such torture that enough nourishment could not be taken . . . to sustain nature."

His visit to Betty's deathbed was delayed because he was bedridden for three months by the typhus he had contracted while serving as a war chaplain. General "Stonewall" Jackson then pressed him into service as his chief of staff, but typhus returned. While he was recovering, diphtheria attacked his children again. Five-year-old Tom, his fourth son, died. Not long afterward he wrote a poem, "Tried, but Comforted," expressing how immensely difficult it can be even for someone so anchored in God's word to remain confident of the Christian story in such circumstances. When he would hear the doxology, he wrote, his "sad heart" could not in "joyful praises bear its part" because it could do nothing but "mourn its loss and tell its woe." When he tried to picture Tom among the heavenly host singing "Glory to thee, Eternal King," he found himself asking,

> But is not this a hope too sweet?
> Faith is too weak the joy to meet;

Oh! might my bursting heart but see
If true the blissful thought can be![n]

If he could but once see or hear Tom among the heavenly throng, then,
he wrote,

would my burdened heart, I know,
With none but tears of joy o'erflow—
But ah! when faith would strain her eyes
For that blest vision, there arise

The shadows of my dreary home;
'Twixt Heaven and my heart there come
That dying bed, that corpse, that bier;
And when I strive that song to hear,

Sad memory echoes but the wail
My love to soothe could naught avail;
I only hear his anguished cry,
I only see his glazing eye.

Getting Home Safely May Be No Easy Task

Dabney's experience underscores how life's sadder, more somber, mysterious, and ominous keys can hinder us from confidently embracing the full Christian story. His loved ones' deaths struck some of life's most dissonant chords and plunged him into one of life's most horrifying minor keys, disrupting his life's story in profoundly disorienting ways. As the neuroscientist Antonio Damasio has put it, the "simple reality" is that feelings of pleasure and pain

or some quality in between are the bedrock of our minds[,] . . . the continuous musical line . . . , the unstoppable humming of the most universal of melodies that only dies down when we go to sleep, a

---

n. As I wrote in the Reader's Guide to *When the Stars Disappear*, poetry can be difficult, but it repays our effort because it engages more than our intellects. If you find these verses daunting, then read them slowly aloud, pausing only at the punctuation. So don't pause after the word *see* in this stanza's third line but go right on through the fourth line because it is part of a single sentence. Similar advice holds for reading biblical poetry.

humming that turns into all-out singing when we are occupied by joy, or a mournful requiem when sorrow takes over.[36]

With Jimmy's death, the sad refrain of Dabney's sorrow was loud but not yet loud enough to overwhelm his faith and hope—as he put it, "the actings of faith, the embracing of consolation, [and] the conception of all the cheering truths which ministered consolation were proportionably vivid." When Bobby died, his sorrow swelled to a crescendo that stunned and benumbed him, rendering him unable to be cheered and consoled by these truths. After Tom's death the dissonances blared, riveting Dabney's thoughts on the scenes of his loss, intensifying his horror and thus raising the specter that Christianity's blissful hope might not be true.

Profound suffering, as a form of elemental and persistently painful feeling, impacts us directly and immediately, dominating our minds and thus overwhelming our awareness of anything else.[37] Its horror can also compel us to ask, How can the Christian story be true, when life includes something like *this*?

Dabney closed his poem by affirming the need for faith and hope. Yet as he wrote to his mother after his sister's death, the "feeling . . . that surely God must be our enemy" since he has permitted us and our loved ones to suffer so horrendously is "all too apt to arise under great sorrows." It is "in refutation of this feeling," Dabney noted, that the apostle Peter wrote to tell the Christians who were suffering in his day that their suffering shouldn't surprise them, "as though something strange were happening" (1 Pet. 4:12). Peter would remind us, Dabney wrote,

> that for God's own children to suffer, even though it be severely, is no novel thing. "Whom the Lord loveth he chasteneth, and scourgeth every son whom he receiveth." This road of bereavement is one along which all the Bible saints travelled. . . . *Yet they got home safely, and so may we.*

But getting home safely may be no easy task. The final stanzas of Dabney's "Tried, but Comforted" show he was never completely disoriented.[38] He knew what he should believe and hope in spite of his feelings. Yet his suffering was excruciating, striking at his confidence about being able to lead the life he knew God had called him to live. How could his heavenly Father have ordered these sorrows for him in love and wisdom? Why would God, if he is perfectly good and all-powerful, allow disease to ravage and strike down those he loved, leaving him "almost without hope and interest"? Chapter 4 explores the degree to which we can account for these things.

REDEMPTION AND CONSUMMATION

What Suffering Should Prompt Us to Seek

You return man to dust and say, "Return, O children of Adam!" . . .
We are brought to an end by your anger;
by your wrath we are dismayed.
You have set our iniquities before you, our
secret sins in the light of your presence.
For all our days pass away under your wrath;
we bring our years to an end like a sigh.
The years of our life are seventy, or even
by reason of strength eighty;
yet their span is but toil and trouble; they are soon gone,
and we fly away.

Psalm 90:3, 7–10

Under the sun the race is not to the swift,
nor the battle to the strong,
nor bread to the wise, nor riches to the intelligent,
nor favor to those with knowledge,
but time and chance happen to them all.

Ecclesiastes 9:11

Blessed be the God and Father of our Lord Jesus Christ!
According to his great mercy, he has caused
us to be born again to a living hope
through the resurrection of Jesus Christ from the dead,
to an inheritance that is imperishable, undefiled, and unfading,
kept in heaven for you,
who by God's power are being guarded through faith
for a salvation ready to be revealed in the last time.
In this you rejoice, though now for a little while, if necessary,
you have been grieved by various trials, so that
the tested genuineness of your faith
—more precious than gold that perishes
though it is tested by fire—
may be found to result in praise and glory and honor at the revelation of Jesus Christ. Though you have not seen him, you love him.
Though you do not now see him, you believe in him
and rejoice with joy that is inexpressible and filled with glory,
obtaining the outcome of your faith, the salvation of your souls.

Peter 1:3–9

This chapter addresses the questions that came up in the last paragraph of chapter 3 and then proceeds to outline the third and fourth parts of the full Christian story. Most of us will not suffer like Robert Dabney, but any suffering can raise the question, Why doesn't a wholly good and all-powerful God vanquish suffering—and especially profound suffering?

LIFE'S TRUE MORNING STAR

Dabney's story should keep us from assuming that God will shield us from suffering. The loss of his sons and his sister eclipsed many of the brightest stars in his personal story. There is no doubt that Scripture presents suffering, even if not perhaps suffering as profound as Dabney's, as an inevitable part of our personal stories.[1]

Although those losses also threatened to eclipse the stars Dabney had always oriented himself by in Christianity's general story, he invoked the resolute faith of the apostle Peter's original readers to remind himself that Christians may suffer profoundly and yet finish their earthly journeys faithfully. Their faith and hope enabled them to weather the trials that tested the genuineness of their faith as Dabney's faith enabled him to endure his bereavements. And our faith and hope can enable us to bear whatever suffering we may face.

Biblical faith is anchored in God's acts. Peter opens his letter by blessing God for causing those whom he has chosen "to be born again [into] a living hope through the resurrection of Jesus Christ from the dead" (1 Pet. 1:3; cf. Acts 5:30; Gal. 1:1).[2] "Christian hope is everliving," Karen Jobes explains, "because Christ, the ground of that hope, is everliving. The present reality of the Christian's life is defined and determined by the reality of the past—the resurrection of Jesus Christ—and is guaranteed into the future because Christ lives forevermore."[3] Christ's resurrection should produce in us, as it did in Peter's readers, a keen and vital hope for "a priceless inheritance" that is being kept in heaven for us, "pure and undefiled, beyond the reach of change and decay" (1 Pet. 1:4 NLT). This helps us bear whatever suffering we may face. We can rejoice with a glorious and inexpressible joy that we will one day receive "the salvation of [our] souls" (1:9)[4]—that is, an "unfading crown of glory" when our Lord appears and welcomes us to enjoy perfect and everlasting communion with him (5:4).

The First Glimmer of Life's True Morning Star

On that day (the day of consummation, as we shall see), Jesus will rise as life's true morning star (see Rev. 22:16). Yet until that day dawns, Peter wrote in his second letter, we "will do well to pay attention" to Scripture's prophetic word, which is "as to a lamp shining in a dark place" (2 Pet. 1:19).

Life's true morning star first glimmered in the garden of Eden at Genesis 3:15, when God declared to the serpent:

> And I will put enmity
> > between you and the woman,
> > and between your offspring and her [offspring];
> he will crush your head,
> > and you will strike his heel. (NIV)

This is the *protevangelium*, the first hint of the Bible's Good News.[5] By pronouncing it at the beginning of his judgments on our first parents' disobedience, God was offering them hope that ultimately everything could still be made right for them. From that moment forward, they could, in the very midst of their suffering, place their hope in the prophetic word of Genesis 3:15, when God had declared that a woman would bear a child who would crush the serpent's head.

Adam and Eve believed God, trusting his word. Recognizing that God's words implied that his wife would bear children,[6] Adam expressed his faith by naming her Eve, "because she would become the mother of all the living" (3:20 NIV).[a] When Eve gave birth to Cain, she said, "I have gotten a man *with the help of the LORD*" (4:1). During her temptation, Eve didn't call God "LORD," so her doing so at Cain's birth showed she was placing her faith in the personal, covenant-making God.

Adam and Eve's faith sustained them through the horror of Cain killing Abel and of God then driving Cain from the land to be a restless wanderer hidden from God's face (see Gen. 4:1–24). Eve reaffirmed her faith after bearing another son, Seth, by declaring that "God has granted me another offspring in place of Abel, . . . because Cain killed him" (4:25 NAB).[7] From then on some of Adam and Eve's descendants gave voice to their faith by calling on the name of the Lord (see 4:26).

As a final act of kindness while they were still in the garden, the Lord met some of Adam and Eve's immediate needs by making clothes

---

a. "*Eve* probably means *living*" (NIV's marginal note on Gen. 3:20).

for them (see Gen. 3:21). "The couple are not expelled nude from the garden," Victor Hamilton writes. "They are not sent beyond the garden totally vulnerable."[8] Their garments, Kidner observes, "are forerunners of the many measures of welfare, both moral and physical, [that] . . . sin makes necessary." The way forward to our full salvation is cluttered with complications unnecessary in Eden. Genesis 2's innocent nakedness was lost forever. We require clothing "not so much as an act of grace" (although in relieving some of our shame it is that too), "but as a reminder of [our] sinfulness," of the fact that humankind now stands exposed to God's judgment.

> Then the LORD God said, "Behold, the man has become like one of us in knowing good and evil. Now, lest he reach out his hand and take also of the tree of life and eat, and live forever—" therefore the LORD God sent him out from the garden of Eden to work the ground from which he was taken. He drove out the man, and at the east of the garden of Eden he placed the cherubim and a flaming sword that turned every way to guard the way to the tree of life. (Gen. 3:22–24)

The pathway to redemption was now open, leading away from Eden's innocence toward and through our Lord's sacrifice. In fact, the way to full communion with God runs through the "fiery trial" that Peter wrote of, which tests our faith through suffering (see 1 Pet. 1:6–7; 4:12). It does not go around it.

LIFE'S CONSTANT REMINDERS

Allen Ross suggests that careful reflection on God's words to Eve in Genesis 3:16 yields two important insights. First, the Hebrew word usually translated as "childbearing" in that verse is actually the word for *conception*. It is translated as *conception* everywhere else in the Old Testament. So it should be translated the same way here. Of course, conception is a biologically veiled event that in itself involves neither pleasure nor pain. Consequently, Ross concludes, the first half of verse 16—"I will surely multiply your pain in childbearing"—should be taken to represent the whole process that begins with conception and extends through a mother's child-rearing years. Motherhood involves suffering. It involves unpleasant and harmful experiences that mothers wish would end. Second, the Hebrew word for *pain* in verse 16 means "painful toil" and thus refers to more than the relatively brief although remarkably intense physical pain of childbirth. It includes the emotional toll that inevitably accompanies a mother's experience of family life. God's sentence regarding the woman in Genesis 3:16 involves, then, much more than just the excruciating pain of childbearing. It includes the care, toil, and distress common to mothers throughout their lives.[9]

God repeated the same Hebrew word for *pain* in addressing Adam. By cursing the ground, God ensured that Adam's painful toil would remind him and his descendants of humanity's desperate plight. Human life is now a treadmill requiring us to sustain ourselves by doing work that we would often rather not be doing and which we often find unpleasant enough that we would like it to end.

Adam and Eve's disobedience brought them immediate spiritual death that would inevitably result in biological death. Cut off from human life's true source of communion with God, they and we, their descendants, can only linger in a world that is now itself, through God's curse, a source of frustration and futility.[10] Life's pain and toil confirm God's warning in Genesis 2:17 that if Adam ate from the forbidden tree, then "DYING he would die."

The painful toil that now dogs humanity echoes throughout Scripture, as we shall now see.

Israel's Lament

Psalm 90 applies this lesson to God's Old Testament people. As Ross remarks, this community lament[b] "is written from the intense awareness of mortality and sin."[11] Verses 3, 5–6 echo God's words to Adam in Genesis 3:19:

---

b. See Mark Talbot, *When the Stars Disappear: Help and Hope from Stories of Suffering in Scripture* (Wheaton, IL: Crossway, 2020), 44–46, for more on lament in the psalms.

You return man to dust
and say, "Return, O children of Adam!"ᶜ . . .
You sweep them away as with a flood; they are like a dream,
like grass that is renewed in the morning:
in the morning it flourishes and is renewed;
in the evening it fades and withers. (Ps. 90:3, 5–6)

It seems likely that the Israelite community had undergone some crushing event that had stripped them of any illusions about who they were. They were now vividly aware of being Adam's children, subject with him to God's death sentence, which made their lives as unsubstantial as dreams and as transient as grass.[12]

Verses 7–10 explain why their lives were so brief:

For we are brought to an end by your anger;
by your wrath we are dismayed.
You have set our iniquities before you,
our secret sins in the light of your presence.
For all our days pass away under your wrath;
we bring our years to an end like a sigh.
The years of our life are seventy,
or even by reason of strength eighty;
yet their span is but toil and trouble;
they are soon gone, and we fly away.

These verses, Claus Westermann writes, see "the frailty of human life as the result of divine action. . . . Our transitoriness is the outcome of God's anger, . . . his reaction to our iniquities. . . . It is obvious," Westermann continues, "that behind these verses lies the primaeval story of man's expulsion from the garden of Eden," and so "in the background of . . . these verses and Genesis 3 lies the awareness, *which all men have*, of the necessary connection between guilt and punishment."[13]

---

c. The ESV margin notes that the final words of this verdict can be translated "Return, O children of Adam" rather than as "Return, O children of men." The same Hebrew phrase is repeated several times in Ecclesiastes where I will render it as "children of Adam," just as I am doing here.

These Israelites understood that even though they were God's people, all their days were passing away under his wrath until they would finally fritter out "like a sigh" (v. 9). They knew that the constancy of God's wrath meant that even if they lived unusually long lives, the best of their years would be but trouble and sorrow that quickly passed, and then they would fly away (see v. 10).[14]

Some Degree of Frustration and a Sense of Futility Is Now Everyone's Lot

The echoes of God's words to Adam and Eve in Genesis 3:16–19 are louder and more frequent in Ecclesiastes. In fact, the relationship between Ecclesiastes and the first several chapters of Genesis "is best understood," David Clemens writes, "as an arresting but thoroughly orthodox exposition of Genesis 1–3." In particular, "in both texts, the painful consequences of the fall are central."[15]

The echoes begin with the Preacher's opening cry: "Vanity of vanities, says the Preacher, vanity of vanities! All is vanity" (1:2). The Hebrew word for *vanity* is *hebel*. It means *vapor* or *breath*. "A wisp of vapour, a puff of wind, a mere breath—nothing you could get your hands on; the nearest thing to zero," Kidner comments. "That is the 'vanity' [Ecclesiastes] is about."[16]

This cry echoes Abel's Hebrew name, grounding life's vanity in biblical history. Just as Adam named his wife Eve because God had said she was to be the mother of all living, so all of human life is *hebel*—that is, vanity—because, like *Hebel* or Abel, "it is scarred by the madness of sin and swept away without warning by death." The Preacher's cries of *hebel* remind us of Abel's murder at the hand of Cain. Nothing is more vapor-like than "the fleetingness of [Abel's] godly young life," who "enters the biblical narrative only to die."[17]

This holds for us all: we are all "like a breath"—literally, "like *hebel*," like Abel—with our days "like a passing shadow" (Ps. 144:4; cf. 39:5, 11). A human life, no matter how long or how great its achievements, is *hebel*. All is vanity and a striving after wind, with nothing permanent to be gained under the sun (see Eccles. 2:4–11).

Psalm 90 recognizes the painful transitoriness of life even for God's chosen people. Ecclesiastes considers what happens to everyone who lives "under the sun" (see 1:2–3 to 12:8). Death's inevitability and apparent finality show life's futility to be universal. From an "under the sun," exclusively secular standpoint, everything human appears as "evanescent—a mere nothingness."[18]

From that standpoint, wisdom is ultimately no better than foolishness (see 2:12–15; 6:8; 8:16–17), righteousness than wickedness (see 9:2–3), or love than hate (see 9:6), for death swallows them all. "Even at its best wisdom cannot outrun death."[19] "Under the sun"—that is, in terms of the humanly opaque causal processes that shape our fortunes[20]—

> I saw that . . . the race is not to the swift, nor the battle to the strong, nor bread to the wise, nor riches to the intelligent, nor favor to those with knowledge, but *time and chance happen to them all.* . . . Like fish that are taken in an evil net, and like birds that are caught in a snare, so the children of Adam are snared at an evil time, when it suddenly falls upon them. (9:11–12)

We are no more able than fish or birds to understand when calamity is about to strike and so keep ourselves out of its way.

When Ecclesiastes was translated into Greek, the Hebrew word *hebel* was rendered as the Greek word *mataiotēs*, meaning that Genesis 3 and Ecclesiastes would eventually echo in the New Testament. Commenting on the phrase "For the creation was subjected to futility" (Rom. 8:20), John Stott writes:

> This reference to the past must surely be to the judgment of God, which fell on the natural order following Adam's disobedience. The ground was cursed because of him. In consequence, it would "produce thorns and thistles," so that Adam and his descendants would extract food from it only by "painful toil" . . . until death claimed them and they returned to the dust from which they had been taken. Paul . . . sums up the result of God's curse by the . . . word *mataiotēs*. . . . It means . . . emptiness, whether of purpose or of result. It is the

word chosen by the [Greek] translators [of the Old Testament] for "Vanity of vanities! . . . All is vanity." . . . As C. J. Vaughn comments, "the whole Book of Ecclesiastes is a commentary on this verse. For it expresses the existential absurdity of a life lived 'under the sun,' imprisoned in time and space, with no ultimate reference point to either God or eternity."[21]

Death casts a pall over all of human life, even for us who "call upon the name of the LORD" (Gen. 4:26; cf. Acts 2:21; Rom. 10:13). God's warning in Genesis 2:17, that if Adam and Eve ate from the forbidden tree, then "DYING they would die," included all of the debilitating processes that end in death.[22] In fact, all of our experiences of perplexity, frustration, pain, sickness, aging, loneliness, discord, strife, alienation, and separation are part of "a kind of funeral procession."[d] The Preacher emphasizes those aspects because he recognizes that it is better for us "to spend [our] time at funerals than at parties. After all, everyone dies—so the living should take this to heart" (Eccles. 7:2 NLT).

Christians need to take this to heart, for we may assume that we will not suffer much.[23] We may even feel that because we are Christians, God owes us lives without much suffering.

Why?—Why Me? Why This? Why Now?

We may even suffer profoundly. And that may perplex us, prompting us to ask, Why? Why am I suffering? And why am I suffering this way? Sometimes the answers to these questions are clear. Adam and Eve knew why she was going to find labor painful and he would find providing food for his family laborious. Cain knew why God had condemned him to be a vagabond who would no longer know God's presence (see Gen. 4:12–14). Likewise, the Israelites of Psalm 90 knew that their suffering was caused by their sin, even if some of the particular ways in which they were suffering may have startled and dismayed them.

But often we don't know. We can't say why we suffer as we do. And this may tempt us, as it tempted Dabney, to wonder if God is against us.

---

d. See chap. 2, 69.

Why did God allow disease to ravage Dabney's loved ones, leaving him "almost without hope and interest"? Why did he suffer so much—and why do some of us suffer so little?[24]

Answering these questions requires us to understand what it means for God to have created the world as a humanly inhabitable place.

At Isaiah 45:18, the prophet described God's creative work by four Hebrew verbs: he *created* the heavens, he *fashioned* (that is, *planned*) and then *made* the earth, and thus *established* it (that is, *made it stand firm*)—all so that the world would not be an unintelligible chaos but a humanly livable place.[25] God created the world to be a hierarchically structured environment filled with created realities acting according to stable causal processes so we can understand how it works.[26] Genesis 1 emphasizes this by being "so tightly ordered, its rhetoric so laden with rhythmical repetitions, that almost regardless of what the chapter says, the impression it leaves us with is one of great orderliness and regularity."[27] *Perfect* order and regularity. As Henri Blocher comments, God saw his finished creative work to be "very good" because he saw a cosmos—that is, "a diverse totality that is properly arranged, organized and differentiated"—where the earth's living creatures "followed as perfect an order as the order of the heavens," and where the whole constituted a model "of perfect obedience and of regular motion."[e]

By creating us in his image, God enabled us to think some of his thoughts after him and thus be capable of discovering, at least in part, some of the world's divinely designed structures and processes. He then gave us a mandate to investigate its beings, patterns, and processes so that we can subdue the earth and reign benevolently over it and its living creatures.[28]

If Adam and Eve had obeyed God's command not to eat from the forbidden tree, then the process of investigating God's creation could have proceeded apace. But they disobeyed, prompting God to subject creation to corruption and futility. This so affected the good that God had created that, while everything remains, everything is changed.[29]

---

e. See chap. 1.

Everything remains: even after their disobedience, God has preserved creation's general order and regularity, pledging that until the consummation it will stand fast (see Gen. 8:22). So the world's structures and processes remain somewhat discoverable by us and we are still to rule over the rest of creation. Yet *everything was changed* because now those structures and processes convey not only health and psychological wholeness and life, but also sickness and psychological brokenness and death. Anything painful, perplexing, frustrating, or abnormal that we encounter "under the sun," anything that makes life "under the sun" ultimately futile if there is no resurrection (see 1 Cor. 15:1–34), has its root in Adam and Eve's one disobedient act.

The Preacher understood this. As Clemens observes, "Few, if any, other Old Testament texts provide so succinct and precise an account of the fall as Ecclesiastes 7:29"[30]—"This alone have I discovered: God made humankind[f] upright, but they have sought many evil schemes" (NET). Adam's disobedience may also echo in Ecclesiastes 9:18—"one sinner destroys much good"—which echoes in Romans 5:12–19, where Paul states that "one man," explicitly Adam (see 5:12, 14), by his primal act of disobedience brought us death (see 5:12–21; 1 Cor. 15:22).

Ultimately, the Preacher knows, nothing—nothing good and nothing bad—falls out of God's hand (see Eccles. 2:24; 3:13; 5:19; 9:1). The world, including all its suffering, is providentially ordered.[g] So we should accept what God has actually done:

> Accept the way God does things,
> > for who can straighten what he has made crooked?
> Enjoy prosperity while you can,
> > but when hard times strike, realize that both come from God.
> > Remember that nothing is certain in this life. (7:13–14 NLT)

---

f. *Humankind* translates the Hebrew word *adam* with a definite article preceding it, which indicates that while it refers primarily to humankind, it can still be read as referring especially to the first man.

g. As I explained in *When the Stars Disappear*, 21, God's providence involves his seeing the future and providing in advance for the needs of his people—that's what the Latin word *providēre* means: to foresee, provide, provide for. This includes his providentially so ordering our lives' events that we should fear him and thus remain humble and dependent on him.

The Preacher also knows that God generally administers his providence through the world's regular causal processes (see, e.g., Eccles. 1:4–7, 9). Fools and sluggards generally get what they deserve because they refuse to conform to creation's ordered patterns and processes and thus fall victim to the consequences that follow on their violation (see Eccles. 4:5 with Prov. 6:6–11; 20:4; 24:30–34). Wisdom is generally better than folly because the wise understand those patterns and processes and thus can see where they are going, while fools stumble around in the dark (Eccles. 2:13–14).

"But time and chance happen to them all" (Eccles. 9:11). In other words, what God, in the course of his ordinary providence, permits creation's structures and processes to bring us is not only outside our control but can appear to us as inexplicable and thus as a product of pure chance. Yet "whatever God does endures forever; nothing can be added to it, nor anything taken from it. God has done it, *so that people fear before him*" (3:14; cf. 8:12–13). A healthy fear of what God's providence may bring keeps us humble and dependent as we acknowledge that he has so ordered what goes on "under the sun" that however much we may toil in seeking to understand what is or will be, we won't understand much. "No one can comprehend what goes on under the sun. Despite all their efforts to search it out, no one can discover its meaning. Even if the wise claim they know, they cannot really comprehend it" (8:17 NIV). This means we cannot know "from the way things turn out, whom God truly loves since the same treatment is dealt out to the just and the wicked alike."[31] "Under the sun," "the customary signs of blessing or curse" have been displaced. It rains on the just and the unjust (see Matt. 5:45). In this fallen and thus sometimes upside-down world, righteousness is not always rewarded, and wickedness does not always receive what it deserves: "There is a vanity that takes place on earth, that there are righteous people"—like Abel—"to whom it happens according to the deeds of the wicked, and there are wicked people to whom it happens according to the deeds of the righteous. I said that this also is vanity" (Eccles. 8:14; see 3:16; 7:15; 10:5–7). God's ways, including his apportionment of good and bad, joy and sorrow, ease and difficulty, to each of us in our earthly lives, are "past finding out" (see Job 9:1–12; cf. Luke 13:1–4; Rom. 11:22–23 KJV).

Medical science has helped us track some of creation's processes. So we can now give a bit of an answer to the question, Why did Dabney suffer so much—and why do some of us suffer so little? Diphtheria is caused by a bacterium that is controlled by a vaccine. We won't suffer like Dabney if we have gotten that vaccine. Yet many of creation's processes remain opaque to us. Perhaps the lifelong illness suffered by the psalmist who wrote Psalm 88 could now be cured, perhaps not. We may suffer less than Dabney since we have gained a bit more control over some of the world's stable causal processes. Yet we may still suffer as profoundly, even if not in exactly the same way. Since God is providentially in control of all things, we should—indeed, we are commanded to[h]—pray that he will deliver us from evil, including profound suffering (see, e.g., 1 Chron. 16:8–36; Matt. 6:13; 2 Cor. 1:8–10). Yet "under the sun" we cannot know to what degree he will spare us from bad things.

REDEMPTION AND CONSUMMATION

Perplexity, frustration, futility.[i] This is some of the fruit of our first parents' eating from the forbidden tree.[32] It is some of what actually followed after the serpent falsely claimed that if they ate of it, then they would become like God. It involved a loss in godlikeness, a degradation of our God-given capacities.

These are all aspects of the funeral procession that began when Adam and Eve broke their spiritual lifeline by their disobedience. And thus began the litany of human sin and woe. As that litany swelled in the Old Testament's historical books, its psalmists' laments, in Ecclesiastes's stark "under the sun" realism, and in its prophets' denunciations, it became clear, as the great fourth-century bishop Athanasius put it, that corruption and death were gaining an ever firmer hold on human

---

h. See Luke 18:1–7; 1 Thess. 5:16–18; and Talbot, *When the Stars Disappear*, especially p. 53.

i. Ironically, being perplexed, frustrated, or feeling everything is futile when we are suffering is often what tempts us to conclude that God is not good. But the problems stem from us, not him.

beings and thus that we, who were "created in God's image and in [our] possession of reason reflected the very Word Himself, [were] disappearing." So if God's creative work was not to be lost, that Word needed to become flesh.[33]

The Word became flesh. Jesus was born to do his Father's will. He lived a life of perfect obedience that climaxed in his giving himself up for us, "a fragrant offering and sacrifice to God," so that we could be redeemed and God's work not lost (Eph. 5:2; see Titus 2:14; Heb. 10:5–7). This is the Bible's good news. "At just the right time, when we were still powerless, Christ died for the ungodly" (Rom. 5:6 NIV). He then "was raised for our justification" (Rom. 4:25). His life, death, and resurrection are the historical climax that the Old Testament witnesses to and prepares us for. It's what the biblical story is all about. Our Lord's redeeming work is, as C. S. Lewis wrote, the chapter in the full Christian story "on which the whole plot turns."[34] It is the world's decisive event, when God himself entered time and space to do what no one else could do to rectify our rebellion by conquering death and thus take the essential step toward making everything right again.

Understanding what God has done in Christ requires us to consider the final two parts of the Christian story together. For Christianity is an unfinished but completely plotted story where the meaning of redemption is clear only in the light of consummation. The last two parts of the full story mustn't be pulled apart.

Redemption

Redemption involves our release from the deleterious effects of Adam and Eve's rebellion by means of the sacrificial death of our Lord. We can get this, the pivotal chapter of the full Christian story, in focus by concentrating on three New Testament passages.

1. The Heart of the Gospel

In Romans 3:21–26 Paul spells out why he is "not ashamed of the gospel." He is unashamed of it because "it is the power of God for salvation to everyone who believes" (Rom. 1:16). It is God's way of satisfying his righteous wrath against all the ungodliness and unrighteousness of human beings.

It is clear, Paul maintains, that the whole world is accountable—that is, guilty and condemned—before God (see 1:18–3:20, and especially 3:19). This is what the universal presence of suffering and death shows (see Rom. 5:12, 18–19; 6:21, 23). The gospel is the humanly incredible good news[j] that we need no longer be accounted guilty and thus condemned: "*But now* God's righteousness has been manifested, a righteousness to which the Old Testament law and prophets bear witness—the righteousness that comes through faith in Jesus Christ for all who believe" (3:21–22, my paraphrase).

This righteousness comes to us "by [God's] grace as a gift, through the redemption that is in Christ Jesus" (3:24). God has released us from condemnation by presenting Jesus as a propitiatory sacrifice that we receive by faith (3:25). Jesus's death demonstrates God's righteousness, "so that he might be just and the justifier of the one who has faith in Jesus" (3:26). "Because [Christ] shed his blood . . . in a sacrificial death for us sinners, God is able justly to justify the unjust."[35]

This is the heart of the gospel: if we put our faith in Christ's work, then we are *justified*—that is, we are *declared righteous* by God in spite of our sin. Our status before God changes because Jesus's death on the cross has *propitiated* God's wrath—in other words, it has placated God's anger against our sin. God the Father sent his Son to take our place, to bear our sins, and thus to die the death we deserve. By not sparing his own Son (see Isa. 53:4–6; John 3:16; Rom. 8:32), God *demonstrates* his righteousness by publicly displaying his holy hatred of sin.[36] In forgiving us, God has acted righteously by directing "against His very own Self in the person of His Son the full weight of that righteous wrath" we deserve.[37] As Stott puts it, "God himself gave himself to save us from himself"—and for himself (see Titus 2:14).

All this is ours, Paul insists, *only by faith* (see especially Rom. 3:27–4:25). Our redemption depends on nothing but our looking to him to

---

j. It is literally humanly incredible—that is, such that we in our sinfulness cannot believe it—unless the Holy Spirit regenerates our hearts so that we can believe (see John 3:1–8; Titus 3:3–7).

do for us what we cannot do for ourselves. So "there is nothing meritorious about faith. . . . When we say that salvation is 'by faith, not by works,' we are not substituting one kind of merit ('faith') for another ('works'). Nor is salvation a sort of cooperative enterprise between God and us, in which he contributes the cross and we contribute faith." Faith's value "is not to be found in itself, but entirely and exclusively in its object, namely Jesus Christ and him crucified."[38] Richard Hooker put it this way: "God justifies the believer—not because of the worthiness of his belief, but because of [the worthiness of Christ as the one] who is believed." In short, "faith's only function is to receive what grace offers."

2. Fellowship and Life Restored: The Blissful Consequences of Faith

When we receive God's grace by looking to Christ's work, two "blissful consequences" become ours, as Paul tells us in Romans 5.[39]

First, "we have peace with God through our Lord Jesus Christ" (Rom. 5:1). Our faith in Christ's propitiatory work reconciles us to God (see Rom. 5:10–11; Col. 1:19–22). Our spiritual lifeline is thereby restored, and we are reinstated into God's "favour and fellowship."[40]

C. E. B. Cranfield comments that the first eleven verses of Romans 5 "affirm the amazing truth that God's undeserved love has through Christ transformed [us] from being God's enemies into . . . being His friends." This is because from God's standpoint "justification and reconciliation . . . are inseparable." Human judges may have no personal relationship at all with those who appear before them, neither "personal hostility if the accused be found guilty, [nor] . . . friendship if the accused is acquitted." Yet God's relationship with us is always personal. "God's justification involves a real self-engagement [with] the sinner on [God's] part. *He does not confer the status of righteousness upon us without at the same time giving Himself to us in friendship.*"[41]

By means of the cross, God has reopened the way for us to enjoy fellowship with him (see John 14:23; Rev. 3:20). Through Christ's redeeming work, "we have obtained our introduction into this grace in which we have taken our stand" (Rom. 5:2a, Stott's translation). This, Stott tells us, refers to "our privileged position of acceptance by him."[42] We take our stand "in or on this grace," recognizing that as justified believers we now "enjoy a blessing far greater than a periodic approach to God. . . . Our relationship with God, into which justification has brought us, is not sporadic but continuous, not precarious but secure. We do not fall in and out of grace like courtiers who may find themselves in and out of favour with their sovereign." We are not on probation. By means of the new covenant established by our Lord's blood (see Luke 22:20; Heb. 8:6; 9:15; 12:24), we know we will receive the eternal inheritance that God has promised to those who believe. And since nothing is now "able to separate us from the love of God in Christ Jesus our Lord" (Rom. 8:39), we can "rejoice in hope of the glory of God" (5:2b).

Second, we receive life because of our Lord's obedience. For just as "one trespass"—one deliberate act of rebellion against an explicit command[43]—"resulted in condemnation" and death "for all people," so "one righteous act"—our Lord's doing his Father's will by enduring the cross and despising the shame (see Matt. 26:39; Phil. 2:8; Heb. 12:2)—"resulted in justification *and life*" for all who believe (Rom 5:18 NIV).[44]

Yet "the free gift is not like the trespass" (Rom. 5:15a):

> For if many died through one man's trespass, much more have the grace of God and the free gift by the grace of that one man Jesus Christ abounded for many. And the free gift is not like the result of that one man's sin. . . . For if, because of one man's trespass, death reigned through that one man, much more will those who receive the abundance of grace and the free gift of righteousness reign in life through the one man Jesus Christ. (vv. 15b–17)[45]

"Anyone who 'receives the gift' that God offers in Christ," Douglas Moo states, "finds security and joy in knowing that the reign of death has been completely and finally overcome by the reign of grace, righteousness, and eternal life (cf. vv. 17, 21)."[46] For alongside the condemnation that came through Adam's sin, "there is the grace of God. And since it is precisely God's grace . . . there is . . . a superabundance connected with God's gift in Christ that has the power not only to cancel the effects of Adam's work but to create, positively, life and peace."

And, again, we receive this gift only by faith. For, as Moo notes, there is "an important difference between the reigns of death and life." Death "has the character of fate." Adam and Eve did not explicitly choose death. It—and the suffering that precedes it—followed on their choice to disobey. "The reign of life, on the other hand, is experienced through choice and personal decision; it is for those who 'receive' the gift. . . . Righteousness and life are for those who *respond* to God's grace in Christ and . . . they are *only* for those who respond." This response is the "obedience of faith" (Rom. 1:5; see 1 John 3:23). To disbelieve is to disobey (see Rom. 10:16–17).

Romans 1 through 4 emphasize our reception of Christ's redeeming work through faith. Chapters 5 through 8 emphasize the life that is ours when we receive Christ's work. As I wrote in chapter 3, after Adam and Eve "opened the door to human suffering by their disobedience, the way forward to the restoration of full communion with God became a pathway strewn with suffering and death, culminating in the suffering and death of our Lord." In Adam we are all "children of wrath" who are spiritually dead in our trespasses and sins (see Eph. 2:1–3). *But now*, because of our Lord's redeeming work, the way back to life and the future establishment of full, face-to-face communion with him has reopened if we choose to be "in" him, rather than "in" Adam (see Rom. 6:11, 23; 8:1). "For as *in* Adam all die, so also *in* Christ shall all be made alive" (1 Cor. 15:22). "He gives Life—*his* Life—for the wages of our sin was *his* death."[47]

3. Christ's Resurrection as Firstfruits of All Who Belong to Christ

Paul juxtaposes Adam and Christ again in 1 Corinthians 15.

In Romans 5, Paul contrasts the disastrous consequences of Adam's disobedience with the blessed consequences of our Lord's obedience: "For as by the one man's disobedience the many were made sinners, so by the one man's obedience the many will be made righteous" (v. 19). In Adam's disobedience, all of us have turned our backs to God and not our faces (see Jer. 2:27; 32:33). Like Adam, we have all transgressed God's law and been faithless to him. We have given God the cold shoulder, stiffened our necks, stopped our ears, and made our hearts diamond-hard rather than listen and obey (see Neh. 9:29; Zech. 7:11–12).

By contrast, our Lord was utterly obedient from the moment of his miraculous conception (see Luke 1:35).[48] When he came into the world, he said: "'Sacrifice and offering you did not desire, but *a body you prepared for me.* . . . Then I said, 'Here I am. . . . *I have come to do your will*, my God'" (Heb. 10:5, 7 NIV; see vv. 5–14). God the Son became incarnate so that he could do his Father's will (see Matt. 26:39, 42; John 5:30; 6:38). His posture was one of obedience "to the point of death, even death on a cross" (Phil. 2:8). That posture *is* righteousness (see Deut. 6:25). And by Christ's posture, all who believe the gospel—all who choose to be in Christ rather than in Adam—will be made righteous.

First Corinthians 15 emphasizes the fruit of these postures. The fruit of Adam's disobedience was universal condemnation and death (see 1 Cor. 15:21 with Rom. 5:15–16, 18). But the fruit of Christ's obedience is justification and resurrection life for all who believe (see 1 Cor. 15:1–3, 22 with Rom. 5:18–19). Through our Lord's earthly work, God the Father has delivered us "from the domain of darkness and transferred us to the kingdom of his beloved Son, in whom we have redemption, the forgiveness of sins" (Col. 1:13–14). Because of Christ, grace reigns "through righteousness leading to eternal life" (Rom. 5:21; see John 17:1–2; Heb. 5:9). And Christ will reign, Paul tells us, "until he has put all his enemies under his feet," where "the last enemy to be destroyed is death" (1 Cor. 15:25–26; cf. Heb. 2:14).

"Under the sun," as the Preacher has hammered home, death's dominion seems complete. It appears to be the final victor, the last word that exposes the vanity and futility of everything. It appeared to be the final victor for a few days even with our Lord, as two of his disciples lamented on the road to Emmaus after his crucifixion: "We had hoped that he was the one to redeem Israel" (Luke 24:21).

Yet death is not the last word. As Paul insists, the fact that our Lord was raised from the dead is proof that death will be swallowed up in victory (see 1 Cor. 15:54; also Isa. 25:8). This is why believing that Christ was raised is the core of true Christian faith. "For I delivered to you as of first importance what I also received: that Christ died for our sins in accordance with the Scriptures, that he was buried, that he was raised on the third day in accordance with the Scriptures" (1 Cor. 15:3–4). Indeed, this is the message on which we must take our stand and by which we are being saved (see vv. 1–2; Rom. 10:9).[49]

But it is not merely or even primarily our Lord's resurrection that constitutes the first Easter morning's good news. For Paul's thinking is resolutely future-oriented, always keeping in mind our resurrection as one of this world's final events.[50] So to confess that our Lord was raised on that first Easter morning is to believe that in raising his Son, God the Father "has thereby set in motion a series of events that have to do with . . . the defeat of death" for all of us who believe in our Lord's redeeming work.[51]

God the Father's raising his Son from the dead was the fruit of Jesus's perfect, unswerving obedience.[52] His resurrection is "the firstfruits of those who have fallen asleep" (1 Cor. 15:20)—of Christians who have died—and thus serves "as a kind of guarantee for the full harvest."[53] For those of us in Christ, death is only an interim word and not the last word. God "has identified us as his own by placing the Holy Spirit in our hearts as the first installment that guarantees everything he has promised us" (2 Cor. 1:22 NLT). We can rest assured that "if the Spirit of him who raised Jesus from the dead dwells in [us], he who raised Christ Jesus from the dead will also give life to [our] mortal bodies through his Spirit" (Rom. 8:11).

The Spirit bears witness not only to the fact that we have become God's children (see Rom. 8:15–16), but also to the fact that on the day when our Lord returns—the day of consummation, or the future "day of the Lord" (1 Thess. 5:2)—God will release creation from its bondage to corruption and the futility to which he has subjected it (see Rom. 8:20–21 with Gen. 3:17). Then creation itself will "obtain the freedom of the glory of the children of God" (Rom. 8:21). So creation itself eagerly awaits our revelation as God's children. It groans with us, "who have the firstfruits of the Spirit," as we "wait eagerly for . . . the redemption of our bodies. *For in this hope*"—the hope of the redemption of our bodies as

God's adopted children—"*we were saved*" (Rom. 8:23–24). The fruit of our Lord's obedience is everlasting, embodied life for us along with the restoration of all things (see Acts 3:21).

In the beginning, at creation, all was pristine. Because of Adam and Eve's disobedience everything is now marred by suffering and death. Yet by his life and death, our Lord conquered death, and thus will halt life's funeral procession (see Isa. 51:11; 65:19; Rev. 7:17; 21:4). So for those in Christ, everything will be pristine once again at the end in the consummation (see Isa. 65:17).

Consummation

In 1 Corinthians 15, Paul is responding to the fact that some Corinthians were denying the resurrection of the dead (see v. 12). By now it should be clear that Paul is referring to our resurrection, meaning the future bodily resurrection of those of us who belong to Christ (see v. 23). In order to counter this disastrous denial, Paul begins by stressing what all true Christians believe—that Christ was raised from the dead.[k] He does this by recounting the public evidence for Christ's resurrection. The first eight verses of 1 Corinthians 15 are thus crucial to our grasp of the gospel:

> Now, brothers and sisters, I want to remind you of the gospel I preached to you, which you received and on which you have taken your stand. By this gospel you are saved, if you hold firmly to the word I preached to you. Otherwise, you have believed in vain.
>
> For what I received I passed on to you as of first importance: that Christ died for our sins according to the Scriptures, that he was buried, that he was raised on the third day according to the Scriptures, and that he appeared to Cephas, and then to the Twelve. After that, he appeared to more than five hundred of the brothers and sisters at the same time, most of whom are still living, though some have fallen asleep. Then he appeared to James, then to all the

---

k. "If you confess with your mouth that Jesus is Lord *and believe in your heart that God raised him from the dead,* you will be saved. For with the heart one believes and is justified, and with the mouth one confesses and is saved" (Rom. 10:9–10).

apostles, and last of all he appeared to me also, as to one abnormally born. (NIV)

The gospel on which the Corinthians had taken their stand is grounded in Christ's death, burial, and bodily resurrection.[54] These verses demonstrate "what it means to stand in the Christian tradition. . . . It means going back to the Church in Palestine; it means going back to Christ crucified and raised from the dead."[55] It means going back in space and time to a place and time where, after his resurrection, Jesus was seen by many on several occasions and, *were it not for what they saw*, "there would have been no Christian faith at all."[56] This is what Paul preached, "and this," he reminds the Corinthians, "is what you believed" (15:11 NIV).

Paul then argues that on the basis of this proclamation, the Corinthians must not say that there is no resurrection of the dead:

> [For] if there is no resurrection of the dead, then not even Christ has been raised. And if Christ has not been raised, then our preaching is in vain and your faith is in vain. . . . And if Christ has not been raised, your faith is futile and you are still in your sins. . . . *If in Christ we have hope in this life only, we are of all people most to be pitied.* (15:13–14, 17, 19)

For Paul, the future resurrection of those who belong to Christ and Christ's own resurrection are inextricably linked. To deny the future bodily resurrection of believers is tantamount to denying Christ's resurrection. And if Christ has not risen, then Christian preaching is *kenos*—that is, empty of any true content, of having any purpose or goal.[57] Moreover, Christian faith is also *kenos*, for without Christ's resurrection the gospel's core has been gutted so that there is nothing left to believe. If Christ has not risen, then he has not triumphed over death, and we will never be delivered from the vanity and futility that echoes throughout the Old Testament. The Greek word for *futile* at 1 Corinthians 15:17 is the same word the Greek translators of the Old Testament used to translate the Hebrew word *hebel* in Ecclesiastes and which Paul uses at Romans 8:20. So to deny that we will be bodily resurrected is tantamount to maintaining that all of the kinds of perplexity, frustration, pain, sickness, aging, loneliness, discord, alienation, and strife that the Old Testament laments will always persist. It is tantamount to saying that nothing has changed from what the Preacher asserted about the futility of life "under the sun." It would be to acknowledge that we have not been redeemed and are still being condemned for our sins. It is to say that in the end death wins.

Our first parents disobeyed "under the sun," and ever since it has been humanity's lot to suffer and die "under the sun." So it was only fitting that our redemption should also take place "under the sun."[58] The second person of the Trinity became incarnate and lived a life of perfect obedience to his Father "under the sun" so that humanity, as God created and intended it, would not disappear. Our suffering and death are in space and time, so our redemption must also be (see Luke 24:26–27; Acts 17:2–3; 1 Cor. 15:20–26).

This volume began by recounting a time when there was no suffering, when God created a perfectly pristine world for our first parents to inhabit. He created them to be the crown of a hierarchically structured world filled with created realities governed by stable causal processes that they were to rule over intelligently and lovingly as his proxies and visible images.

He set them in a garden and commanded them to roam through it, tasting all but one of its fruits. He prohibited them from eating the fruit of only one tree. Yet that prohibition was a revelation and an invitation, for by it the transcendent God of creation was revealing himself also to be the immanent, personal God who desires to be in communion with human beings. He was inviting our first parents to make a decisive, wholehearted, lifelong commitment to fellowship with him. He was inviting them to commit themselves to the greatest and most fulfilling love that can be known by human beings.

If they had responded as he asked, they would have known truly abundant life in the everlasting presence of God's smiling face. But they rebelled, choosing to disobey and thus rupturing their spiritual lifeline to God. This brought death into our world, along with all of the kinds of human woe.

The gospel is the incredibly good news that while we were still rebels, God reconciled us to himself by the death of his Son (see Rom. 5:10; Col. 1:21–22). When we put our faith in Christ's redeeming work, our spiritual lifeline with God is restored (see Rom. 5:5; Gal. 4:6), our communion with him begins again (see John 14:23; 2 Cor. 6:16), and we are sealed with God's Holy Spirit, who is the guarantee of our promised eternal inheritance in the resurrected Christ's everlasting kingdom (see Eph. 1:14; 4:30).

Yet for now our communion with God is imperfect and incomplete. We still struggle against sin (see Heb. 12:1–4). We must walk by faith rather than by sight (see 2 Cor. 5:7). "Now we see things imperfectly, like puzzling reflections in a mirror, but then we will see everything with perfect clarity. All that [we] know now is partial and incomplete, but then [we] will know everything completely, just as God now knows [us] completely" (1 Cor. 13:12 NLT).

At the consummation those of us who have put our faith in Christ's redeeming work will be raised with our natural bodies transformed by God into spiritual bodies like our Lord's resurrected body so that we can forevermore grow in the grace and knowledge of him.[59] As God the Father lives in the divine equivalent of face-to-face relationships with his Son and Spirit, so, for those of us who accept God's invitation (see Isa. 55:1 with John 7:37–39 and Rev. 22:17) and endure to the end (see Mark 13:13; James 5:7–11), our reflection of his image will one day advance from one perfection to another through Christ's face-to-face everlasting presence with us as the church, his bride (see Rev. 21:1–3; 22:4).

Christians confess that Jesus Christ was God incarnate, whose earthly life, death, and resurrection reveal human life's true meaning. The gospel is "the word of truth" that illuminates all else (see Eph. 1:11–14; Col. 1:3–7). It tells us "the true story of the whole world."[1] Having received that word by faith, we eagerly await our Lord's second coming,

---

1. See the prologue, 15.

when we will hear his greeting, "Come, you who are blessed by my Father, *inherit the kingdom prepared for you from the foundation of the world*" (Matt. 25:34; cf. Eph. 1:4).

What is first in intention is last in execution. From eternity past, God the Father has always intended that his Son, Jesus, would gather to himself a great multitude of people from every nation, tribe, and language (see Rev. 7:9–10). The Christian story is and always has been a fully plotted story, providentially moving through its four parts from its beginning toward its end. From before time began, God the Father has always intended everything to converge on the moment when, by our faith in his promises, the redeeming work of his Son, and rebirth and renewal by his Holy Spirit (see John 3:5; Titus 3:4–7), he will bless us in Christ with the love that he has for his blessed Son—a love that knows no bounds in time or space.[60]

Beyond this prospect of perfect, everlasting communion with God himself, Scripture does not reveal much about life in the consummation. There will be other joys—for instance, the joy of the righteous inhabiting a new creation (see Isa. 65:17–25; 2 Pet. 3:13; Rev. 21:27) and the joy of reunion with those who have died in Christ (see 1 Thess. 4:13–18)—but concentrating on them could distract us from anticipating the joy of God the Father giving us, through the redeeming work of his Son, the face-to-face, unhindered, full communion with himself that our first parents refused.

So the gospel as God's "word of truth"[m] is unrelentingly future oriented. It unequivocally proclaims Christ's bodily resurrection as the event that, by the grace of God, causes us "to be born again to a living hope" for a consummation that looks forward to "an inheritance that is imperishable, undefiled, and unfading," which is being kept in heaven for us "who by God's power are being guarded through faith for a salvation ready to be revealed in the last time" (1 Pet. 1:3–5). This salvation will take place in space and time, like all of the other parts of the full Christian story, for it is an integral part of that story. The God

---

m. See Eph. 1:13; Col. 1:5; 2 Tim. 2:15.

who spoke creation into existence, who spoke to our first parents in the garden, now speaks through "Jesus, the mediator of a new covenant, and to the sprinkled blood that speaks a better word than the blood of Abel" (Heb. 12:24). And he will speak once more, "shaking not only the earth but also the heavens" to remove what can be shaken so that "the things that cannot be shaken may remain" (vv. 26–27).

This, the hope for consummation, is the final metaphorical star that the full Christian story puts in place so that we can be properly oriented in these our earthly days.

AWAITING THE DAWN

In the meantime, we must walk by faith and not by sight, reminding ourselves that suffering is an inevitable part of fallen human life. From Ecclesiastes we have learned that it is unlikely we will be spared any of the kinds of suffering common to human beings. We may get cancer or other terminal illnesses. We will almost surely grieve the loss of some of those whom we love. Sinful temptations that we must resist may plague us, perhaps for our whole lives. Sometimes we will suffer from loneliness or difficult relationships. We may spend our lifetimes in wearisome, unfulfilling jobs. Some of us will be beset with physical, mental, or psychological maladies that undermine our ability to live ordinary lives.

As Christians we must, in addition, bear the burden of identifying with our Lord in order to fulfill his last mandate:

> All authority in heaven and on earth has been given to me. Therefore go and make disciples of all nations, baptizing them in the name of the Father and of the Son and of the Holy Spirit, and teaching them to obey everything I have commanded you. And surely I am with you always, to the very end of the age. (Matt. 28:18–20 NIV)

"It was fitting," the author of the book of Hebrews tells us, "that [God], for whom and by whom all things exist, in bringing many sons to glory, should make the founder of their salvation perfect through suffering" (Heb. 2:10). And it is fitting that we identify with our Lord by suffering with him (see Matt. 10:24–25; John 13:12–17 with 15:20).[61] We must take up our crosses and die daily (see Luke 9:23–26) knowing that our speaking God's word of truth to the lost may cost us our friends, our jobs, our homes, our freedom, and perhaps even our lives (see Heb. 10:32–12:13).

In the face of this, we eagerly await the consummation when we will see our Lord Jesus Christ rise as creation's bright morning star (see Rev. 22:4, 16). Then the star that Balaam could only see afar off will come out of Jacob to crush all evil (see Num. 24:17). Then the Son of righteousness will rise with healing in his wings (see Mal. 4:1–2). Then we will no longer need the stars of faith and hope to guide us because we will forevermore gaze upon his loving face.

EPILOGUE

Give Me Understanding That I May Live

People who have wealth but lack understanding
are like the beasts that perish.

Psalm 49:20 NIV

You have dealt well with your servant,
O Lᴏʀᴅ, according to your word. . . .
Before I was afflicted I went astray,
but now I keep your word. . . .
I know, O Lᴏʀᴅ, . . . that in faithfulness you have afflicted me.

Psalm 119:65, 67, 75

Blessed is the one who finds wisdom,
and the one who gets understanding,
for the gain from her is better than gain from silver
and her profit better than gold.
She is more precious than jewels,
and nothing you desire can compare with her.
Long life is in her right hand;
in her left hand are riches and honor.
Her ways are ways of pleasantness,
and all her paths are peace.
She is a tree of life to those who lay hold of her;
those who hold her fast are called blessed.

Proverbs 3:13–18

Give me understanding that I may live.

Psalm 119:144

As creatures of instinct, animals are, as Derek Kidner says, "in contented bondage to their surroundings, their behaviour a product of inborn and incoming urges." But as creation's crown who are made in God's image, we have the freedom "to set a course and hold to it."[1] In other words, we were created to lead our lives by ruling over ourselves and the rest of creation. The stories we hear and tell enable us to do this.

Storytelling lifts us above all of the earth's other creatures, as even those who understand us to be no more than evolutionary accidents can see. So Lisa Cron opens her book *Wired for Story* like this:

> Once upon a time really smart people were completely convinced the world was flat. Then they learned that it wasn't. But they were still pretty sure the sun revolved around the Earth . . . until that theory went bust, too. For an even longer period of time, smart people have believed story is just a form of entertainment. They've thought that beyond the immense pleasure it bestows . . . story itself serves no necessary purpose. . . .
>
> Wrong again.
>
> Story, as it turns out, was crucial to our evolution—more so than opposable thumbs. Opposable thumbs let us hang on; story told us what to hang on to. Story is what enables us to imagine what might happen in the future, and so prepare for it—a feat no other species can lay claim to, opposable thumbs or not. Story is what makes us human, not just metaphorically but literally. Recent breakthroughs in neuroscience reveal that our brain is hardwired to respond to story; the pleasure we derive from a tale well told is nature's way of seducing us into paying attention to it.

In other words, we're wired to turn to story to teach us the way of the world.[2]

Most stories are about something happening to specific people in particular places over limited periods of time, so, as people living in space and time, we can use them to help us get oriented in our own lives. They are, as Cron claims, "the language of [human] experience." And given the freedom from bondage to our immediate surroundings that our storytelling ability helps to give us, Cron is right: our ability to tell stories is more crucial to human life than any of our distinctively human physical features because stories alone enable us, of all the earth's creatures, to imagine the future and thus act with it in mind. She's also right that our brains are hardwired to respond to stories and thus that we are predisposed to rely on them to learn the ways of the world.

But an evolutionary, exclusively bottom-up story isn't just different from the Christian top-down story; it is an entirely different kind of story. It is in fact a kind of story that excludes from the outset the possibility of personal communication and communion between God and us—and thus precludes our gaining any real understanding about our suffering.

Usually when we encounter someone doing something unfamiliar, the quickest and surest way to understand what they are doing is to ask them. Small children often ask their parents these sorts of questions:

"Mommy, what are you doing?"
 "I'm getting ready to go to work."
"What are you doing, Daddy?"
 "I'm taking out the trash."

Over time, children begin to recognize their parents' routines. When Mommy is putting the car seat in the SUV, she is getting ready to take me somewhere. When Daddy turns on the night-light in my bedroom, he is getting ready to tuck me in for another night's sleep.

When someone is doing something unusual like changing a flat tire, quite often the question "Why?" follows the question "What are you doing?" As incredible as it may seem, we now know that even six-month-old infants recognize when people are acting purposefully—when someone is doing something intentionally (that is, for some reason that can answer the question "Why?")—and can differentiate purposeful action from the causal regularities that govern physical objects. As Justin Barrett puts it, they distinguish the *whos* from the *whats*.[3]

Stories portraying someone doing something purposefully are top-down stories that explain what is happening in terms of a person's intentions and choices. The full Christian story is a top-down story that takes everything about us and our world to be explained in terms of God's intentions and choices. As such, it is shot through with purpose: from eternity past,[a] God intended to create creatures enough like himself that they could freely enter into communion with him, and so he chose to create a world of space and time for us to inhabit where we could exercise that freedom. After our first parents abused their freedom by disobeying his command and thereby brought suffering into the world, God still sought to give them hope through his announcement of the *protevangelium*. Then at just the right time, God the Father sent Jesus Christ, who, as God's incarnate Son, chose to live a life of perfect obedience to his Father and then to die a completely undeserved death in order to atone for the sins of those who put their faith in him (see Rom. 5:6; 1 John 4:9–10, 14). God the Father then raised his Son from the dead and together they sent the Holy Spirit to dwell in us who put our faith in Christ's redeeming work (see John 14:26; 15:26; Gal. 4:6). The Spirit witnesses to the fact that we are now God's children who will be resurrected to everlasting life when Jesus returns to judge the living and dead (see Acts 10:42; 1 Pet. 4:5). God will then consummate his purposes by releasing creation from the futility to which he has subjected it and those of us who have put our faith in Christ's redeeming work will finally enter into the full and everlasting communion with him that God has intended from the start (see Eph. 1:3–10; Rev. 21:3). God will then wipe every tear from our eyes, and death will be no more, nor

---

a. See Eph. 1:4; 2 Tim. 1:9.

will there be any mourning, crying, or pain, for all suffering will have ceased (see Rev. 21:4).

All of this, including our suffering, takes place because it fulfills God's purposes. And so this top-down story is filled with meaning because it is a story about a person—three persons, in fact—who have intended and chosen to bring to completion all that happens as parts of the full Christian story.

An evolutionary, exclusively bottom-up story attempts to understand everything in ultimately impersonal terms, holding that "the laws of physical cause and effect can somehow ultimately account for" every aspect of reality.[4] The eminent sociobiologist E. O. Wilson claims that humankind should embrace such a story, building knowledge up "from reality and reason alone, cleansed of all superstition," in order to form what the great Renaissance thinker Francis Bacon termed "the empire of man." This quest is to be "driven by the belief that *entirely on their own, human beings can know all that needs to be known,* and in knowing understand, and in understanding gain the power to choose more wisely than ever before."

An exclusively bottom-up story denies that reality has any sort of overarching purpose. Since everything has arisen from the impersonal, purposeless interaction of matter according to fixed causal laws, the universe has only accidentally produced creatures like us. C. S. Lewis summarizes this view this way:

> People who take [this view] think that matter and space just happen to exist, and always have existed nobody knows why; and . . . the matter, behaving in certain fixed ways, has just happened, by a sort of fluke, to produce creatures like ourselves who are able to think. By one chance in a thousand something hit our sun and made it produce the planets; and by another thousandth chance the chemicals necessary for life, and the right temperature, occurred on one of these planets, and so some of the matter on this earth came alive; and then, by a very long series of chances, the living creatures developed into things like us.[5]

When Wilson summarizes what he says is the scientific meaning of our existence in his book *The Meaning of Human Existence*, he makes precisely these points:

> In ordinary usage the word "meaning" implies intention, intention implies design, and design implies a designer. Any entity, any process, or definition of any word itself is put into play as a result of an intended consequence in the mind of the designer. This is the heart of the . . . worldview of organized religions, and in particular their creation stories. Humanity, it assumes, exists for a purpose. Individuals have a purpose in being on Earth. Both humanity and individuals have meaning.[6]

Yet, he tells us, thanks to Darwin, there is now

> a second, broader way the word "meaning" is used and a very different worldview implied. It is that the accidents of history, not the intentions of a designer, are the source of meaning. There is no advance design, but instead overlapping networks of physical cause and effect. The unfolding of history is obedient only to the general laws of the Universe. Each event is random yet alters the probability of later events. During organic evolution, for example, the origin of one adaptation by natural selection makes the origin of certain other adaptations more likely. This concept of meaning, insofar as it illuminates humanity and the rest of life, is the worldview of science.

Science, Wilson claims, establishes that "humanity . . . arose entirely on its own through an accumulated series of events during evolution. We are not predestined to reach any goal, *nor are we answerable to any power but our own.* Only wisdom based on self-understanding, not piety, will save us. *There will be no redemption or second chance vouchsafed to us from above.*" In the end, human suffering is just a by-product of our evolutionary origin, with no meaning beyond its sometimes being an instrument that, by steering us away from some kinds of harmful situations, helps humanity survive.

Ultimately, each of us must adopt one of these worldviews.[7] Is our world a place of ultimate meaning, where God intends and indeed commands us to live in particular ways, and where our eternities are determined by our choices in this life? Or is it a place where meaning is simply something we make (so to speak) locally in the cosmically brief moment when human beings exist? Is whatever meaning we make—"all the labours of the ages, all the devotion, all the inspiration, all the noonday brightness of human genius"—ultimately "destined to extinction in the vast death of the solar system, and . . . [will] the whole temple of Man's achievement inevitably be buried beneath the debris of a universe in ruins"?[8]

Wilson claims that the top-down view, where history is interpreted as "the unfolding of a supernatural design," is preferred by most people because it is "comforting."[9] Sigmund Freud went further, claiming in *The Future of an Illusion* that religion is infantile, a product of wish-fulfillment.[10] Both Wilson and Freud assume that as science has advanced, we have gained the cognitive tools that enable us to free ourselves from the crutch of religion.[11]

Yet the full Christian story as we have seen it in Scripture is neither in any ordinary sense comforting nor the product of wish fulfillment. In claiming that God created us to fulfill a particular role in creation that our first parents then chose to abandon, it portrays us as constantly under the eye of a righteous judge whose holiness must be manifested in his wrath against our sin. His anger is manifested in all of life's perplexities, frustrations, and futilities, the chief of which is death. On our own, we can do nothing to appease God or rectify our situation. We must accept redemption on God's terms, who leaves us subject to all the kinds of suffering that can befall humankind, and we must then, additionally, deny ourselves, take up our crosses daily, and follow the path of suffering inaugurated by our Savior (see Matt. 10:38–39; Luke 9:23; 1 Cor. 15:30–31). Because we identify with him, the world will hate us, excluding, reviling, and spurning us as evil (see Matt. 10:16–23; Luke 6:22; 1 Pet. 4:12–14). Yet we mustn't lose heart. In fact, we must endure to the end in order to be saved (see Matt. 10:22; Heb. 3:14; 10:32–38).

And even then, on the day of consummation, the true worth of our earthly works will be revealed by fire, manifesting to everyone exactly what each of us has and hasn't done (see 1 Cor. 3:10–15; 2 Cor. 5:10).

"Science," Wilson declares, "builds and tests competitive hypotheses from partial evidence and imagination in order to generate [whatever] knowledge [it has] about the real world."[12] It is "totally committed to fact without reference to religion or ideology" and thus, by Wilson's lights, "cuts paths through the fever swamp of human existence." By restricting the potential sources of our knowledge of ultimate reality to what we can discover working "entirely on [our] own," Wilson, Freud, and others like them commit themselves to a belief in the exclusively materialistic basis of all of reality in its "overlapping networks of physical cause and effect." This seals them off from needing to consider whether there are any obligations that press upon us because of the intentions and purposes of a Creator.[13] Freed from such considerations, they can devote themselves to forming "the empire of man." They can be godlike in determining humanity's future, since, as Wilson notes, we have now reached "the most important . . . threshold in the technoscientific era," namely, the threshold where "we are about to abandon natural selection, the process that created us, in order to direct our own evolution by volitional selection—the process of redesigning our biology and human nature as we wish them to be. No longer," he asseverates,

> will the prevalence of some genes . . . over others be the result of environmental forces, most of which are beyond human control or even understanding. The genes and their prescribed traits can be what we choose. So—how about longer lives, enlarged memory, better vision, less aggressive behavior, superior athletic ability, pleasing body odor? *The shopping list is endless.*[14]

If we restrict knowledge to no more than what we can in principle discover on our own, then that opens the way for us to conclude, as Wilson does, that "human existence [is] simpler than we thought. There is no predestination, no unfathomed mystery of life. Demons and gods do not vie for our allegiance. Instead, we are self-made, independent, alone, and fragile, [no more than] a biological species adapted to live in a biological world." We are not then accountable to anything or anyone except ourselves.

Yet is science our only access to ultimate reality? Is the restriction on our potential sources of knowledge to what we can at least in principle discover for ourselves warranted?

It is not warranted in everyday life. We often rely on what others tell us rather than on what we can discover for ourselves. This ranges from little Sally asking, "Mommy, who is your mommy?" to my asking, "Where can I reach you next week?" Sally might be able over time to discover the answer to her question, but I cannot discover the answer to mine since it depends on your intentions and plans, which you must reveal to me (cf. 1 Cor. 2:10–11). Moreover, we are often obliged to act according to someone else's intentions: If you have hired me to fill a specific role in your company, I am obliged to learn from you what that role is. As your employee, I am not free to do whatever I want without consulting you. I am not free to form an empire devoted to myself and employees like me.[b]

Wilson declares that "the capacity to decide, and how and why the capacity came into being, and the consequences that followed, are the broader, science-based meaning of human existence." He maintains that "premier among [these] consequences is the capacity to imagine possible futures, and to plan and choose among them."[15] This emphasis on science, insofar "as it enables us to imagine what might happen in the future, and so prepare for it," is legitimate. Pursuing scientific knowledge to secure a better future is part of what God commissioned us to do in issuing the creation mandate (see Gen. 1:28). We should welcome legitimate scientific advances that help us exercise our God-given dominion over creation appropriately. But to take our capacity to choose to be no more than an evolutionary accident—in other words, to take science as the whole story—amounts to our taking a mere *story fragment* for the whole story, which means it isn't really a story at all.

---

b. See von Rad's comment on Gen. 2:15 in chap. 2, note 7.

When the elements of the story that can be known only by revelation are stripped away, we may feel free to choose any future we desire, but our feeling then fails to acknowledge what is actually the case. It is only "by faith [that] we [can] understand that the universe was created by the word of God, so that what is seen was not made out of things that are visible" (Heb. 11:3). And it is only by faith that we know that "just as people are destined to die once, and after that to face judgment, so Christ was sacrificed once to take away the sins of many; and he will appear a second time . . . to bring salvation to those who are waiting for him" (Heb. 9:27–28 NIV). The story's true beginning and end must be revealed to us and thus can be known only by faith.

Acknowledging that we can know the full story only by faith is crucial for understanding who we are and what we were made for. It is why the psalmist declared, "People who have wealth but lack understanding are like the beasts that perish" (Ps. 49:20 NIV). He addressed his psalm to all human beings: "Hear this, all peoples! Give ear, all inhabitants of the world, both low and high, rich and poor together!" (vv. 1–2). His message is one that all human beings need to hear and heed. That message, like Ecclesiastes, emphasizes "the futility of worldliness," although "it brings out into the open the assurance of victory over death which Ecclesiastes leaves concealed."[16] It drives home that those who trust in their wealth—and by extension all who lack the kind of understanding that comes only by faith—are clueless about who they are meant to be. God has "set eternity in the human heart" (Eccles. 3:11 NIV)—meaning that we, unlike the beasts, have an "aspiration for eternity [that] constitutes indirect evidence for our divine placement within a larger narrative framework of meaning."[17] Yet we all too readily abridge the story, considering just the part that lies immediately before us and thus failing to orient ourselves by the past and future that God has revealed. As Daniel Treier sums it up, "God configures humans to be eternity-seeking not so they despair over earthly futility in itself, but so that restless hearts might rest in their ultimate Good alone—*at the pace made possible by divine revelation.*" We live fully human lives only when we acknowledge that we inhabit the story that God is progressively revealing.[c] Otherwise we are, as the psalmist says, like mere beasts.

Yet Psalm 49 does more than simply remind us what distinctively human life consists in. By reminding himself of the ultimate futility of trusting in anything other than God, the psalmist reminds us of what we were made for. His faith-filled wisdom and understanding enable him actually to grasp the true meaning of human existence (see vv. 3–4).

He reminds himself that he should not fear "in evil times when beset by the wickedness of treacherous foes" who trust in their wealth and boast of their great riches (vv. 5–6 REB). For their foolish confidence is misplaced. Faithless living must ultimately fail. For even the wealthiest human beings, despite all "their pomp"—despite the splendor of their wealth, fame, power, and worldly influence—"cannot abide" (v. 12 NRSV). Right when they seem to be in control and others are praising them, they find they are not as death overtakes them and shepherds them away (vv. 13–14). When their time comes, there is no "overnight lodging," no way station between life and death that their money can buy.[18] Moreover, their end "is described impersonally, as an unmaking," when their forms just waste away (see v. 14 NRSV).[19]

"But," the psalmist declares, "God will redeem me from the realm of the dead; he will surely take me to himself" (v. 15 NIV). Here God "suddenly and for the only time," becomes the psalm's subject right at the point where the foolishness of faithlessness becomes apparent.[20] And verse 15's *me* and *he* "confirm that this [will not be] salvation at arm's length."[21] God will *take* his faithful to himself as he *took* Enoch and Elijah.[22] The end of the faithful, unlike the end of the faithless, is personal through and through.[23]

In other words, when the right time comes, we as God's faithful will finally meet him face-to-face. As Allen Ross observes, this is just one Old Testament passage among many that expresses confidence that a believer's "communion with God"—which begins when we accept God's

---

c. See Herbert McCabe's "Why God?" reprinted as an appendix.

offer of salvation by faith—"will survive the oppression of this world and the experience of death. . . . The end of the wicked is dark and destructive; the end of the righteous is life with God, now and forever."[24] After having guided us with his counsel, God will take us to glory, where he himself will be our portion forevermore (see Ps. 73:24–26).

And so the saga of Scripture comes full circle. The opportunity for communion with God that our first parents spurned has been, through our Lord's redeeming work, offered to us again. In receiving that offer by faith, we are called to be witnesses to his resurrection (see Matt. 28:19–20; Acts 1:8, 22; 4:33). The primary purpose of our lives must then be to "proclaim the excellencies of him who called [us] out of darkness into his marvelous light" (1 Pet. 2:9). We do so as we boldly and openly live out the full Christian story, keeping in mind especially its beginning and end.

In the first chapter of *When the Stars Disappear*, I recounted the perils Paul and his companions faced in his journey by sea from Adramyttium to Rome to appear before Caesar. At one point during a terrible storm at sea, all of the stars that could guide them disappeared. They lost all hope of being saved. But then God appeared to Paul in a dream, assuring him that he would indeed stand trial before Caesar and that everyone aboard Paul's ship would be saved. When the storm passed and the sun and stars reappeared, Paul sailed on to proclaim the gospel in Rome, just as God had ordained (see Acts 23:11).

As Luke recounts it, Paul's journey had a specific, intentionally meaningful beginning and end. Even in the midst of the storm, Paul was destined to accomplish a particular task in a specific place in order to fulfill God's purposes. Storm or no storm, he was not free to sail wherever he wished. His journey was truly *a journey*—"travel or passage *from one place to another*."[d] It was the specific journey it was because it had a specific beginning—Adramyttium—and a specific end—Rome. It was no improvisation, where Paul and his companions could make it up as they went along. It was not a lark or a junket.[25] It

---

d. *Merriam-Webster*, s.v. "journey," accessed November 9, 2021, https://unabridged.merriam-webster.com; my emphasis.

was not even a serious, self-chosen project, adopted by Paul perhaps after much thought and deliberation.[e] It was a journey providentially ordained by God.

If the full Christian story is indeed "the true story of the whole world," then it, like Paul's journey to Rome, has a specific, intentionally meaningful beginning and end. It is also a true journey, over a much more expansive stretch of space and time, from humanity's real beginning in the garden of Eden to its final end when the heavenly Jerusalem will descend from heaven so that God may dwell with those redeemed by his Son (see Rev. 21–22). If we have accepted our Lord's redeeming work by faith and are thus numbered among God's people, then we are on that journey, and our personal stories—the storylines of our earthly lives—are to play some particular part in accomplishing God's eternal purposes (see Eph. 4:11–16). They are to be parts—indeed, integral parts[f]—in the full Christian storyline. Consequently, we are not free to do whatever we wish. Our lives are not to be improvisations, where we just make up the life we like as we go along. They are not to be larks or junkets or even serious, self-chosen projects. They are to be part of God the Father's project for bringing many sons and daughters to glory through the suffering and death of Jesus, his Son (see Heb. 2:10 with Heb. 5:9 and 2 Pet. 1:17).

When we abridge the full Christian story by deemphasizing its divinely revealed beginning and end, we make it into a different kind of story—one where we can focus on our own happiness and comfort, with little thought about God's project and humanity's true beginning and ultimate end. The fact that God has called us to "proclaim the excellencies of him who called [us] out of darkness into his marvelous light" (1 Pet. 2:9) then fades from our consciousness, and we become virtually indistinguishable from the world around us. We cease to be the world's salt and light (see Matt. 5:13–16).

---

e. Although Paul had for quite a while planned at some point to visit Rome (see Acts 19:21; Rom. 15:24, 28).

f. See the epilogue of Mark Talbot, *When the Stars Disappear: Help and Hope from Stories of Suffering in Scripture* (Wheaton, IL: Crossway, 2020), with its emphasis on the way in which God's Old Testament saints actually *made real* the substance of God's promises by their obedience, 90.

In the end, at the final judgment, our Lord will judge us to have lived our lives wisely and skillfully to the degree that we have sought divine wisdom and understanding in the Scriptures in order to align the trajectories of our individual life stories with the trajectory of the world's true general story (see Ps. 119:99; Rom. 15:4; 2 Tim. 3:14–16).

The stories we hear and tell are what enable us to lead distinctively human lives. At first, it may seem that the only really important stories are our personal stories, the stories we tell about our individual lives. Yet ultimately two general stories compete for our allegiance, affecting our personal stories in radically different ways.

Suffering can disrupt any of these stories and thus affect our lives, sometimes for good and sometimes for ill. When I was seventeen and fell about 50 feet off a Tarzan-like rope swing, breaking my back and becoming paralyzed from the waist down, my personal story was deeply disrupted. My future went dark as I became uncertain about my life's long-range trajectory—Would I ever walk again? Could I hope for a somewhat normal life, even if it might be a life that was wheelchair-bound?

Those questions challenged the general story I had been living, making me rethink what I had been living for. While I was a Christian, I had been living an inane life, more interested in superficial pleasures like riding down sunny, winding roads with my friends while listening to pop music or driving those roads by myself at breakneck speeds. Yet as soon as I hit the ground, almost everything that had been distracting me fell away. And to this day, my paralysis and the kinds of chronic suffering that accompany it focus me, prompting me to concentrate on the one issue that really matters—my relationship with God. I am daily acquainted with the very real pains and uncertainties of infirmity, but they cannot begin to touch the much greater joy of daily and sometimes even moment-by-moment conscious, prayerful dependence on him.

My suffering has drawn me to God and his Scriptures, where I hear his voice telling me the story of salvation again and again. In those Scriptures I find God's divinely revealed wisdom and understanding to be a tree of life by which I live and am blessed (see Prov. 3:18). Its story of what God is doing from creation to consummation has revealed to me a world that gives my life a depth and meaning it could not otherwise possess.

And so with the psalmist I often find myself praying,

You have dealt well with your servant,
　　O LORD, according to your word.
Teach me good judgment and knowledge,
　　for I believe in your commandments.
Before I was afflicted I went astray,
　　but now I keep your word.
You are good and do good;
　　teach me your statutes. . . .
[The] heart [of the arrogant] is unfeeling like fat,
　　but I delight in your law.
It is good for me that I was afflicted,
　　that I might learn your statutes.
The law of your mouth is better to me
　　than thousands of gold and silver pieces.

Your hands have made and fashioned me;
　　give me understanding that I may learn your commandments.
　　. . .
I know, O LORD, . . . that in faithfulness you have afflicted me.
. . .

Give me understanding that I may live. (Ps. 119:65–68, 70–73, 75, 144)

ACKNOWLEDGMENTS

My foremost debt in completing this volume is, once again, to Christian Scholars' Fund, who throughout its development has generously supported my work by helping to reduce my teaching course load at Wheaton College so that I have had more time to think and write.

Wheaton College also sped up the process of completing it by granting me a one-semester sabbatical over the 2020–2021 academic year, along with an additional one-course reduction by awarding me a G. W. Aldeen Faculty Development Grant.

Colleagues in the philosophy and Bible and theology departments at the college have interacted with much of this material. Special thanks are owed to Dan Treier and Dan Block for reading through the entire manuscript to make sure I wasn't making egregious biblical or theological errors. Any remaining errors are, of course, mine.

The students in my PHIL 241: Suffering courses over the last couple of years have read and commented on much of this material. In addition, many other students have worked through most of it in independent-study cohorts and during summer research projects. They include Annikka Bouwsma, Abbie Weaver, Kelly Fitzpatrick, Courtney Baer, and Adriana Moore; Jeremy Chong, Felisa Welkener, Mike Cembala, and Katherine Hoppe; Davis Whyte, Carolyn Weldy, Carlson Chiles, Mia Rynbrandt, Mason Packwood, Karsten Baldwin, and Kira Wimbush. Erik Miles also made detailed comments on portions of it, as did Michael Rau.

Four readers have been especially diligent in reading through multiple drafts: Nancy Duperreault, Dave Zeilstra, Paul Winters, and Jason

Baldwin. Jason deserves special thanks for reading all the endnotes with suggestions concerning which could be cut, which shortened, and even (if only very infrequently) which needed a little expansion. Tory Houriet also read two of the chapters, along with the front and back matter.

Portions of this book have been presented orally, such as in a two-day conference at Immanuel Church in Andover, Minnesota (with special thanks to Jim and Bonnie Hoekstra), over several month-long engagements with the Christian Perspectives adult Sunday school class at the Orchard Church, Arlington Heights, Illinois, over the past several years (with special thanks to Bob and Connie Hansen and Judy and Bill Bradish), as well as in podcasts, radio interviews, and television shows.

Other portions have been previewed in print, such as in the two-part article "The Importance of Vocation" and "The Importance of Calling" in the C. S. Lewis Institute's *Knowing and Doing* journal, Spring and Fall 2018; and in "Broken Wholeness," in *When Suffering Is Redemptive: Stories of How Anguish and Pain Accomplish God's Mission*, ed. Larry J. Waters (Wooster, OH: Weaver, 2016).

Thanks to the estate of Herbert McCabe OP, which holds the copyright for Herbert McCabe's essay "Why God?" from *Faith Within Reason* (New York: Continuum, 2007); used by permission of Bloomsbury Publishing for inclusion as an appendix.

Thanks to Lydia Brownback for being a careful and accommodating editor and to Justin Taylor for all of the ways in which he enhances the author/publisher relationship at Crossway.

Thanks also to Cindy who has always been willing to put down whatever she has been doing to allow me to read portions of my text to her for her response.

MORE ADVICE FOR MY READERS

When we are suffering, we need assurance that things won't always be so bad. As I hope to convince you as you read this book, if the full Christian story is true, then the world is not as it ordinarily seems. To the naked, untrained eye, the world can seem merely to plod on from one day to the next or, as the apostle Peter quotes of the scoffers in his day, "Where is this 'coming' he promised? Ever since our ancestors died, everything goes on as it has since the beginning of creation" (2 Pet. 3:4 NIV). Even in the eyes of someone as godly as Job, suffering can tempt us to conclude that the days just grind on endlessly, meaning life will never be good again.[a]

Christians must trust what they have heard more than what they can see. Scripture tells us that the world's causal regularities depend on the existence of a Word by whom "all things were created" and in whom "all things hold together" (Col. 1:16–17). Because God the Son "upholds the universe by the word of his power" (Heb. 1:3), we know that the world doesn't just grind mercilessly on according to impersonal and uncaring natural laws but that its causal regularities are part of its progression toward a glorious future, a time when, for God's people, suffering and death will be no more (see Rev. 21:1–4). By listening to God speak to us

---

a. "Has not man a hard service on earth, and are not his days like the days of a hired hand? Like a slave who longs for the shadow, and like a hired hand who looks for his wages, so I am allotted months of emptiness, and nights of misery are apportioned to me. When I lie down I say, 'When shall I arise?' But the night is long, and I am full of tossing till the dawn. . . . My days are swifter than a weaver's shuttle and come to their end without hope. Remember that my life is a breath; my eye will never again see good" (Job 7:1–4, 6–7).

through his Scriptures, we come to understand how the world actually is. We learn that God's power and goodness produce and ground those regularities (see Gen. 1:3–19; 8:22; Isa. 45:18; Rom. 1:18–20) as well as guarantee that he will finally bring our suffering to an end (see 2 Cor. 4:16–18; 1 Pet. 1:3–9). This helps us endure—as we must (see Heb. 10:32–38; 12:1–7)—until that end.

Yet becoming deeply and thoroughly convinced that the world is not purposeless takes effort. We must learn to live in ways that are true to the reality rather than conformed to the way things seem (see Hab. 2:2–4; 2 Pet. 3:8–18). This requires immersing ourselves in the full Christian story and then dedicating ourselves to the kind of careful, consistent thinking that resists the world's squeezing us into its own, ultimately hopeless mold.[b] Becoming deeply and thoroughly convinced of the full Christian story requires an unremitting, unconditional commitment to growing in biblical wisdom and understanding, as Solomon urged: "Get wisdom, get understanding; do not forget my words or turn away from them. . . . The beginning of wisdom is this: Get wisdom. *Though it cost all you have, get understanding*" (Prov. 4:5, 7 NIV).

Deep and thorough conviction grows out of familiarizing ourselves with a coherent web of detailed claims. When a perspective is developed in a way that shows how it all hangs together, it becomes more convincing.[c] In this volume, as in *When the Stars Disappear*, the superabundance of endnotes is intended to offer another layer of detail and coherence to the text's claims. The text outlines the basic storyline as clearly and concisely as I can. The footnotes, marked by superscript lowercase letters, refer to other parts of my first two volumes where I have said more about what's in the text or where I need to make a clari-

---

b. See Eph. 2:12, where Paul declares that those living apart from Christ, live "without God and without hope" (NLT) and J. B. Phillips's rendering of Rom. 12:1–2: "With eyes wide open to the mercies of God, I beg you, . . . as an act of intelligent worship, to give him your bodies, as a living sacrifice, consecrated to him and acceptable by him. Don't let the world around you squeeze you into its own mould, but let God re-mould your minds from within, so that you may prove in practice that the plan of God for you is good, meets all his demands and moves towards the goal of true maturity." *The New Testament in Modern English* (New York: Macmillan, 1960).

c. Of course, detailed false narratives can tempt us to embrace untruths. Yet we as Christians are simply working to become more firmly anchored in what we already have good reason to believe is trustworthy and true (see John 1:14; Eph. 1:13–14; Rev. 21:5–7).

fying comment without cluttering up the text. Reading just the text and footnotes your first time through will give you the lay of the land. But good reading is always rereading, and so on your next reading look up the parenthetical biblical references to check whether my claims are properly anchored in God's word.[1] That will also enable Scripture to start echoing through your mind. Then, finally, sample the endnotes, identified by numbered superscripts. They place the text and biblical references in a much more detailed web. Considering them enables the Holy Spirit to help you become fully convinced of truths we must hear because they are not ones we can see. Many readers of *When the Stars Disappear* have told me that reading its endnotes brought them to a much deeper level of insight and conviction. I think they should be especially helpful for pastors and teachers as they preach and teach the full Christian story. In all of this, my strategy is to give these four volumes on suffering and the Christian life layers of meaning that can be explored bit by bit.

When Paul was in Athens, he engaged the foremost intellects of his age (see Acts 17:16–34). Commenting on that meeting, John Stott writes that "Christ calls human beings to humble, but not to stifle, their intellect."[d] We humble our intellects by acknowledging that there are truths that are indispensable to human life that we cannot discover on our own. As I argue in the epilogue, these are truths that God himself must teach us. Learning them enriches, uplifts, and invigorates us beyond anything we could, without God's words, ever attain. The gospel opens us up to a world of profoundly satisfying truth that otherwise we would never know. Listening to God as he teaches us through his Scriptures assures us that our suffering will end. It also reveals truths that will enthrall us throughout eternity, long after our suffering has ceased.

---

d. John R. W. Stott, *The Message of Acts: The Spirit, the Church, and the World* (Downers Grove, IL: InterVarsity Press, 1990), 281.

APPENDIX

"Why God?"

by Herbert McCabe

When Macbeth hears of the suicide of his wife he gives famous expression to a certain view of life, of history, of the world, in which time becomes simply a mindless succession of events. Time, says Macbeth, is not the time of any story; the development of any plot; tomorrows and yesterdays are nothing but successive moments. It is, he says, an illusion to suppose that there is any story, any tale being enacted. What we think is a story is in the end just like the random mouthings of an idiot, with no connected meaning:

> Tomorrow, and tomorrow, and tomorrow,
> Creeps in this petty pace from day to day,
> To the last syllable of recorded time;
> And all our yesterdays have lighted fools
> The way to dusty death. Out, out, brief candle,
> Life's but a walking shadow, a poor player
> That struts and frets his hour upon the stage,
> And then is heard no more. It is a tale
> Told by an idiot, full of sound and fury
> Signifying nothing.[a]

It seems to me that I can best address the title I have given above by arguing that, without God, Macbeth would be in the end quite right.

---

a. William Shakespeare, *Macbeth*, 5.5.19–28.

I say "*in the end* quite right" because I don't mean that my atheist friends are all living in the kind of despair and disintegration that is represented by Macbeth. I mean only that this seems to me the *logical*, not necessarily the *psychological*, consequence of atheism. Unless our lives are a story told by God they are not a story at all, and this means they have no final meaning.

At one time there was a popular romantic picture of the courageous man who had rejected the props of religion and its illusory comforts, who stood erect on the darkling plain, swept with confused alarms of struggle and fight, facing boldly the fact that life does not provide him with any meaning at all. He is prepared with honesty to manage without it. The difficulty with this alluring picture is that concepts like courage and honesty have to belong to a character in a story, and if in the end there is no story then there is no courage or honesty either. You might as well speak of the honesty and courage and integrity of the warrior ant.

Let me try to explain why I think our lives first of all have to be *given* a meaning, and secondly why they have to be given a meaning *by God*. For it might seem that we can make our own meaning or, if that won't ultimately do, we can be given meaning by our society, culture and history, without recourse to a great storyteller in the sky.

In the first place we are constantly providing meaning for our own actions. That is what we mean by saying that they are deliberate and done for a reason. They are episodes in some coherent story. If you chance to discover me early one morning in your garden in lemon-coloured pyjamas throwing flowerpots through your windows, then, like Lord Emsworth, you may enquire what I am doing, or even "What is the meaning of this?" And I will tell you a story of which this incident is a part. It finds its place in a story which I am enacting, a story of which I am a character but also the author. In deliberately deciding what I do, I am giving meaning to my behaviour. Doesn't this mean that I provide my own meaning to my life, that I tell my own life-story? Why do I need to drag anyone else in? More especially, why drag God in?

But it will only take you a moment to recognize that you can only tell such stories and provide your actions with such meanings if you are already acting in the context of a whole lot of institutions, a whole lot of frameworks of meaning that are provided for you. There is the language, to start with, in which you formulate your intentions; but, also, gardens, flowerpots and home-ownership (as well as many other things) are all meanings that belong to the society which produced you and in which you formulate aims and purposes and live out your life. There is a larger story, the history of your society and culture, within which you enact your own individual stories. The life which you lead and within which you make deliberate decisions is already a role, or many roles, in institutions that precede you. Your life is to be a character in a story that was begun before you; and if it were not so, if you were not already part of a story, you could not make your own story, decide how to live out your life. And beyond the framework provided for you by your culture, history and language, there is the framework of the animal species to which you belong. This also is a framework of meaning that determines what counts for you as desire and frustration, contentment and revulsion. And it makes possible a story.

That is what I mean by saying that our lives have been given a meaning to start with. We do not start from scratch (as the existentialists used to imagine) to create the meaning of our lives. From the start, our lives are a matter of having a role and a meaning. You were daughters, sons, citizens, Liverpudlians, Christians perhaps, and linguistic, symbol-using animals with particular biological requirements and possibilities, before you ever made one existential choice.

And it is only in the context of these frameworks of meaning that there are any questions to answer, decisions to make, or any life to live. We cannot, then, start from scratch to create the meaning of our lives, although it *does* seem that we could at least try to create an unmeaning, to deny and reject the inherited frameworks of meaning provided for us by culture and history and nature. And this is exactly what Macbeth is doing in the passage I quoted above.

Matthew Arnold, in an overestimated poem called "Dover Beach" (where the "darkling plain" comes from), finding that the world offers him no frame of meaning, "Nor certitude, nor peace, nor help for pain," cries out, "Ah, love, let us be true / To one another!" Here, in "one another," at least we can find some meaning to life. Shakespeare is more ruthless; he has already blocked off this romantic get-out by the suicide of Lady Macbeth. It is just this that provokes Macbeth's speech. He has nobody left to be true to. It is this that convinces him that there is no meaning to time. In the pattern he has tried to impose on time, his wife should have died only after the completion of their reign: "She should have died hereafter; / There would have been a time for such a word."[b] By her death, Lady Macbeth is untimely ripped from the pattern—as Macduff (that other omen of disaster) was untimely ripped from his mother's womb. Time is not the time of the intelligible story Macbeth has tried to invent, so for him it has to be just a meaningless succession of days and

> Life's but a walking shadow, a poor player
> That struts and frets his hour upon the stage,
> And then is heard no more. It is a tale
> Told by an idiot, full of sound and fury
> Signifying nothing.

This speech marks the disintegration of Macbeth, indeed his damnation. The audience is confronted with an actor on the stage proclaiming that there is no play, no story, only a petty pace from day to day. He is denying the point of his existence. Macbeth is not merely going to be slain by Macduff within the play, he is seeking to annihilate himself, to opt out of the whole scheme of creation. This actor is not a character in a play. There are no characters. There is no play. There is just sound and fury.

As it seems to me, our lives are to a greater or lesser extent *our own.* They are our own to the extent that we are grown-up, to the extent that we have managed to acquire skills in living (what Aristotle called virtues). To this extent we compose the story of our own lives; we play

---

b. Shakespeare, *Macbeth*, 5.5.17–18.

a part in a drama of our own composition. It marks us off from our fellow-animals that we do not just have a stationary lifetime between birth and death, but a life-*story*, determined by our own decisions—not random choices, but decisions that flow out of our own characters, from what we have made of ourselves. But the decisions we make cannot be made in a vacuum. Our individual life-stories are subplots in a larger story. How our individual subplot fits into the larger story, enriching it or disrupting it and anyway modifying it, is, I suppose, what ethics and moral evaluation is about. Macbeth's subplot starting from the murder of the king has been a story of distortion, of deliberately wrecking the meaning of the larger story, disrupting the custom and usage of his society, and defying what is seen as the order not only of human life but of all animal life and of nature itself. As his subplot crumbles into meaninglessness, Macbeth responds by proclaiming that there is no larger story, it is all an illusion, it is not a story, it is a tale told by an idiot, signifying nothing.

All this is what I mean by saying our lives have been *given* a meaning; there has to be already a story within which and to which we contribute our own stories. That is all very well, perhaps, but why bring God into it? Do we need this extra character? Is it not enough that we seek to live our lives in tune with humankind, to tell and enact our own stories within the greater human story, in tune with the appropriate life of our species, in harmony with nature itself?

This is how my humanist atheist friends speak: I mean my grown-up atheist friends, who take seriously the importance of making the best of the only life we have, who want to lead what Socrates or Aristotle would call the good life, who recognize that greed and injustice and cowardice and promiscuity are all things that would diminish them and waste their time, their lifetime. So what has God got to do with it? Isn't God just invented to frighten immature people into behaving themselves because they haven't *seen* that decent human behaviour is valuable in itself? And that's the best case. After all, most gods frighten people into bad and stupid behaviour, into bigotry and cruelty, rather than civilized life in friendship and harmony.

Now I am entirely with my atheist friends in their hostility to the gods. The Jewish tradition from which Christianity comes begins with defiance of the gods; the ten commandments tell us to abandon the gods and live in righteousness, in friendship and justice with each other.

That is fine, but my difficulty with the atheists is this: I cannot see how my life-story can be in tune with humankind, in harmony with my environment and with nature itself, unless my environment and nature itself is musical too. My singing cannot be in harmony, or even out of harmony, with others unless they are singing too. I cannot see how the subplot which is my life can be fitting or even unfitting to the order of nature if that order is not a story too.

My life is *my* own, my *personal* life-story, in so far as I have grown in common sense and practical intelligence, in practical wisdom. This is what makes it a life-story and not just a lifetime. If, then, we are to see the order of nature as a kind of story, then there has to be some kind of intelligence, some kind of wisdom, some kind of a storyteller that makes it a story. There must be some kind of a singer that sings this song. Not, of course, with our particular human, linguistic kind of intelligence and wisdom and singing, but with something analogous to these.

And I want to appropriate the word "God," take it away from those who believe in the gods, which are indeed illusions and dangerous illusions, and use it to refer to the wisdom by which the world is a story, the singer by which nature is not just sound and fury but music.

What I refer to as God is not any character in the drama of the universe but the author of the universe, the mystery of wisdom which we know of but cannot begin to understand, the wisdom that is the reason why there is a harmony called the universe which we can just stumblingly begin to understand. Our lives are a subplot in the story of the universe, but that story is not one we can comprehend, and it is one that often puzzles us and troubles us and sometimes outrages us. But it is a story. And I say this not because I have *faith*, or *believe* it, but simply because I cannot believe that existence is a tale told by an idiot.

If I were to tell you what I believe, I would tell you much more. I would tell you that by the gift of faith I believe that this story is a love-story, that this song is a love-song, that the wisdom which made this drama so loved his human characters that he became one himself to share their lives; he chose to be a character in the story, to share their hopes and fears and suffering and death.

NOTES

Prologue

1. See Michael W. Goheen and Craig Bartholomew's *The True Story of the Whole World: Finding Your Place in the Biblical Drama* (Grand Rapids, MI: Faith Alive, 2009).

2. See Elinor Ochs and Lisa Capps, *Living Narratives: Creating Lives in Everyday Storytelling* (Cambridge, MA: Harvard University Press, 2001). Katherine Nelson, ed., *Narratives from the Crib* (Cambridge, MA: Harvard University Press, 1989), examines in detail a two-year-old's need to develop her own, privately spoken narratives in order to make sense of her life.

3. See Henri Blocher, *In the Beginning: The Opening Chapters of Genesis* (Downers Grove, IL: InterVarsity Press, 1984), 7.

4. Blocher, *In the Beginning*, 15.

5. There are popular accounts, such as Desmond Morris's *The Naked Ape: A Zoologist's Study of the Human Animal* (New York: Dell, 1967), which has sold over ten million copies. Some other relatively popular works, such as Jonathan Gottschall's *The Storytelling Animal: How Stories Make Us Human* (New York: Houghton Mifflin Harcourt, 2012), presuppose an entirely naturalistic evolutionary perspective, even if they concede that there are some evolutionary advantages to religion. More serious academic works include Merlin Donald's *A Mind So Rare: The Evolution of Human Consciousness* (New York: Norton, 2001); Brian Boyd's *On the Origin of Stories: Evolution, Cognition, and Fiction* (Cambridge, MA: Harvard University Press, 2009); and Richard Joyce's *The Evolution of Morality* (Cambridge, MA: MIT Press, 2006). Many of these books contain valuable empirical insights that, freed from their naturalistic setting, can help those of us who believe the biblical account of creation understand how fearfully and wonderfully God has made us to be.

6. Allen P. Ross, *A Commentary on the Psalms*, vol. 2, 42–89 (Grand Rapids, MI: Kregel, 2013), 140.

7. Bruce K. Waltke, *The Book of Proverbs: Chapters 1–15* (Grand Rapids, MI: Eerdmans, 2004): "*Understanding* (or having 'know-how,' *tᵉbûnâ*) is a stock-in-trade correlative parallel with 'wise' in Proverbs. . . . [It] designates the pragmatic,

applied aspect of thought, operating in the field of action; it aims at efficiency and accomplishment. *Bînāh* [the first word for *understanding* that I mention in my text] is the conceptual, interpretive activity of thought, operating in the field of meaning; it aims at perception and comprehension. . . . Perceptive and competent people have insight into the moral order and a social conscience that molds their activity. They have a cool spirit . . . , are patient . . . , hold their tongues . . . , can plumb the depths of another's heart . . . , *and keep a straight course*" (96–97; emphasis added in the final phrase). The word for "understanding" at Prov. 3:13 is *t˘bûnâ*. The word for *understanding* at Ps. 119:144 is *bin*, which is the verbal form of *bînāh*.

Chapter 1: Creation

1. The New Testament doesn't record any instance of someone dying from an illness in the ordinary, although fallen, course of things, so it doesn't offer us any special insights into how we should respond to such illnesses. It does note the death of saints in several places (see, e.g., 1 Cor. 15:16–20; 1 Thess. 4:14–15), and at least one New Testament saint was so ill that he was at death's door. Paul's words about him imply that he had not ruled out the possibility of Epaphroditus dying from his illness (see Phil. 2:25–27). Of course, the New Testament does record instances of Christians dying at the hands of others (see, e.g., Acts 12:1–3; Heb. 11:35–38).

2. C. John Collins points out that our Lord read Gen. 1–2 as one account (see Matt. 19:3–5 and its parallel at Mark 10:2–8) (*Genesis 1–4: A Linguistic, Literary, and Theological Commentary* [Phillipsburg, NJ: P&R, 2006], 121). J. A. Motyer calls Gen. 1:1–2:3 "the Genesis poem of Creation" (*Look to the Rock: An Old Testament Background to Our Understanding of Christ* [Leicester, UK: Inter-Varsity Press, 1996], 67). As such, it is like Ezek. 16:1–15. The passage in Ezekiel is more emotionally evocative of the real travesty of Israel's apostasy from God than the much fuller history of God's dealings with his people as we find it in the Old Testament's historical books. In the same way, Gen. 1–2:3 is meant to be more evocative of the wonder of God's creative acts than a more detailed or scientific account would be. As Daniel I. Block says, "If there is such a thing as a doxological narrative, [Genesis 1:1–2:4a] is it" (*Covenant: The Framework of God's Grand Plan of Redemption* [Grand Rapids, MI: Baker Academic, 2021], 18). Motyer calls 2:4–25 "the emergent narrative of the beginnings of history" (*Look to the Rock*, 68). Block observes that "the literary style changes significantly in the middle of Genesis 2:4, but the narrator has intentionally juxtaposed these chapters so that chapter 2 functions as an expansion or exposition of 1:26–30. . . . Viewed together, these two chapters present complementary images of the divine creation of the universe, especially in their anthropology" (*Covenant*, 51). Earlier, he observed that "the change of verb from 'to create' [*bara'*] cosmic time and space [in Genesis 2:4a] to 'make' (*'āśâ*) a home for humanity [in Genesis 2:4b] suggests that [the account in Genesis 2:4–25] builds on [the account in Genesis 1:1–2:3]" (*Covenant*, 17).

3. Henri Blocher writes regarding the first perspective: "If man *is* the image, the emphasis falls on his *situation*. The metaphor of the *selem* [that is, the image] does not speak firstly of the nature of the human creature. . . . It defines our *constitutive relationships.* Mankind belongs to the visible world, as befits an image. But in particular we are defined in relationship to God" (*In the Beginning: The Opening Chapters of Genesis* [Downers Grove, IL: InterVarsity Press, 1984], 85). He then observes, "The first chapter of Genesis certainly does not specify the attributes by which mankind resembles God. We can only suppose that the transcendence of God, his use of speech and the presence of his spirit will be reflected in the human creature. *Conversely, the second chapter shows us as it were mankind in close-up and directs its interest to the composition of his nature*" (87; emphasis added).

4. See Rom. 4:17; 11:36; 1 Cor. 8:6; Col. 1:16; Heb. 11:3; and Rev. 4:11, with Acts 14:15.

5. Collins, *Genesis 1–4*, 59.

6. Gordon J. Wenham observes, "While the creation of light and the firmament on days 1 and 2 are described quite succinctly, those aspects of the environment described in days 3 to 5 that affect man more closely . . . take up proportionately more narrative space, and the creation of man himself and the definition of his role is the fullest account of all. *The creation of man in the divine image is without doubt the focal point of Gen 1, the climax of the six days' work.*" *Genesis 1–15*, vol. 1, Word Biblical Commentary (Waco, TX: Word, 1987), 37; emphasis added.

7. Paul Beauchamp, *Création et séparation: étude exégétique du chapitre premier de la Genèse* (Paris: Aubier-Montaigne, Cerf, Delachaux & Niestlé, Desclée de Brouwer, 1969), 45. Quoted in Blocher, *In the Beginning*, 75.

8. Gerhard von Rad, *Genesis: A Commentary* (Philadelphia: Westminster, 1972), 47.

9. "The shift from the consistent use of the verb in the jussive (e.g., 'Let there be') to a cohortative ('Let us make') is enough to prepare the reader for something momentous on the sixth day. That momentous element is the creation of man *in our image, as our likeness*" (Victor P. Hamilton, *The Book of Genesis: Chapters 1–17* [Grand Rapids, MI: Eerdmans, 1990], 134). Verbs in the cohortative case express exhortation—and I think that in light of what is revealed in the New Testament era, we can take the "Let us make" of v. 26 to involve the three members of the Godhead exhorting each other to participate in the creation of us in their image.

10. Derek Kidner, *Genesis: An Introduction and Commentary* (Downers Grove, IL: InterVarsity Press, 1967), 52. The once-common suggestion that these pronouns should be taken as a plural of majesty—like Queen Victoria saying of herself, "We are not pleased!"—has been abandoned because God does not speak of himself this way anywhere else in Scripture.

11. Gerhard F. Hasel, "The Meaning of 'Let Us' in Gn 1:26," *Andrews University Seminary Studies* 13 (1975): 65.

12. Why singular verbs are used with this plural noun is unclear. In the article on *elōhîm* in *New International Dictionary of Old Testament Theology and Exegesis*,

Terence E. Fretheim writes that the "use of *elōhîm* in the OT for Israel's God (always with sing. vbs.) probably means that the pl. has reference to intensification or absolutization or exclusivity (say, God of gods). . . . While Trinitarian perspectives are probably not in view, the OT witnesses to a richness and complexity in the divine realm (Gen 1:26; Isa 6:8) such that later Trinitarian developments seem quite natural." Terence E. Fretheim, "*elōhîm*," in *New International Dictionary of Old Testament Theology and Exegesis*, ed. Willem VanGemeren (Grand Rapids, MI: Zondervan, 1997), 1:400.

13. Kidner, *Genesis*, 52.

14. Blocher, *In the Beginning*, 84.

15. Blocher writes: "One may well imagine images that are exact replicas, but the verb 'create' excludes that idea from Genesis. Mankind . . . is a mere creature and nothing more. . . . The spirit conferred on mankind does not emanate as if it were a portion of the Spirit of God. Zechariah 12:1 uses for the creation of the spirit of man within him the same verb 'to form' as Genesis 2 uses for the body, the verb that describes the work of the potter. From this point of view Scripture places mankind firmly alongside the world, before the LORD." *In the Beginning*, 82.

16. Blocher, *In the Beginning*, 82; final emphasis added.

17. "Mankind is to be the created representation of his Creator, and here on earth, as it were, the image of the divine Glory (1 Cor. 11:7; 2 Cor. 3:18), that Glory which mankind both reflects and beholds." Blocher, *In the Beginning*, 85.

18. See D. J. A. Clines, "The Image of God in Man," *Tyndale Bulletin* 19 (1968):

> One essential meaning of the statement that man was created "in the image of God" is plain: it is that man is in some way and in some degree like God. Even if the similarity between man and God could not be defined more precisely, the significance of this statement of the nature of man for the understanding of biblical thought could not be over-emphasized. Man is the one godlike creature in all the created order. His nature is not understood if he is viewed merely as the most highly developed of the animals, with whom he shares the earth, nor is it perceived if he is seen as an infinitesimal being dwarfed by the enormous magnitude of the universe. By the doctrine of the image of God, Genesis affirms the dignity and worth of man, and elevates all men—not just kings or nobles—to the highest status conceivable, short of complete divinization. (53)

19. James L. Mays, "What Is a Human Being? Reflections on Psalm 8," *Theology Today* 50 (1993–1994): 513. This is a superb exposition of Ps. 8.

20. See Ps. 8:3–8. Verse 5, which the ESV translates as "Yet you have made him a little lower than the heavenly beings and crowned him with glory and honor," and the NIV translates similarly, is perhaps better translated as the NLT does: "Yet you made them only a little lower than God and crowned them with glory and honor," since the word the ESV translates as "heavenly beings" is *elōhîm*

and thus may mean either God or heavenly beings. Allen P. Ross comments: "The text affirms that the Lord made man 'a little lower than God.' . . . Since verse 6 refers to Genesis 1:26, to the 'image of God' specifically, it may be best to leave 'God' as the translation. The Creator made man less than divine." *A Commentary on the Psalms*, vol. 1, 1–41 (Grand Rapids, MI: Kregel, 2011), 296.

21. Mays, "What Is a Human Being?," 519. Cf. John Calvin, *Institutes of the Christian Religion*, ed. John T. McNeill, trans. Ford Lewis Battles (Louisville, KY: Westminster John Knox, 1960), 1.35: "Nearly all the wisdom we possess, that is to say, true and sound wisdom, consists of two parts: the knowledge of God and of ourselves. . . . In the first place, no one can look upon himself without immediately turning his thoughts to the contemplation of God, in whom he 'lives and moves.' For quite clearly, the mighty gifts with which we are endowed are hardly from ourselves; indeed, our very being is nothing but subsistence in the one God."

22. Karl Barth, *Church Dogmatics* 3/1, quoted in Hasel, "The Meaning of 'Let Us' in Gn 1:26," 65.

23. Collins, *Genesis 1–4*, 67.

24. The creatures God creates at Gen. 1:21 live, breathe, and move around. The Hebrew word *ruach*—about which I will have more to say later in this chapter—"can be used," Van Pelt, Kaiser, and Block tell us, "to refer to the life-sustaining function called breathing or breath. This breath is the essence of life (Gen 6:17; Job 12:10; Isa 38:16; 42:5; Ezek 37:5–14; Mal 2:15–16). *As such the Old Testament is clear in its teaching that such breath is a direct result of the divine, creative power of Yahweh graciously bestowed upon his creation* (Job 27:3; 33:4; Ps 104:29, 30; Zech 12:1)." Miles V. Van Pelt, Walter C. Kaiser Jr., and Daniel I. Block, "*ruach*," in *New International Dictionary of Old Testament Theology and Exegesis*, 3:1073; emphasis added.

It is one of the properties of science, E. O. Wilson tells us, to believe that everything that exists developed naturally out of everything before it. This is, he says, "the concept of the continuum" (Edward O. Wilson, *The Meaning of Human Existence* [New York: Liveright, 2014], 44). Another way to put this is that those who, like Wilson, hold to an exclusively bottom-up evolutionary story (see chap. 3 and the epilogue) assume as part of their practice of science that reality is a causally closed system—nothing affects it other than the laws of nature acting naturally. So neither animate or human life would be "a direct result of the divine, creative power of Yahweh graciously bestowed on his creation." The use of *bara'* at Gen. 1:21 and 1:27 suggests (or perhaps even implies) that the world as we know it is not a causally closed system.

25. J. A. Motyer, *The Prophecy of Isaiah* (Leicester, UK: Inter-Varsity Press, 1993), 76–77.

26. God is being (Gen. 1:1; Rom. 11:36; Rev. 1:4) and life (Deut. 5:26; Ps. 42:2; Jer. 10:10; 1 Tim. 4:10; Rev. 7:2), which is why all of creation and animate life have only derivative being and depend entirely on him. Collins notes that "the word *created* appears three times [in v. 27], but only the first is [reporting the event]; the second and third are just restatements of the event described

by the first. *Thus the storyline stops advancing, and the reader is allowed to dwell on the event"* (*Genesis 1–4*, 72; emphasis added). "The creation of man is," then, "the peak of the account, with the storyline coming to a halt so that the reader can mull over this event." We are "presented as the crown of God's creation week" (78).

27. Kidner, *Genesis*, 51. The next set of quotations from Kidner is from the same page.

28. "Humans are like God in their ability to go out of themselves and enter into personal relations through communicative activity. The etymology of the Latin term for 'person' is instructive: *per-sonare* literally means 'to sound through.' What it means to be in the image of God is best grasped by an auditory rather than a visual analogy. The human creature is not so much ikon as an *echo* of the divine being and of the trinitarian communicative relations." Kevin Vanhoozer, "Human being, individual and social," in *The Cambridge Companion to Christian Doctrine*, ed. Colin E. Gunton (New York: Cambridge University Press, 1997), 177.

29. For a philological argument that the proper translation of the Hebrew is *as the image of God* rather than *in the image of God*, see Clines, "The Image of God in Man," 70–80. The most convincing considerations are, however, functional, mirroring the sorts of considerations I give in these endnotes. William J. Dumbrell puts it like this: "Human beings do not have the image of God, since God has no image, but are as the image of God." *Covenant and Creation: An Old Testament Covenant Theology* (Milton Keynes, UK: Paternoster, 2013), 26.

30. "In the ancient East the setting up of the king's statue was the equivalent to the proclamation of his domination over the sphere in which the statue was erected (cf. Dan. 3.1, 5f.). When in the thirteenth century BC the Pharaoh Ramesses II had his image hewn out of rock at the mouth of the *nahr el-kelb*, on the Mediterranean north of Beirut, the image meant that he was the ruler of this area. *Accordingly man is set in the midst of creation as God's statue. He is evidence that God is the Lord of creation.*" Hans Walter Wolff, *Anthropology of the Old Testament* (Philadelphia: Fortress, 1974), 160; emphasis added.

31. Longman quotes M. Lanier from the unpublished "Survey of the Old Testament," where Lanier states, "Image was not physical likeness, but rather a responsibility and identity of role and function" (Tremper Longman III, *Genesis* [Grand Rapids, MI: Zondervan, 2016], 37n20). Ross puts it like this: God imparted spiritual capacities to Adam and Eve (see Gen. 2:7) "that endowed them with the ability and responsibility to represent God on earth" (Allen P. Ross, *Creation and Blessing: A Guide to the Study and Exposition of the Book of Genesis* [Grand Rapids, MI: Baker, 1988], 174). These capacities, he notes, are passed on to Adam and Eve's descendants by natural reproduction.

32. Wolff writes:

> Taken by itself the phrase ["the image of God"] points first and fundamentally to a correspondence between man and God. . . . But how are we to understand this relation of correspondence between

God and man more precisely? . . . According to [God's statement at Genesis 1:26, "Let us make man in our image, after our likeness"], man proceeds from God's *address*. We must not view this in the purely formal sense, especially since the address in which God blesses man in 1.28 is similar to the words spoken to the fish and the birds in 1.22. *What is unique is the continuation of the words addressed to man. This confers on man the office that distinguishes him.* . . . When the Creator gave created beings over to man, he also gave him responsible tasks (2.15–17) and powers of decision (2:18–23). . . . The different features of the [Genesis 2:5–25] narrative make the implications of Gen. 1.26–28 graphically evident. According to this *the relation of correspondence to which the phrase "the image of God" points is to be seen first of all in that man, in hearing and then also in obeying and in answering, corresponds to the word of God's address.* (*Anthropology of the Old Testament,* 159–60; emphasis added to all but the first use of *address*)

As Wolff put it earlier, "the Creator of all things . . . enters into dialogue with man and with his wife as with none other of his creatures" (94–95)—and *our basic relationship with our Creator is constituted by this dialogue,* for

not only the creation of mankind as a whole but also the evolution of the individual—indeed of one's own life—is traced back to Yahweh as being a work of art fashioned by his hands. *No man can completely understand himself if he does not remain conscious that he derives from a process in which he had "no say."* Such insight also leads to the dialogue of man with his God, a dialogue which in Job's case takes on the bitterest edge. . . . *Modern man . . . should transpose into the appropriate state of biological knowledge the fundamental assurance that both mankind and the individual originated in the will of God; and . . . he should not neglect the chance of being called to the dialogue of man with his Creator.* (98; emphases added)

33. Clines, "The Image of God in Man," 99.
34. A. R. Millard, "A New Babylonian Genesis Story," *Tyndale Bulletin* 18 (1967): 8. The Merriam-Webster Unabridged Dictionary defines *corvée work* as "unpaid labor (as on roads) for a day or longer period due from a vassal to his lord" (*Merriam-Webster,* s.v. "corvée work," accessed November 9, 2021, https://unabridged.merriam-webster.com). In other words, human beings were created to be the gods' slaves. The quotation in the next sentence is from page 9.
35. Kidner, *Genesis,* 52. He cites Gen. 1:22; 2:3; and the parting blessing of Isaac, Jacob, and Moses as confirming that blessing bestows both a gift and a function; then he cites Num. 6:24–26 regarding God's turning full-face to the recipient and Acts 3:26 for this being an act of self-giving.
36. Wenham, *Genesis 1–15,* 24; emphasis added. Ross's *Creation and Blessing* is a book-length treatment of this theme.
37. Wenham, *Genesis 1–15,* 33.

38. Blocher, *In the Beginning*, 71. All the remaining unattributed quotations in this paragraph come from the same page. The words "does not fight, it parades" are from Beauchamp, *Création et séparation*.

39. Wenham, *Genesis 1–15*, 34.

40. As Willem A. VanGemeren emphasizes, "The story of salvation has its roots in Israel's belief in God's involvement with his creation. *Creation is not merely an article of faith to be believed but, as C. S. Lewis put it, 'an achievement.'*" *Psalms, Proverbs, Ecclesiastes, Song of Songs*, vol. 5, *Expositor's Bible Commentary* (Grand Rapids, MI: Zondervan, 1991), 514; emphasis added.

41. I have substituted the word *person* for the NIV's *being* in the epigraphs and for the ESV's *creature* here to stress our uniqueness among all the earth's creatures. Gen. 1:30 emphasizes what we share with them: "And to every beast of the earth and to every bird of the heavens and to everything that creeps on the earth, everything that has the breath of life, I have given every green plant for food." In that verse the Hebrew for *breath of life* is *nephesh chay*, while the Hebrew for the same phrase at 2:7 is *neshamah chay*. The former phrase encompasses all animate life while the latter refers to the unique sort of life we have as it was specially breathed into us by the Lord God. The NLT translates the latter phrase as *living person*. There was no time when Adam was alive without being a living person.

42. Block writes:

> The image of a garden at the center of creation is tightly linked to ancient accounts of royal gardens associated with the palaces of kings. These gardens represented visual ideals of a world in which the physical environment, human and animal inhabitants, and the divine sovereign/Sovereign functioned harmoniously, and from which the blessing of god/God and the kind of rule of the king would emanate throughout the realm.

So "Genesis 2 paints a picture of a perfect world, where all needs are met, especially for [humankind]." *Covenant*, 25–26.

43. God's "real name," Bonhoeffer wrote, is YHWH; "that is, it is the name of *this* God"—the God of Abraham, Isaac, and Jacob; the God who delivered the Israelites from Egyptian bondage; the God of whom Moses is writing—"the God who is being spoken of [in Gen. 2 and 3]. *Elōhîm* in Genesis 1 is not a proper name but a generic term and so means roughly 'deity'" (Dietrich Bonhoeffer, *Creation and Fall* [Minneapolis: Fortress Press, 2004], 74). "The name Yahweh . . . is used throughout the OT . . . as the personal name of Israel's God" (Fretheim, "*Yahweh*," in *New International Dictionary of Old Testament Theology and Exegesis*, 4:1292). "This is the name God bears when he comes and visits his people and makes a covenant with them; this is his covenant name, *his name for his 'marriage' with Israel*." Blocher, *In the Beginning*, 111; emphasis added.

44. See Gen. 17:1–8 and Ex. 6:2–8. The apparent discrepancy between God's statement to Moses in v. 3 of the latter passage and passages in Genesis such as

2:4; 4:26; 17:1 that refer to God as "Lord" (that is, YHWH) is probably best explained in terms of God having not spelled out the significance of the name YHWH to Moses until Ex. 3:11–17 and 6:2–8.

VanGemeren notes that "the practice of rendering the name of the Lord, Yahweh, by a title ('the Lord') keeps us from sensing the richness of Israel's religious experience and practice. The title lacks the emotive quality affected by the relationship between God and his people." *Psalms, Proverbs, Ecclesiastes, Song of Songs*, 15.

Collins observes that Gen. 2:4–3:24 uses the composite name Lord God first to show that "God [is] working personally with the first man" as well as making it clear "that the God who has yoked himself by promises to the patriarchs and their offspring . . . is the transcendent Creator of heaven and earth." *Genesis 1–4*, 137.

45. Hamilton, *Book of Genesis*, 156. He continues, quoting Sarna (Nahum M. Sarna, *The JPS Torah Commentary: Genesis* [Philadelphia: Jewish Publication Society], 1989): "It is as though for the climactic performance the usual act of will was reinforced by an act of divine effort" (157).

46. "The Hebrew [word for *build*] is a vigorous anthropomorphism and reminds us of the overall picture of God as a workman." Collins, *Genesis 1–4*, 107n31.

47. Bonhoeffer asks of Gen. 2:8–17, "Who can speak of these things except in pictures?" But, he continues, "pictures . . . are not lies; they indicate things and enable the underlying meaning to shine through." *Creation and Fall*, 81.

48. "God is portrayed as a potter (. . . [*yôtser*], which is the participle of the verb used here, . . . [*yatsar*], 'to form') who forms man from moistened dust" (Collins, *Genesis 1–4*, 105n9). Wenham renders *yôtser* as "shaped" and then comments:

> The present participle of [the verb *yatsar*] means "potter" (e.g., Jer 18:2), and it may well be that the image of a potter shaping his clay lies behind this description of man's creation. . . . "Shaping" is an artistic, inventive activity that requires skill and planning (cf. Isa 44:9–10). Usually the verb describes God's work in creation. God has "shaped" the animals (2:19), Leviathan (Ps 104:26), the dry land (Ps 95:5), the mountains (Amos 4:13), and the future course of history (Isa 22:11, Jer 33:2). Preeminently, God's shaping skill is seen in the creation of man, whether it be from dust as here or in the womb (Isa 44:2, 24) or in shaping human character to fulfill a particular role (Isa 43:21, 44:21). (*Genesis 1–15*, 59)

49. Kidner, *Genesis*, 50. My entire sentence reproduces Kidner's sentence, yet with a change in verb tenses. The next quotation from Kidner is from the same page.

50. With only one possible exception, the Hebrew word *neshamah* elsewhere in Scripture refers only to human beings. The possible exception is at Gen. 7:22. T. C. Mitchell makes the case that *neshamah* applies only to humanity in "The Old Testament use of *nešāmâ*" (*Vetus Testamentum*, vol. 11, Fasc. 2 [Apr., 1961]). After examining all twenty-six occurrences of *neshamah* in the Old Testament, his final conclusion runs:

The use of the word [*nᵉšāmâ*] in gen. ii 7, where God's creation of
man is distinguished from that of the rest of the animal creation,
by the act of breathing into his nostrils the breath of life . . . [plus]
the general context of the whole creation account would lead one
to expect [that *nᵉšāmâ* refers to] some particular and exclusive
feature in the creation of man, who was made in God's image,
and given dominion over all the animal creation. None of these
considerations settle the matter, but they make it a tenable view
that the word *nᵉšāmâ*, and its related forms, may be used in the Old
Testament to describe the breath of God, which, when imparted to
man, made him unique among the animals. (186)

And no matter whether Scripture uses *neshamah* exclusively for human
beings, the passages I go on to quote in my text clarify that *neshamah* refers to
uniquely human functions.

Blocher also takes *neshamah* to refer only to human beings: "The Spirit was
at work particularly in the creation of mankind. The second tablet of Genesis
(2:7) represents the special privilege of mankind as the communication of a
'breath.' The term employed [*neshamah*] . . . is used rarely for God *and avoids
any notion of emanation*. It is used for mankind and not for animals, and designates the spirit of mankind created to correspond to the Spirit of God" (*In the
Beginning*, 77; emphasis added), adding in a note, "One single text, Gn. 7:22,
might possibly use the word of animals. Jos. 11:14 excludes the animals. In Pr.
20:27 it is the lamp of the LORD" (77n77).

Blocher's claim that *neshamah* "avoids any notion of emanation" distinguishes the biblical account of creation from the ancient Near Eastern creation
myths, as Robert W. Jenson emphasizes in tracing the disastrous effects of ema-
nationist thinking both within and outside the church. He declares that "in the
world's religions the dominant understanding of our being and the being of the
world is that it derives from deity by *emanation* of one sort or another. By this
interpretation either there finally is no reality other than the divine, or insofar
as it is other it is illusion or degradation" (Robert W. Jenson, *Systematic Theology*, vol. 2, *The Works of God* [Oxford, UK: Oxford University Press, 1999], 5).
The biblical claim is that we (and the whole created world) are real and good.

51. Various passages confirm this. God asks rhetorically at Job 38:36, "Who has
put wisdom in the inward parts or given understanding to the mind?" with the
obvious answer being, only God. David reiterates this regarding himself at Ps.
51:6: "Behold, you [referring to God as *elōhim*] delight in truth in the inward
being, and you teach me wisdom in the secret heart." Prov. 2:6 states, "For the
LORD gives wisdom; from his mouth come knowledge and understanding." Job
39:17 asserts that the ostrich deals cruelly with her young because God "has
made her forget wisdom and given her no share in understanding." See also
James 4:5: "Or do you suppose it is to no purpose that the Scripture says, 'He
yearns jealously over the spirit that he has made to dwell in us'?"

In saying that wisdom and understanding are attributes that depend on
supernaturally bestowed capacities from God, I am not denying a point I made

in the prologue and will reiterate in the epilogue—namely, that we must seek wisdom and understanding if we are to attain them (see, e.g., Prov. 2:1–5 and 4:1–9).

52. Elihu states that he is oriented toward God in exactly the same way as Job is because he "too was pinched off from a piece of clay" (v. 6). He assumes that their sharing the same spirit [*ruach*] and breath [*neshamah*] means that they are both accountable: "Answer me, if you can; set your words in order before me; take your stand" (v. 5).

53. The Hebrew word *ruach* is sometimes translated "breath" (see Gen. 6:17; 2 Sam. 22:16; Ps. 104:29; Eccles. 3:19 ESV, NIV). *Neshamah* is at least once translated "spirit" (see Prov. 20:27 ESV, NIV). So we must not draw conclusions about the scope of these terms from our English translations.

54. Blocher, *In the Beginning*, 82. Blocher says at p. 77 that *neshamah* "is a near synonym for" *ruach*, which is the word for *Spirit* in Gen. 1:2 as well as in each of my quotations in the text. But because *ruach* has a wider semantic range than *neshamah*, it can also refer to the breath of animals.

55. The workmen fulfill God's commands. For the significance of this, see Jeffrey J. Niehaus, *Biblical Theology, Volume 1: The Common Grace Covenants* (Wooster, OH: Weaver, 2014), 41–42.

56. God is the only completely free agent (Ps. 115:3; 135:6; Dan. 4:35) and so necessarily the source of whatever freedom we possess because we are created in his image.

57. Roger Scruton writes:

> As a self-conscious subject I have a point of view on the world. The world *seems* a certain way to me, and this "seeming" defines my unique perspective. Every self-conscious being has such a perspective, since that is what it means to be a subject of consciousness. When I give a scientific account of the world, however, I am describing . . . the way things are and the causal laws that govern them. This description is given from no particular perspective. It does not contain words such as *here*, *now*, and *I*. . . . In short, the subject is in principle unobservable to science, not because it exists in another realm but because it is not part of the empirical world. *It lies on the edge of things, like a horizon.* (*On Human Nature* [Princeton, NJ: Princeton University Press, 2017], 32; emphasis added)

Later he says: "Subjects are not objects, and points of view are not *in* the world but *on* the world" (54). Again, "the subject is a point of view *upon* the world of objects and not an item *within* it. . . . Better to refer to the subject as a horizon, a one-sided boundary to the world as it seems" (57). See also 66–67, 110–11.

58. Scruton, *On Human Nature*, 9. The next quotation comes from p. 30. The first chapter of Scruton's *On Human Nature* is dedicated to showing that human beings belong "to another order of explanation than that explored by biology." Near the end of that chapter, entitled "Human Kind," he writes:

> While we human beings belong to a kind, that kind cannot be characterized merely in biological terms but, rather, only in terms that make essential reference to the web of interpersonal reactions. These reactions bind us to each other and also reach out to (even if they may not connect with) persons who are not of this world and not of the flesh. (46)

Sarna notes regarding Gen. 2:20 that the fact that no fitting helper was found for the man after he had named all of the animals shows that his review of "the subhuman creation" made him "conscious of his own uniqueness, *of his inability to integrate himself into that whole biological order* or feel direct kinship with the other animate beings" (Sarna, *JPS Torah Commentary*, 22; emphasis added). Thus Scripture makes Scruton's point that we belong to a kind that cannot be characterized merely biologically.

59. Scruton's reference to moral concepts in my text's previous block quotation implies the centrality of language to humanity. John Macmurray emphasized our difference in kind from all of the earth's other life forms like this:

> Language is the major vehicle of human communication. Communication is the sharing of experience. If language is fundamental to human existence, it follows that *the human sphere, the sphere of the personal, cannot be understood through organic categories, in functional or evolutionary terms. It means, in other words, that men are not organisms, that the human world is as distinct from the organic as the organic is from the material, though it is built upon the organic as the organic is upon the material.* (John Macmurray, *Persons in Relation* [New York: Harper, 1961], 12; emphasis added)

The phenomenologist Maurice Merleau-Ponty made essentially the same point when he said, "Man is a historical idea *and not a natural species*" (*Phenomenology of Perception* [London: Routledge, 2002], 198; emphasis added). Cf. my discussion of orienting questions in the prologue.

Hamilton observes: "To read faithfully Gen 1–2 is to make certain affirmations about humanity that distinguish it from the rest of creation. Only humankind is created with the divine image and likeness (Gen 1:26–27). *So the differences between humankind and the rest of creation are qualitative, not just quantitative*" (Victor P. Hamilton, "Genesis: Theology," in *New International Dictionary of Old Testament Theology and Exegesis*, 4:671; emphasis added).

60. See C. S. Lewis, *Screwtape Letters* (New York: Macmillan, 1954), chap. 8.

61. "Eden must have suggested first of all to the [Israelite] person listening to the account the Hebrew term of the same form. 'Eden' is often used in the plural for 'delight,' with other related terms and the corresponding verb, to mean a life of luxury and pleasure. . . . God had prepared for the man a place of pleasure, the very environment of happiness. The overtones that we associate with the word 'paradise' are in harmony with the purpose of the text. . . . The LORD immediately proves his generosity by installing his vassal in a

paradise—that in summary is the first intimation of the narrative." Blocher, *In the Beginning*, 113.

62. Sarna, *JPS Torah Commentary*, 18.

63. Most translations render the Hebrew word *shamar* in this passage as "keep" (ESV and NLT) or "take care of" (NIV) or "maintain" (NET). But *shamar* is the word used when the men of Kiriath Jearim came and took the ark of the Lord to Abinadab's house and consecrated Eleazar his son to guard it (see 1 Sam. 7:1 NIV). It often refers to protecting or preserving religiously important objects, like the covenant (see Gen. 17:9), the law (see Isa. 56:1), love and justice (see Hos. 12:6), and especially God's commandments, statutes, and instructions (see Gen. 26:5). Adam was to guard Eden from the entrance of sin by repulsing the serpent's suggestion that he and his wife should eat from the tree of the knowledge of good and evil. Hamilton writes that "the basic meaning of [*shamar*] is 'to exercise great care over,' to the point, if necessary, of guarding. . . . The same root is used in the next chapter to describe the cherubs who are on guard to prevent access to the tree of life in the garden (Gen. 3:24). *The garden is something to be protected more than it is something to be possessed*" (*Book of Genesis*, 171; emphasis added). John H. Sailhamer argues on textual grounds that the Hebrew that the ESV translates as "to work it and keep it" should actually be translated as "to worship and obey." He writes, "The man is put in the Garden to worship God and obey him. The man's life in the Garden was to be characterized by worship and obedience; he was to be a priest, not merely a worker and keeper of the Garden. Such a reading," he says, "suits the ideas of the narrative" (*The Pentateuch as Narrative: A Biblical-Theological Commentary* [Grand Rapids, MI: Zondervan, 1992], 101). Block argues that it is more natural to interpret the garden as "an ancient royal garden" and Adam as a king rather than (as many regard it) as a temple in which Adam was to serve as priest. See *Covenant*, 28–30.

64. "The restriction is blunt and firm. 'Never eat,' literally, 'you shall not eat,' resembles in its form the ten commandments: [*lo'*] 'not' followed by the imperfect is used for long-standing prohibitions; cf. 'Do not steal, murder,' etc. (Exod 20:3–17)" (Wenham, *Genesis 1–15*, 67). This Hebrew construction indicates "permanent prohibitions" (47n17.b). Wenham translates the verse as "but from the tree of the knowledge of good and evil never eat, for on the day you do, you will certainly die" (44).

65. Regarding our capacity to refer to ourselves as "I," Scruton writes:

> "I" thoughts are fundamental to the life of the person, committing us to the belief in freedom and to the appeal to reason. Just as fundamental . . . are "you" thoughts—thoughts about the person to whom I am accountable or to whom my reasons are addressed. The moral life depends on [what is called] the "second-person standpoint"—the standpoint of someone whose reasons and conduct are essentially addressed to others. (*On Human Nature*, 50)

66. In Pss. 19:13 and 119:133 the psalmists petition God to keep sin from having dominion over them. In Romans, Paul writes:

> Let not sin therefore reign in your mortal body, to make you obey
> its passions. Do not present your members to sin as instruments
> for unrighteousness, but present yourselves to God as those who
> have been brought from death to life, and your members to God
> as instruments for righteousness. For sin will have no dominion
> over you, since you are not under law but under grace. (6:12–14)

67. "There is no indication that human dominion over the creation has been re-
scinded [in the curses of Genesis 3], but every indication that humans will
exercise it badly—exploiting and damaging the creation and using it to exploit
and damage other people." Collins, *Genesis 1–4,* 164–65.

68. Blocher, *In the Beginning,* 88. Kidner comments: "Note that man neither 'has'
a soul nor 'has' a body, although for convenience he may be analyzed into two
or more constituents (e.g. 1 Thes. 5:23). The basic truth is here: he is a unity"
(*Genesis,* 61).

   Merleau-Ponty shows that it is by means of our bodies that our experience
is constituted as being a world: "Although our body does not impose definite
instincts upon us from birth, as it does upon animals, it does at least give
to our life the form of generality, and develops our personal acts into stable
dispositional tendencies. . . . The body is our general medium for having a
world" (*Phenomenology of Perception,* 169). In his *Law, Love and Language,*
Herbert McCabe explains what this means: A dog's world is constituted by
the particular set of senses a dog has got, which makes various features in
its environment significant to it. Color is evidently not a factor in a dog's
experience, but smell most definitely is. By smelling something as meat or as
a female dog in heat,

> he is not surrounded by neutral facts but by things that matter to
> him in various ways. He has a *world.* By a world I mean an environ-
> ment organized in terms of significance. What we call the senses of
> the dog are the ways in which this organization takes place. (*Law,
> Love and Language* [1968; repr., London: Continuum, 2003], 71)

An organism's "senses, then, are modes of response to an environment or modes
of determining a world." Color is significant to us, even if it isn't to a dog, and
so our worlds are significantly different: "The world of a dog may be as exciting
or boring in terms of smell as ours can be in terms of color" (71). Our world,
like a dog's world, is constituted by the senses God has given us. Since human
beings normally possess the same senses, we share a common world. Moreover,
our senses—and most particularly our hearing—enable us to get a perspective
on our lives that is historical and not merely natural (see Merleau-Ponty in n59,
above). Our understanding of our world can be radically changed by what we
hear (see, e.g., Deut. 6:4–9; Rom. 10:13–17; Eph. 4:17–24).

69. On "suitable for him" in 2:18, Collins comments:

> As Delitzsch, 140, noted, the relationship expressed by . . . *kenegdô,*
> literally, "according to the opposite of him" . . . differs from that
> of . . . *kamôhû,* "like him" . . . , which the narrator does not use.

Hence the proposed "helper" will be "one who by relative difference and essential equality should be his fitting complement." In the interpretive tradition, she is a "help and support," more than simply one with whom he can make children: see Tob. 8:6; Sir. 36:24. (*Genesis 1–4*, 107n26)

To designate the woman as a *helper* does not diminish her, since elsewhere in the Old Testament the Hebrew words for *help* and *helper* usually refer to divine assistance.

70. Collins, *Genesis 1–4*, 134.

71. The Hebrew word that I have translated as *flesh and bone* is *tzela'*. No one knows exactly what it means in this context. Elsewhere it means "side," as the side of a hill or the side of a house or the sides of the ark of the covenant (see Ex. 25:14). This comment by John E. Hartley strikes me as getting the meaning about right:

> The most crucial passage in which [*tzela'*] appears is, of course, the one explaining the origin of woman (Gen 2:21f.). God created woman by taking "a rib" from Adam while he was in a very deep sleep. . . . Conceivably this means that God took a good portion of Adam's side, since the man considers the woman to be "bone of his bones" and flesh of his flesh (2:21f.). *This picture describes the intimacy between man and woman as they stand equal before God.* Since God made the woman, she is responsible to him in worship. She is not a mere extension of man; she possesses a unique individuality in her own right. There is no indication that woman is inferior. On the other hand, since her body is made from man's, there is a continuity between the two with the result that *they can find a fulfilling relationship only in one another, but never with the same intensity in any other part of creation.* Therefore woman's origin makes it possible for a man and a woman to establish a dynamic relationship in which they become "one flesh" (cf. 2:24). (John E. Hartley, "*ṣēlā*," in *Theological Wordbook of the Old Testament*, ed. R. Laird Harris [Chicago: Moody, 1980], 2:768; emphases added)

72. See David M. Fouts, "*bana*," in *New International Dictionary of Old Testament Theology and Exegesis*, 1:666. For the quotation of Uehlinger in the next paragraph, see 667.

73. Samuel Terrien, *Till the Heart Sings: A Biblical Theology of Manhood and Womanhood* (Philadelphia: Fortress Press, 1985), 12. The next quotation from Terrien is from the same place. See note 48 for the implications of the word *yatsar*.

74. Kidner, *Genesis*, 29; emphasis added.

75. The Merriam-Webster Unabridged Dictionary defines *opposite* as: "Set over against something that is at the other end or side of an intervening line or space: facing" and "being the other of a matching or contrasting pair: corresponding or complementary in position, function, or nature" (*Merriam-Webster*, s.v. "opposite," accessed November 9, 2021, https://unabridged.merriam-webster.com.) C. S. Lewis described his own wife's likeness/oppositeness like this: "The most

precious gift that marriage gave me was this constant impact of something very close and intimate yet all the time unmistakably other, resistant—in a word, real." *A Grief Observed* (New York: HarperCollins, 1994), 18–19.

76. Von Rad comments, "God himself, like a father of the bride, leads the woman to the man" (*Genesis*, 84). This is another indication of how deeply God himself was involved in providing Adam with a good life.

77. Collins, *Genesis 1–4*, 139. The next quotation is from 108n32.

78. Kidner, *Genesis*, 65, commenting on Gen. 2:18–25; emphases added. Blocher says, similarly, "Procreation is a purpose of marriage only indirectly, since sexual union will be the means of obeying the blessing-commandment of the first chapter. Procreation is not the purpose of marriage as such. For his institution the LORD gives only one reason: 'It is not good that the man should be alone'" (*In the Beginning*, 108–9).

79. See Gordon P. Hugenberger, *Marriage as a Covenant: Biblical Law and Ethics as Developed from Malachi* (Eugene, OR: Wpif & Stock, 2014). Hugenberger observes:

> There is an unmistakeable formulaic quality about the expression, "this . . . is bone of my bones and flesh of my flesh," which finds remarkably close parallels in Gen. 29:14; 2 Sam. 5:1; 19:13f. [ET 12f.] and 1 Chr. 11:1. . . . Each of these texts employs "the relationship formula" to affirm familial propinquity, thereby suggesting that Adam's intention goes beyond the mere acknowledgement of Eve's origin . . . to an acknowledgement of Eve as a family member, that is, as his wife. . . . [Moreover], as argued by W. Brueggemann and others, in several of these texts it is clear that the "relationship formula" is not merely an assertion of an existing blood tie, "but is rather a covenant oath which affirms and establishes a pattern of solidarity. . . . In other words, under certain circumstances, . . . "the relationship formula" may constitute a solemn "Declaration Formula," which will be seen to be functionally indistinguishable from a covenant-ratifying oath.
>
> In favour of this interpretation of the "relationship formula" in Gen. 2:23, Adam does not address his "jubilant welcome" to Eve . . . , as one would expect for a mere welcome, but to God as witness. . . . [And so] these words appear to have been intended as a solemn affirmation of his marital commitment, an elliptical way of saying something like, "I hereby invite you, God, to hold me accountable to treat this woman as part of my own body." . . . [Such a] concise statement . . . is entirely in keeping with the elliptical character of ancient oath formulae. (164–65)

See Walter Brueggemann's, "Of the Same Flesh and Bone (GN 2.23a)," *The Catholic Biblical Quarterly*, 32.4 (October 1970), who writes, "The central teaching of the formula concerns fidelity to vows, constancy in purpose, acceptance of responsibility which are appropriate to our humanness. When the formula of 2,23a is understood in this way, the whole fabric of Israel's faith is greatly illuminated in terms of fidelity and solidarity. Israel from the beginning knew she lived in a world where solidarity, fidelity, and responsibility are the essentials of *shalom*" (542). I shall spell out some of the implications of marriage as a covenant in my next chapter, with special emphasis on how it should shape our interpretation of Adam and Eve's refusal to obey God's command not to eat of the forbidden tree.

80. Collins, *Genesis 1–4*, 108n37. Collins is quoting H. C. Leupold in my second quotation.

81. See Leonard J. Coppes's article on *before* (*neged*) in the *Theological Wordbook of the Old Testament*. He notes that the root basically denotes "to place a matter high, conspicuous before a person" (vol. 2, 549) and that its prepositional form (as in Gen. 2:18, 20) "retains the basic thrust of the root. It is this connotation of prominence (being conspicuous)" (vol. 2, 550).

82. Blocher, *In the Beginning*, 102.

83. Blocher, *In the Beginning*, 93. "Sexuality . . . necessitates being-with. The fact that the first company given by God to man in order to break his solitude was of the other sex reminds us that God does not institute an abstract otherness. He gives a *neighbour* . . . a concretely qualified presence. . . . And the 'neighbour-ship' which is defined within God's order by sexual differentiation is of a most radical nature; every human individual, being either masculine or feminine, must abandon the illusion of being alone. The constitution of each of us is a summons to community" (97).

84. "*The difference male/female calls mankind to a personal, face-to-face relation-ship*, as God himself exists in face-to-face relationship. . . . The image of God is fulfilled, ultimately, only in Christ's face-to-face relationship with the church" (Blocher, *In the Beginning*, 81; emphasis added). Earlier he wrote:

> There is no scientific explanation why the sexes are differentiated in the animal realm. [But] this fact involves a necessity which is intelligible *for humanity*, the necessity of the complementary dif-ference for full communion between two incarnate liberties. (76)

This suggests how "the living creatures converge towards the man" (see above, n6).

85. Wenham, *Genesis 1–15*, 71. The next two sentences paraphrase comments from Wenham on p. 72.

86. Philip S. Johnston writes: "The term 'paradise' comes directly from the Greek *paradeisos*, which in turn comes from a Persian word for 'garden.' It is the Greek term used for the garden of Eden" (*New Dictionary of Biblical Theol-ogy* [Downers Grove, IL: InterVarsity, 2000], 540–41, s.v. "heaven"). Cf. Claus Westermann, *Creation* (Philadelphia: Fortress, 1974), 80–81, for what the word *paradise* evokes in Western languages, some of which is biblical and some of which is not.

87. In addition to the passages already cited praising self-control, including control of our passions (see pp. 29–30, above), we find condemnation of unnatural desire

(see 2 Pet. 2:10; Jude 7) and of wantonness (see 2 Pet. 2:17–19; Jude 10–14) in two of the New Testament's final letters. So Scripture emphasizes our responsibility to regulate ourselves according to specific standards at its very beginning (see Gen. 2:16–17; 3:11–13, 17; 4:7), in its middle (see pp. 35–36), and at its end.

88. This is P. F. Strawson's point in his seminal piece "Freedom and Resentment" (in *Proceedings of the British Academy*, 1963, 187–211; and often reprinted). Strawson calls the evaluations by which we hold others and ourselves accountable *reactive attitudes*. These attitudes involve our reactions to the postures we take to each other—whether we are manifesting goodwill and respect for others and their dignity, or indifference, or malevolence (see my "Why Personhood Runs Deeper than Neurology," *Didaktikos* [April 2020]: 12–14, at Didaktikos-Journal.com). Scruton and many others have adopted Strawson's "take" on our accountability. C. S. Lewis's discussion "The Law of Human Nature" in the first chapter of *Mere Christianity* is making a case for the universality of our reactive attitudes long before Strawson coined the term. See my "Theism and Thought" (a review article on Victor Reppert's *C. S. Lewis's Dangerous Idea: In Defense of the Argument from Reason*), 7, vol. 23 (2006): 81–94, for reasons to think that Strawson was influenced by Lewis's discussion in developing his own claims.

Chapter 2: Rebellion

1. In the last century, many scholars argued that Gen. 1–3 should not be classified as myth. For instance, while Gerhard von Rad thought the canonical text was the product of centuries of development, he stated that the creation story "has very little in common with a real myth" (*Genesis: A Commentary* [Philadelphia: Westminster, 1972], 95). C. S. Lewis considers Gen. 1–3 to be a myth, but then writes, "What exactly happened when Man fell, we do not know; but if it is legitimate to guess, I offer the following picture—a 'myth' in the Socratic sense, a not unlikely tale." In a footnote he clarifies what he means by "a 'myth' in the Socratic sense": "i.e., an account of what *may have been* the historical fact. Not to be confused with 'myth' in Dr Niebuhr's sense (i.e., a symbolical representation of non-historical truth" (*The Problem of Pain* [San Francisco: HarperCollins, 2001], 71). So Lewis is not denying the potential historicity of the Genesis account.

Gordon J. Wenham translates Gen. 2:4 as: "This is the history of the heaven and the earth when they were created, on the day the Lord God made earth and heaven," arguing that since all of the later uses of *toledah* in Genesis mean "family history," so here the word also means *history* (see *Genesis 1–15*, vol. 1, Word Biblical Commentary [Waco, TX: Word, 1987], 44, 49, 55–56). He examines in detail the difference between the Genesis account and the ancient Near Eastern myths (see 52–55), concluding that Gen. 2–3 is a "factual report" because its introductory formula—namely, "This is the history of the heaven and the earth"—"implies that the characters who appear in Gen 2 and 3 are as real as the patriarchs" (54), while opining that perhaps it should be called "proto-historical" or "pre-history" rather than history because it describes events that took place "before written records began" (54). Both Derek Kidner and Henri Blocher make insightful comments about the passage's historicity (see Kidner's

Genesis: An Introduction and Commentary [Downers Grove, IL: InterVarsity Press, 1967], 66–67; and Blocher's *In the Beginning: The Opening Chapters of Genesis* [Downers Grove, IL: InterVarsity Press, 1984], 157–60). I will say much more about the importance of origin stories in the epilogue.

2. C. John Collins, *Genesis 1–4: A Linguistic, Literary, and Theological Commentary* (Phillipsburg, NJ: P&R, 2006), 135. This concern to explain our current state is sometimes recognized in secular philosophy. For instance, in attempting to explain "why human beings have to live by rules which can frustrate their desires," Mary Midgley observes that people "tend to look backwards, asking whether there was once an 'unfallen conflict-free state before the rules were imposed, a state where rules were not needed, perhaps because nobody ever wanted to do anything bad" ("The Origin of Ethics," in *A Companion to Ethics*, ed. Peter Singer [Oxford, UK: Basil Blackwell, 1991], 3). She thinks this backward glance is natural for those who are seriously asking why they should be moral now. She thinks we tend to answer these questions in terms of some sort of "origin myth," which describes "not only how human life began, but also why it is so hard, so painful, so confusing, so conflict-ridden" (3).

3. "Genesis 1 portrays the cosmos as a royal world, in which the Creator deputizes *Adam* [by means of the italicization, Block means to signify the first man as humanity rather than merely as the first individual person] as his administrative vassal to secure the smooth operation of that world. . . . The narrator casts *Adam* as a king." Daniel I. Block, *Covenant: The Framework of God's Grand Plan of Redemption* (Grand Rapids, MI: Baker Academic, 2021), 27–28.

4. Wenham, *Genesis 1–15*, 61.

5. Kidner, *Genesis*, 61. Wenham notes that gold and precious gemstones were "widely used in decorating the tabernacle and temple (Exod 25:7; 1 Chr 29:2) and in the high-priestly vestments (Exod 28:9–20)," which means that "Paradise in Eden and the later tabernacle share a common symbolism [including the use of aromatic resins] suggestive of the presence of God" (*Genesis 1–15*, 65). The details of vv. 9–14 suggest "that not only man but God dwelt there . . . , for [a land of delight full of trees, water, and precious stones] are symbols of God's life-giving presence" (87).

6. Hans Walter Wolff, *Anthropology of the Old Testament* (Philadelphia: Fortress, 1974), 128. The remaining quotations in this paragraph are all from Blocher, *In the Beginning*, 120, emphasis added. Gen. 2:5 reads: "When no bush of the field was yet in the land and no small plant of the field had yet sprung up—*for the Lord God had not caused it to rain on the land, and there was no man to work the ground.*" The italicized words imply that Adam's role in creation was to work the ground, since the word *for* is giving us the reason why there were no bushes or trees. It was because there was no human being to attend to them. Yet as Blocher clarifies, work is not to be the be-all and end-all of human life. He writes that God's giving the Sabbath to Israel (see Ex. 20:8–11) "relativizes the works of mankind" by protecting "mankind from total absorption by the task of subduing the earth" and thus "anticipates the distortion which makes work the sum and purpose of human life." The Sabbath "informs mankind that he will

not fulfill his humanity in his relation to the world which he is transforming but only when he raises his eyes above, in the blessed, holy hour of communion with the Creator. . . . The essence of mankind is not work!" (57).

7. Claus Westermann, *Creation* (Philadelphia: Fortress, 1974), 81. Cf. 2 Thess. 3:6–12. The quotation in the next sentence is found on p. 82, while the remaining quotations in my paragraph are from Westermann's *Genesis 1–11: A Continental Commentary* (Minneapolis: Fortress, 1994), 222, 220. I am indebted to Westermann throughout this subsection.

   Gerhard von Rad commented on Gen. 2:15 that "it indicates man's purpose in being in the garden: he is to work it and preserve it from all damage, a destiny that contrasts decidedly with the commonly accepted fantastic ideas of 'Paradise.' . . . Work was man's sober destiny even in his original state. . . . *He was called to a state of service and had to prove himself in a realm that was not his own possession*" (*Genesis*, 80; emphasis added). It is noteworthy that two of the twentieth century's most productive commentators see work in the same way.

8. "Psalm 8 celebrates man's destiny to rule over extra-human creation. . . . It leads to the final, decisive and all-embracing recognition by emphasizing that *the crowning of man to be steward over the world is* (in view of his minuteness in relation to the universe and his pitiable need of providing care) *anything but a matter of course, and certainly does not have its ground in man himself* (vv. 3f.)." Wolff, *Anthropology of the Old Testament*, 227; emphases added.

9. "Immediately after man's creation and the planting of the paradisal garden, Yahweh leads him into that garden, so that he may cultivate it and protect it. When at this point the [text] mentions both the serving of the earth through labour . . . and the protective watching over it . . . , [it is indicating] the two aspects of all man's activity in his various callings. The context of the passage brings out the divine working and giving as the premise of all human activity; when the gifts of creation are made over to man, the care and protection of these gifts is also given him as the task of his life"—a task that he and the soon-to-be created woman would, as long as they kept God's commandment, find very rewarding. Wolff, *Anthropology of the Old Testament*, 128–29.

10. Wenham, *Genesis 1–15*, 87.

11. "The evil of pain depends on degree, and *pains below a certain level of intensity are not feared or resented at all.* No one minds the process 'warm—beautifully hot—too hot—it stings' which warns him to withdraw his hand from exposure to the fire: and, if I may trust my own feeling, a slight aching in the legs as we climb into bed after a good day's walking is, in fact, pleasurable" (Lewis, *The Problem of Pain*, 23; emphasis added). Something similar is true with intellectual work.

12. An animal's world is physical and biological, with its senses and instincts setting its basic trajectory in life. We share the same physical and biological environment because we also are biological beings, but the trajectory of our lives is not to be determined by sense or instinct but by our listening to God's words. When human life is determined by sense or instinct, it is not a properly human life, as 2 Pet. 2:12 and Jude 10–11 make clear.

13. Dietrich Bonhoeffer, *Creation and Fall: A Theological Exposition of Genesis 1–3* (Minneapolis: Fortress, 2004), 83. It is part of the artistry of the Genesis account that the author omits recording the words with which God actually addressed Adam in charging him with working and keeping the garden.

14. Kidner points out that while some of the promises of life and warnings of death in Proverbs understand life as quantitative biological life, the terms that accompany them often "show that 'life' and 'death' are to be understood qualitatively and at various levels." More specifically, "in several places it is not too much to say that *'life' means fellowship with God.*" Derek Kidner, *The Proverbs: An Introduction and Commentary* (Downers Grove, IL: InterVarsity Press, 1964), 53; emphasis added.

15. Blocher, *In the Beginning*, 96. *Mitsein* is the German word for *to be with*. C. S. Lewis writes:

> There is no reason to suppose that self-consciousness, the recognition of a creature by itself as a "self," can exist except in contrast with an "other," a something which is not the self. It is against an environment and preferably a social environment, an environment of other selves, that the awareness of Myself stands out. (*The Problem of Pain*, 19)

He then adds:

> This would raise a difficulty about the consciousness of God if we were mere theists: being Christians, we learn from the doctrine of the Blessed Trinity that something analogous to "society" exists within the Divine being from all eternity—that God is Love, not merely in the sense of being the Platonic form of love, but because, within Him, the concrete reciprocities of love exist before all worlds and are thence derived to the creatures. (19–20)

16. Compare Augustine's definition of a people: "A people . . . is a gathered multitude of rational beings united by agreeing to share the things they love." *The City of God*, bk. 19, chap. 24.

17. The *Online Etymology Dictionary* identifies the etymology of the noun *communication* as deriving "from past participle stem of *communicare* 'to share, divide out; communicate, impart, inform; join, unite, participate in,' literally 'to make common,' related to *communis* 'common, public, general'" (*Online Etymology Dictionary*, s.v. "communication," accessed January 28, 2018, etymonline.com). *Community* shares the same etymological origin in *communis*, as does the word *communion*.

18. See chap. 1, 32–33. In declaring that Eve would be called *ishsha* because she was taken out of *ish*, Adam was also, perhaps unknowingly, acknowledging that his understanding of himself would be dependent on his relation to her.

19. Wolff, *Anthropology of the Old Testament*, 29; emphasis added. For more on this vow, see chap. 1, note 79.

20. Blocher, *In the Beginning*, 97. I have altered the order of Blocher's sentences. Wolff notes that "the woman . . . is only brought to man when she is a complete, independent person" (*Anthropology of the Old Testament*, 172).

21. Philippe Rochat notes that a newborn is calmed by its mother's voice from the moment it is born because for the final trimester of its gestation it could hear her speak. *The Infant's World* (Cambridge, MA: Harvard University Press, 2001), 82–83.

22. Rochat, *Infant's World*, 183. My previous sentence paraphrases a few of Rochat's preceding sentences. The quotations in this and the next paragraph are from the same page. The emphasis is added.

23. Blocher, *In the Beginning*, 96; emphasis added. A *salutation* expresses goodwill or courtesy, so it involves greeting another person respectfully.

24. Rochat, *Infant's World*, 131. Here biblical theology and developmental psychology corroborate each other. Wolff writes:

> A man's "face" is far more important than his "head" in the Old Testament. It is always *called pānīm*, in the plural, thus reminding us of the manifold different ways in which a man can give his attention (*pnh*) to his counterpart; events are reflected in the features of the face (e.g. Gen. 4.5); the partner can be already addressed through the play of expression (e.g. Gen. 31.2, 5). In the "face" as the *pānīm*, man's "turnings towards" another, his organs of communication, are gathered together; and among these the eyes, the mouth and the ears are the most important. Among all the organs and limbs, is it not here that we ought to come close to finding out what man's being consists of, and what distinguishes him from all other created beings? (*Anthropology of the Old Testament*, 74)

Edward Tronick, Heidelise Als, et al., "The Infant's Response to Entrapment between Contradictory Messages in Face-to-Face Interaction," *Journal of the American Academy of Child Psychiatry* 17.1 (1978), start their piece on the centrality of face-to-face interaction for infants like this:

> In face-to-face interactions young infants begin to learn and define the rules of social interaction. In these early affective interchanges with caregivers they learn: (1) the meaning of their own expressive behavior; (2) the characteristics of people who are important to them: and (3) cognitive and affective information which allows them to fit into their culture, to identify with their caregivers, and to identify themselves. (1)

The next quotation is from Rochat, *Infant's World*, 135.

25. See Tronick, "Infant's Response." For the effects of a mother's depression and other causes of what the psychologists call "understimulation," see Daniel N. Stern, *The First Relationship: Infant and Mother* (Cambridge, MA: Harvard University Press, 2002), 145–48.

26. The harm suffered by prisoners in long-term solitary isolation confirms this. See, e.g., Lisa Guenther's phenomenological analysis of how "first-person consciousness is constitutively intertwined with the embodied consciousness of others," in "Subjects without a World? An Husserlian Analysis of Solitary Confinement," *Human Studies* 34 (2011): 257–76.

27. Blocher, *In the Beginning*, 96.

28. Wolff, *Anthropology of the Old Testament*, 214. The last two quotations in this paragraph are from pp. 217 and 219.

29. Gordon J. Wenham, *The Book of Leviticus* (Grand Rapids, MI: Eerdmans, 1979), 200.

30. This isn't to say that God may not call us, as he called Jeremiah, to such a life in order to bring about some greater good, especially in New Testament times (see 1 Cor. 7; 9:5). Christians can be called to celibacy or solitude. Yet those states are "not good" for us as God created us. They should be embraced only when they come from God as gifts, callings (see 1 Cor. 7), or trials (see 1 Cor. 9:5), for they involve forgoing goods that normally should be ours (see 1 Cor. 9:5).

31. At 7:1 the man declares: "Your rounded thighs are like jewels, *the work of a master hand*." See 7:1–9 and 4:1–7 for his aesthetic appreciation of her and 5:10–16 for her aesthetic appreciation of him.

32. Blocher, *In the Beginning*, 97.

33. Blocher, *In the Beginning*, 134.

34. See Victor P. Hamilton, *The Book of Genesis: Chapters 1–17* (Grand Rapids, MI: Eerdmans, 1990), 181. The next quotation is from 181n13.

35. Wenham observes:

    > Explicit characterization of actors in the story is rare in Hebrew narrative, so it seems likely that in noting the snake's shrewdness the narrator is hinting that his remarks should be examined very carefully. He may not be saying what he seems to be saying. Perhaps we should not take his words at their face value as the woman did. (*Genesis*, 72)

36. See Victor P. Hamilton:

    > The translation of Heb. *'ap kî* [which are the words introducing the serpent's remark] is still open to question. If it functions here simply to introduce a question (cf. AV, RSV, NIV, etc.)—then this is the only time in the [Old Testament] that *'ap kî* carries interrogative force. . . . I . . . take it as a feigned expression of surprise. So taken, Eve's words in v. 2 become a correction rather than an answer. (*Book of Genesis*, 186)

    The rendering in my text is Hamilton's translation.

37. Collins, *Genesis 1–4*, 170.

38. Hamilton, *Book of Genesis*, 153. The next quotation from Hamilton is from p. 189.

39. Kidner, *Genesis*, 68. My fourth sentence in this paragraph paraphrases Kidner's next sentence, which reads: "God will henceforth be regarded, consciously or not, as rival and enemy" (68). The quotation in my paragraph's final sentence comes from the same place. Most of us can think of situations—for instance, when as teenagers we were prone to believe that our parents were out to ruin our fun—where a falsehood could pervert our desires and feelings and perhaps our entire approach to life. A widespread falsehood about God in our culture

is the assumption that he is a castrating father who is out to ruin our fun (see below, 57).

40. The biblical text in this passage refers to *the woman* and *her husband* rather than naming them as *Adam* and *Eve* because they are primarily being considered as the first human beings who, through their choices, are determining the trajectory for all of humanity (see Rom. 5:12–19). Yet for convenience's sake, I will still sometimes refer to them by their proper names.

41. "Indeed, because he alone is omniscient and sees all things exactly as they are, his is the only comprehensively objective point of view in the universe" (Jeffrey J. Niehaus, *Biblical Theology, Volume 1: The Common Grace Covenants* [Wooster, OH: Weaver, 2014], 30):

> The tree of the knowledge of good and evil . . . does not appear in the eschatological visions because it has been supplanted in history by the cross of Christ. *The original tree was a judgment tree* at which our first parents ought to have judged the serpent by renouncing him and his claims. The first Adam failed to do this, so there was need of a second Adam who would accomplish that judgment. The second Adam—Jesus—did accomplish it by having all sins judged in his person at the second tree, the cross of his judgment. Both Paul and Peter address the cross as a tree [see Gal. 3:13, quoting Deut. 21:22–23 and 2 Pet. 1:24]. (76; emphasis added)

The tree of the knowledge of good and evil could serve as a judgment tree because when God breathed into Adam the breath of life, he became capable of exercising his judgment, which he then exercised wrongly, but which our Lord as Adam's descendant (see Luke 3:23–38) later exercised rightly.

42. Developmental psychologists call this tendency of toddlers to look to their mothers in strange and potentially dangerous situations "social referencing":

> Social referencing [is] a process in which one person utilizes another person's interpretation of the situation to formulate her own interpretation. . . . In referencing, one person serves as a base of information for another and, in so doing, facilitates the other's efforts to construct reality. . . . In a social species, such as human beings, the availability of other conspecifics as a base of information is both comforting and essential, being one of the fundamental reasons for affiliation and sociality. (Saul Feinman, ed., *Social Referencing and the Social Construction of Reality in Infancy* [New York: Plenum, 1992], 4)

Scripture takes social referencing to be indispensable for developing a true perspective on life (see Gen. 18:19; Deut. 6:4–9; 11:19; 32:46; and Proverbs). Parents should function as godly guides:

> Only take care, and keep your soul diligently, lest you forget the things that your eyes have seen, and lest they depart from your

heart all the days of your life. Make them known to your children and your children's children—how on the day that you stood before the Lord your God at Horeb, the Lord said to me, "Gather the people to me, that I may let them hear my words, so that they may learn to fear me all the days that they live on the earth, and that they may teach their children so." (Deut. 4:9–10)

43. All nonbiblical quotations in this paragraph are from Kidner, *Genesis*, 68.

44. Hamilton, *Book of Genesis*, 181.

45. In Hebrew, the permission and the warning are in what is called the "infinitive absolute." More on the best translation of this grammatical construction in this chapter's section entitled, "Dying You Shall Die."

46. Blocher, *In the Beginning*, 121; emphasis added to the second sentence. All but the last quotation in this paragraph and the next are from the same page. The last quotation in this paragraph is from p. 113. I am indebted to Blocher throughout these paragraphs.

47. In Hebrew, the whole sentence that makes up vv. 16–17 is in the jussive case, which means the permission and the prohibition are part of the command. Although while at this point in the creation narrative God spoke the commandment to Adam alone, it was meant for him and Eve.

48. Commenting on Gen. 2:16–17, Westermann writes:

> V. 16 is not a restriction, but a release; "God begins with a great release," G. von Rad. The release of all other trees in the garden means that the man need suffer no deprivation; there is plenty of food there. *The restriction [in v. 17] cannot mean that the man is going to lack anything.* (*Genesis 1–11*, 222; emphasis added)

Wenham mentions that the fact that the first couple was not ashamed of their nakedness before they fell "reiterates [their] contentment . . . with God's provision" (*Genesis 1–15*, 72). Blocher writes, "The woman in Eden had no grounds for dissatisfaction, nothing within her should have disordered or misdirected her desire" (*In the Beginning*, 141).

49. See Gordon McConville: "The [Old Testament] knows of one god who freely enters into a relationship, at once historical and ethical, with a people of his choosing. That people is not 'determined' by the necessities of an impersonal natural order, but relates freely to the one knowable, personal, holy god, who reveals that the way of life consists in communion with him." Gordon J. McConville, "*berit*," in *New International Dictionary of Old Testament Theology and Exegesis*, ed. Willem VanGemeren (Grand Rapids, MI: Zondervan, 1997), 1:738.

50. Daniel N. Stern, *The Interpersonal World of the Infant: A View from Psychoanalysis and Developmental Psychology* (New York: Basic, 1985), 148. He writes that infants and their caregivers "sharing of affective states . . . is the most pervasive and clinically germane feature of intersubjective relatedness. This is especially true when the infant first enters this domain. Interaffectivity is mainly what is meant when clinicians speak of parental 'mirroring' and 'empathetic responsiveness'" (138).

Merriam-Webster's Unabridged Dictionary defines *commune* as a matter of attaining "an earnest or deep feeling of unity, appreciation, and receptivity—used with *with.*" *Merriam-Webster*, s.v. "commune," accessed December 5, 2021, https://unabridged.merriam-webster.com.

51. Block, *Covenant*, 1. Gordon P. Hugenberger offers the following very similar "working definition" for the Hebrew word *berit*: "A covenant, in its normal sense, is an elected, as opposed to natural, relationship of obligation under oath." *Marriage as a Covenant: Biblical Law and Ethics as Developed from Malachi* (Eugene, OR: Wipf & Stock, 2014), 11. Block adds that "the Scriptures present marriage relationships as covenantal: two unrelated persons commit to each other and to the long-range goal of establishing a new family through a formal procedure (Prov. 2:17; Mal. 2:14)." Block, *Covenant*, 2.

52. *Oxford English Dictionary*, s.v. "covenant," accessed November 17, 2021, https://www.oed.com/.

53. The communion thus achieved between parents and children is intended to be moderated and in a sense superseded by the communion of husband and wife if and when someone marries: "Therefore a man shall leave his father and his mother and hold fast to his wife, and they shall become one flesh" (Gen. 2:24; cf. Ps. 45:10; Matt. 19:4–6).

54. Both Old and New Testaments emphasize the naturalness of parent/child relationships (see, e.g., Matt. 7:11; Heb. 11:24–25) and the obligations that that natural relationship should nevertheless involve (see, e.g., Ex. 20:12; Eph. 6:1–3; 1 Tim. 5:4, 7).

55. John Murray, *Collected Writings of John Murray*, vol. 2, *Select Lectures in Systematic Theology* (Carlisle, PA: Banner of Truth, 1977), 47. My use of "full-orbed communion" in the last sentence of this paragraph is also from the same page.

The correct translation of Hos. 6:7—which can be rendered (as by ESV and NLT) to refer to Adam as the first human being or (as by NIV 2011 and NRSV) as referring to a place named "Adam"—is uncertain enough to leave the question of whether God struck a covenant with Adam in Gen. 2 uncertain. Likewise, Dumbrell's argument that God's claim that he will "establish" his covenant with Noah and his descendants at Gen. 6:18 and 9:8–11 involves his confirming that the covenant he made with Adam is not dispositive. See W. J. Dumbrell, *Covenant and Creation: An Old Testament Covenant Theology* (Milton Keynes, UK: Paternoster, 2013), 15–26.

56. See, e.g., Murray, *Collected Writings*, 49:

This [the Adamic] administration has often been denoted "The Covenant of Works." There are two observations. (1) The term is not felicitous, for the reason that the elements of grace entering into the administration are not properly provided for by the term "works." (2) It is not designated a covenant in Scripture. . . . Scripture always uses the term *covenant*, when applied to God's administration to men, in reference to a provision that is redemptive or closely related to redemptive design. Covenant in Scripture denotes the oath-bound confirmation of promise and involves a security which the Adamic economy did not bestow.

57. This is a central claim in Block's *Covenant*, where he calls the world of Eden a "precovenant world" (3). He states, in accordance with his characterization of biblical covenants that I have quoted above, that

> if a covenant involves a ritual that creates a relationship that does not exist naturally, then a covenant would have been unnecessary and superfluous in the scenes described in Genesis 1–2. It would have been superfluous because the entire cosmos was functioning as God intended. Even though Genesis 1–2 casts *Adam* [by italicizing the word Block means it to signify not the individual person but humanity] in the role of "vassal" vis-à-vis God, the divine "Suzerain," this does not make the relationship covenantal. (15)

Gen. 1–2 then "offer a glimpse into the reality that was lost" by Adam and Eve's rebellion "and hint at the realities that God would seek to reconstruct through the covenants that will form the framework of the divine drama of cosmic judgment and redemption" (16). None of this denies that there were covenant-like elements in God's relationship with our first parents before they disobeyed: God's relationship with our first parents was always a suzerain/vassal relationship where God as the suzerain unilaterally set the conditions for their being blessed.

58. The Old Testament's most significant covenants involve solemn, formal commitments between God and his people. Those covenants were made necessary by the fact that our first parents broke their natural relationship with God by eating from the forbidden tree. But God then took the initiative by addressing humankind and defining his relationship with those who were to be called by his name—for instance, "I am the LORD your God, who brought you out of the land of Egypt, out of the house of slavery. *You shall have no other gods before me*" (Ex. 20:2–3). He told them he would be with them—"I will walk among you and will be your God, and you shall be my people" (Lev. 26:12; cf. 2 Cor. 6:16)—and would let his face shine on them (Ps. 80:3, 7, 19; cf. 2 Cor. 4:6) if they kept his commands.

59. Cf. Nahum M. Sarna, *The JPS Torah Commentary: Genesis* (Philadelphia: Jewish Publication Society, 1989), states:

> The difference between the formulation here [at Gen. 1:28] and God's blessing to the fish and fowl in verse 22 is subtle and meaningful. Here God directly addresses man and woman. *The transcendent God of Creation transforms Himself into the immanent God, the personal God, who enters into unmediated communion with human beings.* (13; emphasis added)

There is something profoundly right about Sarna's claim, for God has created us for face-to-face communion with himself, but Sarna's Jewish perspective doesn't permit the nuance that we Christians need here, as it is expressed in

1 Tim. 2:5: "For there is one God, *and there is one mediator between God and men, the man Christ Jesus.*" For Christians, it is more accurate to say that *the transcendent God of creation transforms himself into the immanent, personal God, who in the person of his Son, Jesus Christ, desires to be in face-to-face communion with human beings.*

Westermann notes:

> There are three basic ways in which man's conduct in community can be limited: by the taboo, the command (or prohibition), and the law. Each of these three is institutionally conditioned: the taboo is pre-personal, the command is personal, the law is post-personal. *There can only be command where there is speech*; the voice of him who commands must be there so as to command. *There cannot be command and the consequences of command without a personal relationship to the one who issues the command. Address in the second person is inseparable from the command.* (*Creation*, 91; emphases added)

I am indebted to Westermann's analysis of commands here and in his *Genesis 1–11* throughout this section.

60. Throughout Scripture, those who are in fellowship with God are said to walk with him (see, e.g., Gen. 5:22, 24; 6:9; 2 Cor. 6:16; Col. 2:6). Abraham was commanded to walk before God and be perfect (see Gen. 17:1). Those who are faithful to the end are promised that they will walk with their Lord (see Rev. 3:4). Moreover, those who obey God's commands are called his friends (see John 15:13–15; James 2:23; cf. Ex. 33:11).

61. Kidner, *Genesis*, 62. As Kidner goes on to say, the fact that this tree is called the tree of "the knowledge of good and evil"

> is perhaps best understood in this living context. In isolation [this phrase] could mean a number of things. . . . [But in context] the emphasis falls on the prohibition rather than the properties of the tree. It is shown us as forbidden. *It is idle to ask what it might mean in itself; this was Eve's error. As it stood, prohibited, it presented the alternative to discipleship*: to be self-made, wresting one's knowledge, satisfactions and values from the created world in defiance of the Creator. . . . In all this *the tree plays its part in the opportunity it offers*, rather than the qualities it possesses. (63; emphases added)

This emphasis on the prohibition rather than the properties of the tree is one more indicator that the Genesis account is not myth: this is not a magical tree, with a magical fruit, no matter what someone like C. S. Lewis may think (see *The Problem of Pain*, 65–66). Throughout Scripture God requires his people's obedience if they are to remain in communion with him. For instance, the Lord declared to his new people, Israel:

> If you walk in my statutes and observe my commandments and do them, . . . [then] I will turn to you and make you fruitful and mul-

tiply you and will confirm my covenant with you. . . . I will make
my dwelling among you. . . . And I will walk among you and [I]
will be your God, and you shall be my people. (Lev. 26:3, 9, 11–12)

His commandments test our hearts (see Deut. 8:2; Prov. 17:3).

62. See note 48.

63. See Ps. 49. The Lord placed a similar choice before Israel right before they were
to cross the Jordan to enter the promised land when Moses said:

See, I have set before you today life and good, death and evil. If you
obey the commandments of the LORD your God that I command
you today, by loving the LORD your God, by walking in his ways,
and by keeping his commandments and his statutes and his rules,
then you shall live and multiply, and the LORD your God will bless
you in the land that you are entering to take possession of it. But if
your heart turns away, and you will not hear, but are drawn away
to worship other gods and serve them, I declare to you today, that
you shall surely perish. You shall not live long in the land that you
are going over the Jordan to enter and possess. I call heaven and
earth to witness against you today, that I have set before you life
and death, blessing and curse. *Therefore choose life, that you and
your offspring may live, loving the LORD your God, obeying his voice
and holding fast to him, for he is your life* and length of days, that
you may dwell in the land that the LORD swore to your fathers, to
Abraham, to Isaac, and to Jacob, to give them. (Deut. 30:15–20)

64. As Blocher observes, God's covenant name is "his name for his 'marriage' with
Israel" (Blocher, *In the Beginning*, 111). Comparing Adam and Eve's potential
ratification of their love for their Lord with our wedding vows is, then, what
Scripture itself suggests:

Behold, the days are coming, declares the LORD, when I will make a
new covenant with the house of Israel and the house of Judah, not
like the covenant that I made with their fathers on the day when
I took them by the hand to bring them out of the land of Egypt,
my covenant that they broke, *though I was their husband, declares
the LORD.* (Jer. 31:31–32; cf. Isa. 54:5; Hos. 2:19–20)

This foreshadows the marriage supper of the Lamb to his bride, the church, at
Rev. 19:6–9 (see above, p. 50). Collins notes that marriage is "well suited as an
image for the relationship of the Lord and his people. . . . Paul uses that image
in 1 Corinthians 6:16–17; he also employs it in Ephesians 5:31–32 ([the] text [is]
very close to the Septuagint of Gen. 2:24)" (*Genesis 1–4*, 145), and then refers
his readers to Raymond Ortlund's *Whoredom: God's Unfaithful Wife in Biblical
Theology* (Grand Rapids, MI: Eerdmans, 1996).

Blocher argues (correctly, I think) there is no reason to take God's commandment as establishing a probationary test (*In the Beginning*, 133f.). It is no
more probationary than the bride and groom's vow to be faithful to each other as
long as they both shall live. It is a vow forever to forsake all others and be faithful

to each other, which is the sort of commitment to their Lord that Adam and Eve were to live out through their entire lives. The fact that the command at Gen. 2:17 is a command that our first parents were never to eat from the forbidden tree clarifies that all God was asking them to do was respond with a resounding, "Yes, we will never!" (see chap. 1, 34, and its accompanying endnote, 64).

65. Bonhoeffer, *Creation and Fall*, 85:

> The prohibition contained two complementary aspects. On the one hand it indicated that Adam was human, was free (free "for" and "from")—it is Adam, the human being, who is addressed concerning Adam's own human existence, and Adam understands this. On the other hand it indicates to this human being who is addressed as a free person their limit or boundedness, that is, the human being's creatureliness. The prohibition addresses Adam concerning Adam's freedom and creatureliness and binds Adam to this existence, the existence that belongs to Adam's own being. The prohibition means nothing other than this: Adam, you are who you are because of me, your Creator; so now be what you are. You are a free creature, so now be that. You are free, so be free; you are a creature, so be a creature. And this "—so be . . ." is not a second thing besides the first but something always given already in and with the first and guaranteed by the first. It is about being human—about the human existence that Adam receives from God at any given time—that Adam is addressed.

66. The context is illuminating:

> Meanwhile the disciples were urging him, saying, "Rabbi, eat." But he said to them, "I have food to eat that you do not know about." So the disciples said to one another, "Has anyone brought him something to eat?" Jesus said to them, "My food is to do the will of him who sent me and to accomplish his work." (John 4:31–34)

The priority of the spiritual over the physical is clear earlier in John 4 when Jesus tells the woman at the well that he can give her living water (see vv. 1–15) and later in chap. 6 when he tells those seeking more miraculous feedings: "Truly, truly, I say to you, you are seeking me, not because you saw signs, but because you ate your fill of the loaves. Do not work for the food that perishes, but for the food that endures to eternal life, which the Son of Man will give to you" (vv. 26–27; see vv. 25–65). Near the end of that chapter, Jesus declares: "The words that I have spoken to you are spirit and life" (v. 63). Similarly, Job declared, "My feet have closely followed his steps; I have kept to his way without turning aside. I have not departed from the commands of his lips; *I have treasured the words of his mouth more than my daily bread*" (Job 23:11–12 NIV); and the psalmist said, "How sweet are your words to my taste, sweeter than honey to my mouth!" (Ps. 119:103).

67. My paraphrase follows C. S. Lewis's at the head of chap. 5 of his *Problem of Pain*. Montaigne wrote, "To obey is the principal function of a reasonable soul." Mi-

chel de Montaigne, "Apology for Raymond Sebond," in *Essays,* bk. 2 (New York: Alfred A. Knopf, 2003), 436f. Cf. Westermann, *Creation,* in note 59, above.

68. See, e.g., Prov. 3:18, where wisdom from God is called "a tree of life to those who lay hold of her," and Rev. 22:2, 14, and 19, where the tree of life is part of the holy city in which God dwells with his redeemed people.

69. Bonhoeffer, *Creation and Fall,* 83–84. All quotations but the Blocher quotation in the next two paragraphs are from pp. 86–87.

70. Blocher, *In the Beginning,* 122; emphasis added.

71. "Though somewhat ineffective, these actions [sewing fig leaves together] suggest urgency and desperation; the innocent serenity of 2:25 is shattered." Wenham, *Genesis 1–15,* 76.

72. Wenham comments:

> "Now the snake was more shrewd than all the wild animals." "Shrewd" [*'arum*] is an ambiguous term. On the one hand it is a virtue the wise should cultivate (Prov 12:16; 13:16), but misused it becomes wiliness and guile (Job 5:12; 15:5; cf. Exod 21:14; Josh 9:4). The choice of the term "shrewd" [*'arum*] here is one of the more obvious plays on words in the text; for the man and his wife have just been described as [*'arom*] "nude" (2:25). *They will seek themselves to be shrewd (cf. 3:6) but will discover that they are* "nude" (3:7, 10). (*Genesis 1–15,* 72; emphasis added)

73. John H. Sailhamer, *The Pentateuch as Narrative: A Biblical-Theological Commentary* (Grand Rapids, MI: Zondervan, 1992), 104. My next sentence echoes Kidner's observation that "man saw the familiar world and spoilt it now in the seeing, projecting evil on to innocence (cf. Tit. 1:15) and reacting to good with shame and flight." Kidner, *Genesis,* 69.

74. Blocher, *In the Beginning,* 173. The quotation from Kidner that follows is from *Genesis,* 69.

75. Von Rad, *Genesis,* 85, 91. In contrasting the sort of knowledge of good and evil that Adam and Eve would have experienced in not eating from the forbidden tree or in eating from it, John Murray writes:

> How diverse the states of consciousness! By the fall there invaded man's consciousness elements that would never have crossed the threshold [if they had not eaten], the sense of guilt, of fear, of shame. There entered a new dispositional complex of desires, impulses, affections, motives, and purposes. We may never conceive of knowledge as a state of mind apart from the total condition of heart and will. (*Collected Writings,* 2:53)

76. Wolff, *Anthropology of the Old Testament,* 172.

77. Herman Bavinck, *Reformed Dogmatics,* vol. 3, *Sin and Salvation in Christ* (Grand Rapids, MI: Baker, 2006), 198. The next quotation is from p. 173 (emphasis added), and the last one is from p. 198.

78. Von Rad, *Genesis,* 91. Cf. Heb. 2:15, which states that we for "all our lives are held in slavery by the fear of death" (I am paraphrasing the NRSV).

79. Kidner, *Genesis*, 68. He continues: "If modern denials of [judgment] are very differently motivated, they are equally at odds with revelation: Jesus fully affirmed the doctrine (e.g. Mt. 7:13–27)."

80. "Guilt and shame reveal both God's wrath and his grace, but the latter is shown especially when God seeks out Adam and Eve and interrogates them." Bavinck, *Reformed Dogmatics*, 193.

81. Blocher, *In the Beginning*, 171.

82. Blocher, *In the Beginning*, 171. The next quotation is from p. 172. Emphases in both quotations are added. The first nonbiblical quotation in the next paragraph is from p. 172. The emphasis of *repay* in the verse that completes that quotation is Blocher's.

83. For this way of rendering Hebrew's infinitive absolute, see Blocher, *In the Beginning*, 172 and 121; and Hamilton, below. About the claims in Gen. 2:16–17, Blocher writes:

> What rigorous symmetry! Twice the same grammatical procedure is used, which in Hebrew allows the greatest force: the infinitive absolute. To the phrase 'EATING you shall eat' responds the phrase 'DYING you shall die'. In the first case the tone must be that of the fullness of the permission: you shall eat *freely*, eat your fill without lacking any of the good things that I have created.
>
> Likewise, it is stipulated in the creational agreement: "you shall not eat"; otherwise "DYING you shall die." That is the condition that is the basis and safeguard of the happiness of the human race. . . . The warning, "DYING you shall die" hammers home the absolute certainty: on the monstrous, unthinkable hypothesis of [disobedience], *surely* you will die; the consequence is inescapable. (121–22)

Hamilton writes: "The last part of v. 17 reads literally 'in the day of your eating from it dying you shall die,' understanding the infinite absolute before the verb to strengthen the verbal idea." *Book of Genesis*, 172.

84. Kidner, *Genesis*, 64.

85. Alienation from God cuts us off from life's true source. Wenham says:

> The garden of Eden narrative is full of symbols suggesting the presence of God and his life-giving power—trees, gold, rivers, and jewels used to adorn the holy of holies. *In Israelite worship, true life was experienced when one went to the sanctuary. There God was present. There he gave life. But to be expelled from the camp, as lepers were, was to enter the realm of death.* Those unfortunates had to behave like mourners, with their clothes torn and their hair disheveled (Lev 13:45). *If to be expelled from the camp of Israel was to "die," expulsion from the garden was an even more drastic kind of death. In this sense they did die on the day they ate of the tree: they were no longer able to have daily conversation with God, enjoy his bounteous provision, and eat of the tree of life; instead they had to*

> *toil for food, suffer, and eventually return to the dust from which they were taken.* (*Genesis*, 74; my emphases)

A bit later he adds:

> Only in the presence of God did man enjoy fullness of life. To choose anything else is to choose death (Prov. 8:36). The expulsion from the garden of delight where God himself lived would therefore have been regarded by the godly . . . [in] ancient Israel as yet more catastrophic than physical death. The latter was the ultimate sign and seal of the spiritual death the human couple experienced on the day they ate from the forbidden tree. (90)

Collins says regarding the death threat in Gen. 2:17, "In the light of what happens (the actions and changed attitudes of the humans), we can see that part of the semantic range of 'death' that is present . . . is spiritual death, estrangement from God. *Physical mortality, which 3:19 predicts, is a consequence of the humans' disrupted condition*" (*Genesis 1–4*, 175; emphasis added). For created persons like us, biological death follows inevitably on spiritual death.

Chapter 3: Suffering

1. Derek Kidner comments on Gen. 3:6 that after the woman took and ate, "so simple the act, so hard its undoing. God [himself] will taste poverty and death before 'take and eat' become verbs of salvation" (*Genesis: An Introduction and Commentary* [Downers Grove, IL: InterVarsity Press, 1967], 68). He adds: "There [was] no road back. . . . God's way is forward, for when the body is redeemed (Rom. 8:23) and love is perfect we shall be not back in Eden but clothed with glory (2 Cor. 5:4)" (69).

2. In Western tonal music, a musical chord involving three or more tones played together is *dissonant* when it sounds unstable and thus tense or restless. The tension we hear in dissonance requires resolution and thus dissonant chords "lean" forward, seeking consonance in chords that are stable and restful. Our experience of chords as dissonant is somewhat (but not entirely) person-, culture-, and circumstance-relative. So we feel the need for resolution to varying degrees. We shall see that a person's experience of suffering involves similar sorts of relativity.

   The minor keys can convey sadness because they share some of the properties of sad or subdued speech. Happy and sad speech have different acoustic characteristics in most cultures. For more on this, see Philip Ball, "Does a minor key give everyone the blues?," *Nature* (January 8, 2010), https://nature.com/. I will say a lot more about how music enables us to understand how suffering relates to God's goodness in my third and fourth volumes.

3. Karen Jobes writes that "we intuitively know that suffering is somehow not the way life is meant to be":

   > Misfortune and death are certainly "normal" in the sense that they are universally experienced, *but they are not normal when viewed from God's intention in creation and his plan in redemption.* The

idea that normal life should always be harmonious and free from suffering, despite universal suffering and death, remains a lingering echo of life in Eden as God created it before the fall. It is also a longing for the time when there will be no more tears, suffering, pain, and death (Rev. 21:4). *From either the prefall or the eschatological perspective, suffering and death are abnormal.* (Karen H. Jobes, *1 Peter* [Grand Rapids, MI: Baker, 2005], 285–86; emphases added)

4. *Random House Dictionary of the English Language,* 2nd ed. (1987), defines *affront* as "a *personally* offensive act or word; *deliberate* act or display of disrespect; *intentional* slight; insult." It defines *offend* as "to irritate, annoy, or anger; cause resentful displeasure in" and "to violate or transgress (a criminal, religious, or moral law)." An *offense,* then, violates or transgresses some law, rule, or norm. But only *persons* are accountable to keep such norms, and so only persons can violate or transgress them. So only persons can affront or offend us. The vast chasm between taking reality as ultimately personal or merely material is driven home by C. S. Lewis in *Mere Christianity,* Book 1(San Francisco: HarperCollins, 2001). He argues that the fact that we are persons who know we ought to obey the moral law and are affronted or offended when others do not obey it strongly suggests that a person made the universe.

5. Of course, atheists can be affronted or offended by particular bits of pain or suffering if they take them to result from individuals or groups not acting as they should. For instance, an atheist can be affronted by the pain you have caused him by stepping on his foot if he believes you did it either deliberately or carelessly. And he can be offended by his cellphone not working if he thinks its malfunctioning is due to the manufacturer's carelessness. But those cases are very different from atheists being affronted or offended by the world's total amount of pain and suffering when they don't believe there is any person who can be held accountable for that pain and suffering.

The fact that many atheists and agnostics *do* feel affronted and offended by the world's pain may be grounds for affirming the truth of Rom. 1:20: God's invisible attributes, "namely, his eternal power and divine nature, have been clearly perceived, ever since the creation of the world, in the things that have been made." Paul claims in vv. 18–19 that human beings "by their unrighteousness suppress the truth" because "what can be known about God is plain to them, because God has shown it to them." So when atheists and agnostics find themselves affronted and offended by the world's suffering, their attitudes may betray that they know more than they are willing to admit—namely, that God exists (see Rom. 1:21)—even if they then blame the world's pain on the wrong person. See my "Is It Natural to Believe in God?," *Faith and Philosophy,* 6.2 (April 1989): 155–71.

6. Proponents of what I am labeling as bottom-up stories are often acutely aware that accepting their story as the final explanation for everything should radically affect how we think about ourselves. For instance, in his general introduction to his edition of Darwin's four most influential works, E. O. Wilson writes:

To the extent [the theory of evolution by natural selection] can be upheld, . . . we must conclude that *life has diversified on Earth autonomously without any kind of external guidance. Evolution in a pure Darwinian world has no goal or purpose*. . . . The revolution in astronomy begun by Nicolaus Copernicus in 1543 proved that Earth is not the center of the universe, nor even the center of the solar system. The revolution begun by Darwin was even more humbling: it showed that *humanity is not the center of creation, and not its purpose either*. [This has freed] our minds from our imagined demigod bondage. (Edward O. Wilson, *From So Simple a Beginning: The Four Great Books of Charles Darwin* [New York: Norton, 2006], 12–13; emphases added)

In his "General Summary and Conclusion" in *The Descent of Man, and Selection in Relation to Sex* (first published in 1871), Darwin himself wrote:

He who is not content to look, like a savage, at the phenomena of nature as disconnected, *cannot any longer believe that man is the work of a separate act of creation*. . . . It must not be supposed that the divergence of each race from the other races, and of all the races from a common stock, can be traced back to any one pair of progenitors. (1237–38; emphasis added)

He then denies that there is a difference in kind between humanity and the higher animals: "Every one who admits the general principle of evolution, must see that *the mental powers of the higher animals . . . are the same in kind with those of mankind, though so different in degree*" (1239; emphasis added). He concludes:

We must acknowledge, as it seems to me, that man with all his noble qualities, with sympathy which feels for the most debased, with benevolence which extends not only to other men but to the humblest living creature, with his god-like intellect which has penetrated into the movements and constitution of the solar system— with all these exalted powers—Man still bears in his bodily frame the indelible stamp of his lowly origin. (1248)

Darwin admits that accounting for "the development of our moral qualities is a more interesting and difficult problem" (1240) than accounting for our mental powers, but he thinks he has done so adequately in chap. 3 of *The Descent of Man*.

It is difficult to decide how the top-down biblical story of creation should be integrated with the scientific findings that are usually the basis of bottom-up stories. Kidner's comments in his section "Human Beginnings" in his Genesis commentary are helpful (see pp. 26–31). His final observation is crucial and articulates the way I have been interpreting the first chapters of Genesis:

The interests and methods of Scripture and science differ so widely that they are best studied, in any detail, apart. Their accounts of the world are as distinct (and each as legitimate) as an artist's portrait and an anatomist's diagram, of which no composite picture will be satisfactory, for their common ground is only in the total reality to which they both attend. *It cannot be said too strongly that Scripture is the perfect vehicle for God's revelation . . . ; and its bold selectiveness, like that of a great painting, is its power. To read it with one eye on any other account is to blur its image and miss its wisdom. To have God's own presentation of human beginnings as they most deeply concern us, we need look no further than these chapters and their New Testament interpretation.* (31; emphases added)

Ultimately, the question is, Which perspective should have the final word? Roger Scruton argues that the distinctive features of human personhood can't really be accounted for adequately by a rigorously scientific, bottom-up perspective. As he puts it, "As persons we inhabit a life-world that is not reducible to the world of nature. . . . [And] if that is true, then there must be something left for a [non-scientific kind of thinking] to do, by way of making sense of the human condition." Roger Scruton, "If We Are Not Just Animals, What Are We?," *New York Times*, March 6, 2017.

7. Rebecca Goldstein, *Incompleteness: The Proof and Paradox of Kurt Gödel* (New York: Norton, 2005), 27. Goldstein subscribes to the evolutionary story and characterizes it like this:

Natural selection invokes randomness and contingency as fundamental explanatory factors. At the level of microevolution (generation-to-generation changes), the theory gives a central role to random mutation and recombination. At the level of macroevolution (patterns in the history of life), it gives a central role to historical contingency, such as the vagaries of geology and climate, or such chance events as a meteorite's crashing to Earth, blackening out the Sun, wiping out the dinosaurs, thus allowing mouselike mammals to inhabit the vacated ecological niches. (32n6)

An exclusively bottom-up evolutionary story has plausibility insofar as it seems to acknowledge the good and the bad in human nature and society just as the Christian top-down story does. It just gives the good and the bad a different explanation. Here is E. O. Wilson's way of explaining this feature of our humanity:

We are all genetic chimeras, at once saints and sinners, champions of the truth and hypocrites—not because humanity has failed to reach some foreordained religious or ideological ideal, but because of the way our species originated across millions of years of biological evolution. (Edward O. Wilson, *The Meaning of Human Existence* [New York: Liveright, 2014], 28)

8. George Birkbeck and L. F. Powell, eds., *Boswell's Life of Johnson, vol. 4: The Life (1780–1784)* (Oxford, UK: Clarendon Press, 1934), 313. In context:

Johnson having argued for some time with a pertinacious gentle-
man; his opponent, who had talked in a very puzzling manner,
happened to say, "I don't understand you, Sir:" upon which Johnson observed, "Sir, I have found you an argument; but I am not
obliged to find you an understanding."

Johnson's quip is based on an important insight. As the next sentence in my
text suggests, an explanation can be unsatisfying not because it is inadequate
but because of some inadequacy in the person receiving that explanation. As
Bonaventure observed in his *Disputed Questions on the Mystery of the Trinity*, a
proof or explanation may fail because of "a defect in the knower rather than a de-
ficiency in the object known" (Question 1, Article 1, Replies to Objections 1.2.3).
For instance, blind persons cannot see what is directly in front of them because
of their blindness, not because what is directly in front of them cannot be seen.

As Paul put it, we Christians "have renounced secret and shameful ways; we
do not use deception, nor do we distort the word of God. On the contrary, by
setting forth the truth plainly we commend ourselves to everyone's conscience
in the sight of God. And even if our gospel is veiled, it is veiled to those who are
perishing. The god of this age has blinded the minds of unbelievers, so that they
cannot see the light of the gospel that displays the glory of Christ, who is the
image of God" (2 Cor. 4:2–4 NIV). Our task is to pray that the Holy Spirit will
regenerate the hearts of those to whom we witness (see John 3:1–8; Titus 3:3–5)
and thus cure their blindness so that they can receive God's words as true.

9. John H. Sailhamer, *The Pentateuch as Narrative: A Biblical-Theological Commentary* (Grand Rapids, MI: Zondervan, 1992), 103 (see Deut. 28:48). The final
quotation of this paragraph is from the same page.

Victor P. Hamilton notes that "with the exception of [Gen. 2:25], nakedness in the Old Testament is always connected with some form of humiliation"
and that "a full documentation of all passages would show that nakedness as a
symbol of guilt is most frequent" (*The Book of Genesis: Chapters 1–17* [Grand
Rapids, MI: Eerdmans, 1990], 181). Cf. Hebrews 4:11–13:

Let us therefore strive to enter that rest, so that no one may fall by
the same sort of disobedience. For the word of God is living and
active, sharper than any two-edged sword, piercing to the division
of soul and of spirit, of joints and of marrow, and discerning the
thoughts and intentions of the heart. And *no creature is hidden
from his sight, but all are naked and exposed to the eyes of him to
whom we must give account.*

10. Gordon J. Wenham, *Genesis 1–15*, vol. 1, Word Biblical Commentary (Waco,
TX: Word, 1987), 47, note 25.a; emphasis added. The next quotation of Wenham in my next paragraph is from p. 76.

11. Gabriele Taylor, *Pride, Shame, and Guilt: Emotions of Self-Assessment* (Oxford,
UK: Clarendon, 1985), 53. The quotation in the next sentence is from p. 57.

12. Rom. 8:6 implies that by their disobedience Adam and Eve could no longer know
life and peace. Life depends on living according to the Spirit and putting to death

what Paul calls "the deeds of the body" (8:13)—the first, most tragic, and most decisive of which was Adam and Eve's decision to eat from the forbidden tree.

13. See Henri Blocher, *In the Beginning: The Opening Chapters of Genesis* (Downers Grove, IL: InterVarsity Press, 1984), 180–81:

> "MULTIPLYING I shall multiply your pain in childbearing; in pain you shall bring forth children" (Gn. 3:16a). . . . By announcing that he will "multiply" [the sufferings of pregnancy and of childbirth], or "make them numerous," God does not mean that there were already sufferings in the former dispensation. He is simply saying that henceforth they will be abundant.

He continues:

> The [woman's] sentence seems to presuppose the woman's vocation to bring forth children, as included under the creation mandate of the sixth day (Gn. 1:28a). Mankind retains the blessing and the power to procreate. But with it there is mingled bitterness, so that the blessing becomes a burden. The great disorder of sin so affects the good that God had brought forth, that everything remains and yet everything is changed. Here the gift of generation becomes, so to speak, a caricature of itself. (181)

14. About this second word to the woman, the Jewish commentator Umberto Cassuto says: "Measure for measure: you influenced your husband and caused him to do what you wished; henceforth, you and your female descendants will be subservient to your husbands. You will yearn for them, but they . . . will rule over you" (Umberto Cassuto, *A Commentary on the Book of Genesis, Part 1: From Adam to Noah* [Jerusalem: Magnes, 1961], 165f.). His "Measure for measure" makes clear that he takes this second word to be talionic—a retributive sentence, prescribing what is fitting and not a mere prediction or description. See also Allen P. Ross, *Creation and Blessing: A Guide to the Study and Exposition of the Book of Genesis* (Grand Rapids, MI: Baker, 1988), 146–47, who spells out exactly how this sentence would be talionic as well as how the sting of it would be removed for Christians.

    Hamilton, however, says, "In God's second word to the woman one does hope that God is speaking descriptively and not prescriptively. For this consequence deals with a marriage relationship that will go askew: the woman shall desire her husband but he shall lord it over her" (*Book of Genesis*, 201). All of God's other words from vv. 14–19, however, are prescriptive and talionic. And the very point may be that God is being merciful in frustrating the woman's dream of finding marital bliss. Her disappointment and difficulties should turn her to God.

15. Kidner writes:

> The phrase *your desire shall be for your husband* (RSV), with the reciprocating *he shall rule over you*, portrays a marriage relation in which control has slipped from the fully personal realm to that

of instinctive urges passive and active. "To love and to cherish" becomes "To desire and to dominate." While even pagan marriages can rise far above this, the pull of sin is always towards it. (*Genesis*, 71)

16. "Working the ground became a burdensome task after the rebellion of humankind (3:17–19). The alienation of Cain from the land . . . furthered this alienation (4:12), because the earth would no longer yield the reward for cultivating . . . it. So the 'profane' use of the [Hebrew] word [for *to work*] takes on a profound theological significance when set within a larger canonical context in Gen 1-4. *The response of the ground itself is ultimately dependent on humankind's spiritual relation to God* and, hence, to the ground." Eugene Carpenter, "'*abad*," *New International Dictionary of Old Testament Theology and Exegesis*, ed. Willem A. VanGemeren (Grand Rapids, MI: Zondervan, 1997), 3:304–5; emphasis added.

17. "The sentences on the man and woman take the form of a disruption of their appointed roles," Wenham writes:

> The woman was created to be man's helper and the mother of children. . . . The first part of her judgment is that maternity will be accompanied by suffering. . . . "To be a joyful mother of children" (Ps. 113:9), preferably a large family, was a sure sign of God's blessing (cf. Pss 127, 128). Yet the pain of childbirth, unrelieved by modern medicine, was the most bitter known then (cf. Mc 4:9–10; Isa 13:8; 21:3). . . . [With the second part of her judgment it] is more difficult [to discern] the author's precise intention. . . . It is . . . usually argued that "rule" here represents harsh exploitative subjugation, which so often characterizes woman's lot in all sorts of societies. (*Genesis 1–15*, 81)

He adds, "Though woman was created to be man's companion, she is told that her desire for independence will conflict with his demand for submission" (89). And then—returning to his earlier comments—he says that the man's sentence

> is the longest and fullest, since he bore the greatest responsibility in following his wife's advice instead of heeding God's instruction personally given to him. . . . Man's offense consisted of eating the forbidden fruit; therefore he is punished [talionically] in what he eats. The toil that now lies behind the preparation of every meal is a reminder of the fall and is made the more painful by the memory of the ready supply of food within the garden (2:9). . . . "As for man, his punishment consists in the hardship and skimpiness of his livelihood, which he must now seek for himself. The woman's punishment struck at the deepest root of her being as wife and mother; the man's strikes at the innermost nerve of his life: his work, his activity, and provision for sustenance." (Wenham, *Genesis 1–15*, 82–83, on vv. 17–19)

A bit later Wenham says:

Each is condemned to some permanent disadvantage in life. So characteristic of human existence are these features that modern man tends to regard them as simply inevitable. . . . But against the background of Gen 1, which ended by stating that everything that God had made was very good, these phenomena pose problems and demand explanation. (*Genesis 1–15*, 89)

He also says, regarding the man's sentence, that "physical death is . . . man's eventual destiny, however hard he tries to avoid the fact. *The divine curse thus explains man's mortality*" (89; emphasis added).

18. As Hamilton notes:

To each of the trespassers God speaks a word which involves both *a life function* and *a relationship*. . . . The woman shall experience pain at the point of childbearing, and in relationship to her husband. The man will confront disappointments as a worker through his estrangement from the soil. (*Book of Genesis*, 196)

He observes, regarding the ruptured relationship between the woman and the man in v. 16, "The two who once reigned as one attempt to rule each other." Regarding 3:19b–c, he says:

For the man . . . work [will be] toilsome. The further qualification is . . . that such circumstances shall be with the man for his whole life. *He will never be free of fatigue and toil. There is no evidence in the text that any repentance by the man can lift or remove these circumstances. They will be part and parcel of his life until he returns to the ground.* (203f.; emphases added)

19. Sailhamer corroborates that Genesis 3 foretells what we shall all experience when he writes:

Although much can be said about the curse on the snake, the woman, and the man, it is important to note that the text says very little. . . . *The snake, the woman, and the man are not depicted as individuals involved in a personal crisis; rather, they are representatives. We are left with the impression that this is not their story so much as it is our story, the story of humankind.* . . . The snake on the one hand and the man and the woman on the other are as two great nations embarking on a great struggle, a struggle that will find its conclusion only by an act of some distant and as yet unidentified "seed." (*Pentateuch as Narrative*, 106; emphasis added)

20. For instance, you may find spending an evening listening to Richard Wagner's *Tristan und Isolde* either pleasant or unpleasant depending on whether you like Wagnerian opera. If you were to dislike it enough to be squirming until it ended, then you would probably say you were suffering, although quite mildly.

21. See the real-life case of Megan Meier, a thirteen-year-old who hung herself after she was told by people posing as a sixteen-year-old boy on MySpace that the world

would be better off without her. Rebecca Cathcart, "MySpace Is Said to Draw Subpoena in Hoax Case," *New York Times*, January 10, 2008, https://nytimes.com/.

22. The phrase "disciplinary suffering" captures the connotations of the Greek at Heb. 12:5–11. I borrow it from William L. Lane, *Hebrews 9–13*, vol. 47B, Word Biblical Commentary (Dallas: Word, 1991), 313. The range of Greek words Hebrews' author uses to describe this discipline suggests it covers not only divine rebuke and severe physical or mental correction but also vigorous physical or moral training as well.

23. The Greek noun for "painful" here is *lupē*. The noun translated as "pleasant" is *chara*, which Louw and Nida characterize as "a state of joy and gladness—'joy, gladness, great happiness.'" Johannes P. Louw and Eugene A. Nida, eds., *Greek-English Lexicon of the New Testament: Based on Semantic Domains*, 2nd ed. (New York: United Bible Societies, 1989), 1:302.

24. This is also the conclusion of some careful psychological research. See Ed Diener, Richard E. Lucas, and Christie Napa Scollon, "Beyond the Hedonic Treadmill: Revising the Adaptation Theory of Well-Being," *American Psychologist* 61.4 (May–June 2006): 306. As Diener writes in another piece, "most people are not elated most of the time—they are just mildly happy" (Ed Diener and Carol Diener, "Most People Are Happy," *Psychological Science* 7.3 [May 1996]: 181). In other words, their lives are pleasant.

The branch of empirical psychology that investigates how people evaluate their lives is called "subjective well-being." Cognitively, this includes our judgments of how satisfactory our lives are; affectively, it involves our experiencing our lives as either pleasant or unpleasant. Colloquially, if you evaluate your life positively, then you say you are happy.

Counterintuitively, this research has found that "people living in negative circumstances report well-being scores that are above neutral" and, in fact, *"people who have experienced a negative life circumstance [such as complete quadriplegia] report well-being scores that are higher than what other people would think they should report"* (Diener, Lucas, and Scollon, "Beyond the Hedonic Treadmill," 310; emphasis added). Even the mentally and physically disabled and those with chronic mental problems usually find their lives satisfactory, although others, viewing those lives from outside, tend to evaluate them as vastly less satisfactory than those living them find them to be (see Diener and Diener, "Most People Are Happy," 181, 183f.). This should caution us about drawing conclusions about how much someone is suffering. Most people find life pleasant most of the time, including those living in less-developed countries.

Diener, Lucas, and Scollon cite research showing that "even in such diverse populations as the Amish, African Maasai, and Greenlandic Inughuit, most people are above neutral in well-being" ("Beyond the Hedonic Treadmill," 306). In fact, "In the most recent World Values Survey . . . , 80% of respondents said that they were very or quite happy" (306–7). This corroborates the apostle Paul's claim that God has not left himself without witness, for he has done good for all of us "by giving [us] rains from heaven and fruitful seasons, satisfying [our] hearts with food and gladness" (Acts 14:17).

25. Susan Sontag opens *Illness as Metaphor* (New York: Farrar, Straus & Giroux, 1978) like this: "Illness is the night-side of life, a more onerous citizenship. *Everyone who is born holds dual citizenship, in the kingdom of the well and in the kingdom of the sick.* Although we all prefer to use only the good passport, sooner or later each of us is obliged, at least for a spell, to identify ourselves as citizens of that other place" (3; emphasis added).

26. Each of the eight verses of each stanza of this psalm starts with the same Hebrew letter, beginning with *aleph*, the first letter of the Hebrew alphabet, and ending with *taw*, the last. Once his suffering had led the psalmist to reorient his entire life, writing this psalm was his way of celebrating "the gift of God's Torah, or covenant instruction, as the perfect guide for life." *ESV Study Bible*, ed. Wayne Grudem (Wheaton, IL: Crossway, 2008), Ps. 119 note.

27. For a surprising secular recognition of the ubiquity of such assumptions, see Adam Smith's *Theory of the Moral Sentiments*, 4.1.

28. Søren Kierkegaard, *The Gospel of Suffering*, trans. David F. Swenson and Lillian Marvin Swenson (Minneapolis: Augsburg, 1948), 123. I have reproduced John Piper's alteration of the Swensons' punctuation and paragraphing since it clarifies Kierkegaard's point.

29. C. S. Lewis, *The Problem of Pain* (San Francisco: HarperCollins, 2001), 91.

30. See C. S. Lewis, *Yours, Jack: Spiritual Direction from C. S. Lewis*, ed. Paul F. Ford (New York: HarperCollins, 2008), 157.

31. We must distinguish between two kinds of punishment: *retribution* and *chastisement*. Retribution is a matter of getting what we deserve in the way of suffering. It means getting paid back for our sins. Chastisement is a matter of being disciplined in a way that improves and sanctifies us. Christians are never the subjects of God's retribution because Christ has suffered retributively in their place. But all Christians are subject to his chastisement because, as we have already seen (see above, 84), it is a sign that God is treating us as his children. At one point in my life, I got through significant depression by realizing that it was chastisement for sin.

32. C. S. Lewis, "Answers to Questions on Christianity," in *God in the Dock: Essays in Theology and Ethics* (Grand Rapids, MI: Eerdmans, 1970), 51–52.

33. See Deut. 32:15 with Isa. 6:10 and Jer. 5:28. Daniel I. Block comments that Deut. 32:15 "paints a picture of a prize calf whose senses have been dulled by the glut of food" (*Deuteronomy, NIV Application Commentary* [Grand Rapids, MI: Zondervan, 2012], 756). The Hebrew word that the ESV renders as "dull" and the NIV as "calloused" at the end of the first line of Isa. 6:10 is actually the word for *fat*, as it is translated in the KJV and the RSV ("Make the heart of this people fat, and their ears heavy, and shut their eyes; lest they see with their eyes, and hear with their ears, and understand with their hearts, and turn and be healed.").

34. For instance, in "Narrative and the Emergence of a Consciousness of Self" (in *Narrative and Consciousness: Literature, Psychology, and the Brain*, ed. Gary D. Fireman, Ted E. McVay Jr., and Owen J. Flanagan [New York: Oxford University Press, 2003], 18), Katherine Nelson mentions the "uniquely human capaci-

ties for affiliation, communication, social relations, cultural conventions, and linguistic genres." As we have seen in chap. 2, all of these receive a very rich explanation in Scripture and Christian theology that base them in the world's deepest reality—God's triune personhood.

35. All the Dabney quotations over the next few pages come from Thomas Cary Johnson, *The Life and Letters of Robert Lewis Dabney* (1903; repr., Edinburgh: Banner of Truth, 1977), 168–73, 249–56, and 296–97. Any emphases in those quotations are mine. Dabney was convinced, along with most other southern Christians of his time, that chattel slavery was sanctioned by Scripture. Our condemnation of slavery may then make us less likely to feel moved by Dabney's suffering. Yet I am closing this chapter with Dabney's story for three reasons. First, I know of no more articulate or poignant account by a Christian of what we have seen Blocher call "the funeral procession" of sorrows that can befall us in this life (see above, p. 69). Second, Dabney's suffering was a kind of suffering that, as we shall see in chap. 4, Ecclesiastes shows any human being may experience. And, third, since we have good reason to judge that Dabney was indeed a Christian, we cannot consider his profound suffering to have been sent by God as retribution for his views on slavery. Our Lord's crucifixion covered his sins in the same way that it covers ours.

36. Antonio Damasio, *Looking for Spinoza: Joy, Sorrow, and the Feeling Brain* (Orlando, FL: Harcourt, 2003), 3.

37. In Hans Walter Wolff's *Anthropology of the Old Testament* (Philadelphia: Fortress, 1974), he notes that the heart—*lēb*, the "most important word in the vocabulary of Old Testament anthropology" (40)—is the seat of certain states of feeling, such as joy and grief. In this sense the heart is described as being good . . . or bad . . . , when a man is feeling well disposed . . . or ill-tempered. . . . *The state of the heart dominates every manifestation of life* (Prov. 15.13 RSV):

> A glad heart makes a cheerful countenance,
>   but by sorrow of heart the spirit is broken. (44f.; emphasis added)

These inner states affect our perceiving, thinking, and understanding as well as our wishing, desiring, and willing, which is why the psalmists so often focus on life's emotional aspects.

38. Here are the final five stanzas:

> But yet be still, tumultuous heart,
> And bravely bear thy destined part,
> Yet will I say, stay there, my son;
> And to my Lord, Thy will be done.
>
> 'Tis not for sight and sense to know
> Those scenes of glory here below;
> But be it ours to walk by faith,
> And credit what our Saviour saith.
>
> Let patience work till we be meet
> To dwell in bliss at Jesus' feet;

Then death, once dreaded, friendly come,
And bear us to our lost one's home.

Then shall that glorious hour repay
The woes of all that dreary way,
And I shall hear forever more
My seraph boy his God adore.

Yea, he shall teach this voice to raise,
As angels taught him, Heaven's lays;
And I, who once his steps did lead,
Shall follow him to Christ, our Head.

Chapter 4: Redemption and Consummation

1. Karen H. Jobes comments that Peter's comment at 1 Pet. 4:12, "Dear friends, do not be surprised by the fiery ordeal among you that is taking place to test you, as [if this were] something strange happening to you" is a "startling claim" that

   > runs counter to modern sensibilities that consider suffering and hard times to be an abnormal state of life that should be avoided if at all possible. And if they can't be avoided, they should be dealt with expeditiously so that "normal" life can resume as quickly as possible. In some first-century Greek thought, however, consolation could be found in the knowledge that whatever the misfortune one encountered, "nothing unexpected has happened." . . . *In this way of thinking, misfortune is more bearable if it is understood to be a normal part of the workings of the universe.* (*1 Peter* [Grand Rapids, MI: Baker, 2005], 286; emphasis added)

   Jobes notes that "Peter's letter is pastoral, addressing the needs of people who live in this world, where evil, sin, and suffering are pressing realities of life. Therefore such fiery trials are not to take Christians by surprise but to be expected" (286), adding that

   > Christ's suffering, rejection, and execution *normalize suffering for the Christian in this world.* But to suffer because one is a Christian is at the same time to be blessed, because it marks one as belonging to God's obedient followers, upon whom his Spirit rests (4:14). *As Jesus himself taught, "Woe to you when everyone speaks well of you" (Luke 6:26 TNIV), for such universal acclaim suggests that one has in some way compromised the testimony of God's truth in order to please.* (286; emphases added)

2. Our Lord told Nicodemus, "Truly, truly, I say to you, unless one is born again he cannot see the kingdom of God" and made clear that this is birth by the Spirit, which requires that God himself gives us life (see John 3:1–8; cf. John 1:9–13; 6:44). When we are spiritually reborn, we begin to experience communion with God again.

3. Jobes, *1 Peter*, 85.

4. "Peter refers to the salvation of 'your souls.' In this he is using 'soul' . . . not as a contrast to the body nor, as Paul often does, in a negative way for the natural fallen human self as opposed to a spiritual person . . . but, as is typical of Hebrew . . . , for the total person, the self (Gen. 2:7; Matt. 16:25; Rom. 13:1; Heb. 10:39). . . . Thus one could translate the phrase accurately as simply 'the goal of your faith, your salvation.'" Peter H. Davids, *The First Epistle of Peter* (Grand Rapids, MI: 1990), 60.

5. Victor P. Hamilton says of Genesis 3:15:

> We may want to be cautious about calling this verse a messianic prophecy. At the same time we should be hesitant to surrender the time-honored expression for this verse—*the protevangelium*, "the first good news." The verse is good news whether we understand *zera'* [that is, *offspring*] singularly [referring to an individual child] or collectively [referring to a large group of descendants]. The following words of God to the woman and the man include expressions both of divine grace and of divine judgment. Yes, there will be pain for Eve, but she is promised children. Sterility will not be one of her problems. Yes, there will be frustration for Adam because of intractable soil, but he will eat and not starve to death. One may surmise, therefore, that God's speech to the serpent contains both judgment and promise. Indeed, the serpent is banned and he becomes a crawler. He is under judgment. The promise is that some unspecified member(s) of the human race will one day lash out against this serpent's seed. More than a change in the serpent's position is involved here—it is now a question of his existence. (*The Book of Genesis 1–17* [Grand Rapids, MI: Eerdmans, 1990], 199–200)

It is characteristic of Old Testament prophecies that their fulfillments involve aspects that the original prophecy, considered by itself, did not reveal. Consequently, no matter exactly how our first parents would have understood it, we can, as an illustration of *sensus plenior*, take Gen. 3:15 as fulfilled in the coming of our Lord Jesus Christ. Kidner notes that it is remarkable that

> this first glimmer of the gospel, . . . makes its debut as a sentence passed on the enemy (*cf.* Col. 2:15), not a direct promise to man, *for redemption is about God's rule as much as about man's need* (*cf.* Ezk. 36:22, "not . . . for your sake"). (Derek Kidner, *Genesis: An Introduction and Commentary* [Downers Grove, IL: InterVarsity Press, 1967], 70; emphasis added)

He then goes on to observe that

> the [woman's seed], like the seed of Abraham, is both collective (*cf.* Rom. 16:20) and, in the crucial struggle, individual (*cf.* Gal. 3:16), since Jesus as the last Adam summed up mankind in Himself.

RSV's personal pronoun *he*, allowed but not required by the Hebrew, has a pre-Christian precedent in the LXX here (71).

He adds in a footnote that "'Seed' refers to an individual also in Gn. 4:25; 1 Sa. 1:11 (Heb.)."

6. As most English translations show, the first man is called "Adam" just once before the fall (see Gen. 2:20), and Eve didn't receive her proper name until after the fall. Usually just referred to as "the man" and "the woman," this indicates that they were real individuals who were representing all of humanity and determining the trajectory for the whole human race. One way to interpret the tense of the verbs in the sentence—Adam "*called* his wife's name Eve, because she *was* the mother of all living" (ESV)—is to take the past tense as implying that even before she had any children, Adam took the life-giving role that God addressed to Eve in Gen. 3:16 as already being as good as fulfilled (as the NIV and NLT do), which would indicate that Adam was trusting God's word. Here is Blocher's way of making the same point:

> The mention of Eve brings to our attention the overwhelming confession of hope which is expressed by her name (Gn. 3:20). The name comes from the Hebrew root meaning "to live," as the Bible's own comment indicates: "because she was the mother of all living." In order to convey the word-play in English we should have to give her a new name like Livia. So Adam called his wife "Life," whereas in fact through her fault death has just entered the world! Where did he get such a bold idea, which almost seems blind to reality? Not from unawareness, but from a very precise awareness of the full significance of the words God has spoken. (Henri Blocher, *In the Beginning: The Opening Chapters of Genesis* [Downers Grove, IL: InterVarsity Press, 1984], 192)

7. The Hebrew word *seth* probably means "granted." Contrasting Eve's words at the birth of Cain with her words at the birth of Seth, Hamilton writes: "Eve had called the newborn Cain a 'man' (4:2), but she calls Seth an *offspring* (Heb. *zera'*, lit., 'seed')" (242), which echoes God's declaration in 3:15 (*zera'* appears twice in Gen. 3:15). He continues, "The explanation Eve provided at the birth of Cain focused on herself: 'I have . . .' The explanation Eve provides at the birth of Seth focuses on God: 'God has . . .' This may indicate a spiritual maturation taking place in Eve." Hamilton, *Book of Genesis*, 242.

8. Hamilton, *Book of Genesis*, 207. The final two quotations in this paragraph come from Kidner, *Genesis*, 72, and Gordon J. Wenham, *Genesis 1–15*, Word Biblical Commentary (Waco, TX: Word, 1987), 85.

9. Here are Ross's actual words regarding the likely implications of Gen. 3:16:

> The expositor must study the words used in this part [of the woman's sentence] very carefully. First, since there is no pain in conception, the word "conception" must be taken as a synecdoche representing the whole process that begins with conception. . . . Second the word for "pain" . . . may not be limited to physical suf-

fering in the process of childbirth. It basically means "painful toil" but can be applied to emotional as well as physical pain. (Allen P. Ross, *Creation and Blessing: A Guide to the Study and Exposition of the Book of Genesis* [Grand Rapids, MI: Baker, 1988], 146)

Hence this part of the woman's sentence refers to the whole long process of child rearing, and her susceptibility to physical and emotional pain may be, Ross suggests, why Peter described wives as "weaker vessels" (see 1 Pet. 3:7). In fact, this susceptibility extends beyond a mother's child-rearing years, since mothers and fathers, no matter what their age, continue to care about the welfare of their children, no matter how old those children may be. Of course, much of the pain of motherhood is also shared by fathers. See, for instance, Nicholas Wolterstorff's deeply moving memoir of the grief he experienced on the death of his son Eric in 1983 in his *In This World of Wonders: Memoir of a Life of Learning* (Grand Rapids, MI: Eerdmans, 2020).

10. See Rom. 8:19–22. Although its translation of this passage in Romans is free, the NLT clearly conveys its sense:

> For all creation is waiting eagerly for that future day when God will reveal who his children really are. Against its will, all creation was subjected to God's curse. But with eager hope, the creation looks forward to the day when it will join God's children in glorious freedom from death and decay. For we know that all creation has been groaning as in the pains of childbirth right up to the present time.

Less free translations of this passage preserve its ambiguity concerning who it was—God or Adam or Satan—that subjected creation to futility (e.g., the ESV translates v. 20 as "For the creation was subjected to futility, not willingly, but because of him who subjected it"), but most commentators (e.g., Cranfield, Fitzmyer, Moo, Stott) believe the "him" refers to God's cursing the ground in Gen. 3:17.

11. Allen P. Ross, *A Commentary on the Psalms*, vol. 3, 90–150 (Grand Rapids, MI: Kregel, 2016), 24.

12. The Hebrew word for *dust* in v. 3 is not the word found at Gen. 3:19. This word is stronger, conveying the idea of something being "crushed, and not merely returning to dust" (Ross, *Commentary on the Psalms*, 30). The psalm's heading—"A Prayer of Moses, the man of God"—suggests that the Israelites' wilderness experience, when a whole generation of disobedient and idolatrous Israelites died in the desert before God would allow their children to enter the promised land (see Ex. 32; Num. 14:26–35; Deut. 9:7–22), may have been the profound experience that led the psalmist to write this psalm. As Marvin Tate suggests, the tone of this psalm suggests it was composed as a prayer for people praying "during hard times long endured." Marvin E. Tate, *Psalms 51–100*, vol. 20, Word Biblical Commentary (Dallas, TX: Word, 1990), 439.

A. A. Anderson suggests that v. 6's observation that grass "in the morning . . . flourishes and is renewed" but by "evening . . . fades and withers" may be conveying that it is "soon past its best" (A. A. Anderson, *The Book of Psalms*, vol. 2: *Psalms 73–150* [Greenwood, SC: Attic, 1972], 651). Anderson notes that this agrees with similar descriptions of human existence at Job 14:1–2; Ps. 103:15–16; and Isa. 40:6–7. The latter passage is particularly striking in emphasizing God's part in the inevitable decline of human life:

> A voice says, "Cry!"
>> And I said, "What shall I cry?"
> All flesh is grass,
>> and all its beauty is like the flower of the field.
> The grass withers, the flower fades
>> *when the breath of the* Lord *blows on it;*
> surely the people are grass.

13. Claus Westermann, *The Living Psalms* (Grand Rapids, MI: Eerdmans, 1989), 161; emphasis added. Scripture corroborates that we are all aware of the connection between guilt and punishment (see, e.g., Prov. 20:9; Rom. 3:19–20; 1 Cor. 14:24–25).

14. Westermann adds that these verses also put "the issue of the relation between sin and death . . . where it ought to be, into the light of God's countenance" (*Living Psalms*, 162), reminding us that we on our own independently of Scripture can neither verify nor calculate this relationship. Those who would explain our existence entirely in terms of a natural, evolutionary process do not, in other words, perceive any relation between our offenses against God and our biological deaths.

15. David M. Clemens, "The Law of Sin and Death: Ecclesiastes and Genesis 1–3," *Themelios* 19 (1994): 5. Many commentaries on Ecclesiastes have noted the frequent echoes of the early chapters of Genesis, even when they have disagreed about how Ecclesiastes should be interpreted. One of the best interpretations is Ardel Caneday's "'Everything Is Vapor': Grasping for Meaning Under the Sun," *Southern Baptist Journal of Theology* 15.3 (2011).

16. Derek Kidner, *A Time to Mourn, and A Time to Dance* (Downers Grove, IL: InterVarsity Press, 1976), 22.

17. Daniel J. Treier, *Proverbs and Ecclesiastes* (Grand Rapids, MI: Brazos, 2011). The first quotation in my sentence is Treier's characterization of Abel's life on p. 122. The second is Treier's quotation of Ellen F. Davis's words from her *Proverbs, Ecclesiastes, and the Song of Songs* (Louisville, KY: Westminster John Knox, 2000), 168. The exact meaning of *hebel* as it is used in Ecclesiastes is highly contested, and Treier notes that our fallen attempts to nail down its exact meaning may in fact involve an attempt "to transcend divinely set limits upon human wisdom" (197).

18. Hans Walter Wolff, *Anthropology of the Old Testament* (Philadelphia: Fortress, 1974), 32.

19. Treier, *Proverbs and Ecclesiastes*, 183.

20. John Calvin is among the strongest advocates of the position that nothing falls out of God's providential ordering of all things:

> *All events are governed by God's secret plan.* And concerning inanimate objects we ought to hold that, although each one has by nature been endowed with its own property, yet it does not exercise its own power except in so far as it is directed by God's ever-present hand. These are, thus, nothing but instruments to which God continually imparts as much effectiveness as he wills, and according to his own purpose bends and turns them to either one action or another.

Yet he nevertheless grants that from our limited standpoint things not only appear but are fortuitous:

> Yet since the sluggishness of our mind lies far beneath the height of God's providence, we must employ a distinction to lift it up. Therefore I shall put it this way: *however all things may be ordained by God's plan, according to a sure dispensation, for us they are fortuitous.* Not that we think that fortune rules the world and men, tumbling all things at random up and down, for it is fitting that this folly be absent from the Christian's breast! But *since the order, reason, end, and necessity of those things which happen for the most part lie hidden in God's purpose, and are not apprehended by human opinion, those things, which it is certain take place by God's will, are in a sense fortuitous.* For they bear on the face of them no other appearance, whether they are considered in their own nature or weighed according to our knowledge and judgment. (*Institutes of the Christian Religion,* ed. John T. McNeill, trans. Ford Lewis Battles [Louisville, KY: Westminster John Knox, 1960], 1.16.2, 9; emphases added)

21. John Stott, *Romans: God's Good News for the World* (Downers Grove, IL: InterVarsity Press, 1994), 238–39.
22. Commenting on Eccles. 12:1–8, David Gibson writes:

> The word "before" appears three times: 12:1, 2, and 6, and verse 6 contains repeated images of the finality of death, which is coming to us all. We must remember who God is, who we are, and how we should live, before the curtain comes down and the life we have been given by God is taken from us again by him. . . . Consider the imagery in 12:2 of darkness and gathering clouds. Note the intensity of the picture: all the light givers, sun *and* moon *and* stars, go dark, and the rain does not give way to daylight but only to threatening clouds. As Kidner says, it is a scene to bring home to us the "general desolations of old age." Not only may the lights of the faculties and the senses begin to fade but so too the warm glow of old friends, familiar customs, and long-held hopes. Age steals each away. He writes:

> > All this will come at a stage when there is no longer the resilience of youth or the prospect of recovery to offset it. In one's early years, and the greater part of life, troubles and illnesses are chiefly set-backs, not disasters. One expects the sky to clear eventually. It

is hard to adjust to the closing of that long chapter: to know that now, in the final stretch, there will be no improvement: the clouds will always gather again, and time will no longer heal, but kill. In the next verses the images change from meteorology to a domestic scene. We turn from the natural world's slide into darkness to the fall of a great house into tragic disrepair. The Preacher uses the way in which a once magnificent building becomes dilapidated and ruined to depict what it is like to find our body failing with old age. It is a powerful collection of metaphors and allusions. The "keepers of the house," which now tremble, are your hands, once strong and capable of defending you and providing for others. Men in the gym nearly always focus on their arms, the place of strength. One day they will grow limp and begin to tremble. The "strong men" now stooping are legs, no longer even able to bear your own weight. "Grinders" are teeth, "windows" are eyes, "doors" are ears, and eventually they each fail, no longer able to chew sufficiently, or see completely, or hear perfectly. (David Gibson, *Living Life Backward: How Ecclesiastes Teaches Us to Live in Light of the End* [Wheaton, IL: Crossway, 2017], 141–43. The internal quotation is from Kidner's *A Time to Mourn*, 101–2)

23. In *Recovering Eden: The Gospel according to Ecclesiastes* (Phillipsburg, NJ: P&R, 2014), Zack Eswine points out that the Preacher

admits that often under the sun, folly receives no tangible consequences . . . [and] being wise gives us no immunity under the sun. "The same event happens to the righteous and the wicked. . . . As the good one is, so is the sinner . . . the same event happens to all" (Eccl. 9:2–3). Even more, sometimes "there are righteous people to whom it happens according to the deeds of the wicked, and there are wicked people to whom it happens according to the deeds of the righteous" (Eccl. 8:14). (89, 90)

So "trying to pursue the virtue of wisdom doesn't mean that cancer, dementia, a flood, or a broken heart won't come to us. . . . The wise cannot bribe God for immunity under the sun. . . . Therefore, those who try to be good and wise in order to get God to do favors for them or their kids or their friends under the sun will find disappointment. . . . *Through the Preacher, God is teaching Israel that it lives in the same world as everybody else. God is not theirs so that they can have vacation days while the rest endure the afternoon*" (90–91; emphasis added). This holds for Christians too.

24. J. I. Packer addresses the issue of why we suffer as we do by saying this about the author of Ecclesiastes:

The author speaks as a mature teacher giving a young disciple the fruits of his own long experience and reflection (11:9; 12:1, 12). He wants to lead this young believer into true wisdom. . . . Apparently the young man . . . was inclined to equate wisdom with wide knowledge. . . . Clearly, he took it for granted that wisdom, when he gained it, would tell him the reasons for God's various doings in the ordinary course of providence. What the preacher wants to show him is that *the real basis of wisdom is a frank acknowledgment that this world's course is enigmatic, that much of what happens is quite inexplicable to us, and that most occurrences "under the sun" bear no outward sign of a rational, moral God ordering them at all.* As the sermon itself shows, the text is intended as a warning against the misconceived quest for understanding. The truth is that God in His wisdom, to make and keep us humble and to teach us to walk by faith, has hidden from us almost everything that we should like to know about the providential purposes which He is working out in the churches and in our own lives. (J. I. Packer, *Knowing God* [Downers Grove, IL: InterVarsity Press, 1973], 94, 96; emphasis added)

25. The NIV translates Isa. 45:18 as "For this is what the LORD says—he who created the heavens, he is God; he who fashioned and made the earth, he founded it; he did not create it to be empty, but formed it to be inhabited." The Hebrew word the NIV translates as "empty" is *tohu*—which it translates as "formless" at Gen. 1:2. God's creative acts in Gen. 1—e.g., his *saying* "Let there be light," and then his *separating* the light from the darkness and *calling* the light Day and the darkness Night, and so forth—were steps in his progressively making what was previously formless and empty into a humanly inhabitable place.

As C. S. Lewis notes, the fact that in creating the earth God has established it—made it stand firm and thus be trustworthy—is a reason for delight:

Another result of believing in Creation is to see Nature not as a mere datum but as an achievement. Some of the Psalmists are delighted with its mere solidity and permanence. God has given to His works His own character of *emeth*; they are watertight, faithful, reliable, not at all vague or phantasmal. "All His works are *faithful*—He spoke and it was done, He commanded and it stood fast" (33, *4, 9*). By His might (Dr. Moffatt's version) "the mountains are made firm and strongly fixed" (65, *6*). God has laid the foundations of the earth with perfect thoroughness (104, *5*). He has made everything firm and permanent and imposed boundaries which limit each thing's operation (148, *6*). (C. S. Lewis, *Reflections on the Psalms* [San Francisco, CA: HarperOne, 2017], 96–97)

When Lewis is posing "the problem of pain," he notes that "the inexorable 'laws of Nature' which operate in defiance of human suffering or desert, which are not turned aside by prayer, seem, at first sight, to furnish a strong argument against the goodness and power of God" (C. S. Lewis, *The Problem of Pain* [San Francisco, CA: HarperCollins, 2001], 19). But the correct response to that argument is that, if creation did not possess this sort of stability, then we could not more or less successfully navigate through it.

26. As we shall see in the epilogue, we—in contradistinction to any of the living creatures "below" us—live and must live by understanding. We orient ourselves in terms of the hierarchically structured environment filled with created realities that is governed by stable causal laws. This is the feature of God's creation that elevates creation above being an unintelligible chaos ("a place of empty chaos," Isa. 45:18 NLT) to be a humanly livable place.

    Human disobedience disturbs creation's order, introducing chaos—*tohu*—in its place (see Job 12:24–25: "He takes away understanding from the chiefs of the people of the earth and makes them wander in a trackless waste [*tohu*]. They grope in the dark without light, and he makes them stagger like a drunken man" or, as the NLT renders the first verse: "He strips kings of understanding and leaves them wandering in a pathless wasteland"). Sin is a kind of unmaking that would ultimately destroy God's good creation if he did not intervene (see also chap. 3, note c).

27. Christopher Watkin, *Thinking through Creation: Genesis 1 and 2 as Tools of Cultural Critique* (Phillipsburg, NJ: P&R, 2017), 58. As Frank Thielman observes, in the first four chapters of Genesis (as well as elsewhere in Scripture) the *form* of the biblical words serves the *message*: "Genesis 1:1–2:3 is an intricately crafted narrative" that conveys the message that "one transcendent being, God, designed the world, and his design was ordered, balanced, and good." Frank Thielman, *The New Creation and the Storyline of Scripture* (Wheaton, IL: Crossway, 2021), 17.

28. See Gen. 1:28. Each verb in this mandate is an imperative, driving home that God has commanded us to reign benevolently over creation: "And God said to them, '*Be fruitful* and *multiply* and *fill* the earth and *subdue* it, and *have dominion* over the fish of the sea and over the birds of the heavens and over every living thing that moves on the earth'" (Gen. 1:28). As David reiterated in Ps. 8: "You gave [human beings] charge of everything you made, putting all things under their authority—the flocks and the herds and all the wild animals, the birds in the sky, the fish in the sea, and everything that swims the ocean currents" (Ps. 8:6–8 NLT).

    Thielman remarks that the mandate to rule over all the earth and its animals is "so important that the narrative mentions it twice" (Thielman, *The New Creation,* 19)—Gen. 1:26 and 28. The Hebrew word usually translated in Gen. 1:28 as "subdue" "always means," Wolff tells us, "an action in which man reduces something to his use through the application of force. . . . Thus mankind as God's image is equipped with certain capacities and authorized to have the world at his disposal" (Wolff, *Anthropology of the Old Testament,* 163). To some significant extent, even in this sin-cursed world, we remain capable of mastering or controlling the earth (see Josh. 18:1, NIV, NLT, where the same Hebrew root is best translated as having the land under Israelite control). Yet Gen. 1:28 does not authorize brutality. It merely implies that we are the only earthly creatures who can respond to reason and thus are capable of being instructed, taught, and counseled rather than simply curbed or controlled by force or the threat of force (see Ps. 32:8–9; Prov. 26:3; James 3:3).

29. See Blocher, *In the Beginning*, 181. For the passage in its context, see chap. 3, note 13.

30. Clemens, "Law of Sin and Death," 7. C. John Collins, in "The Place of the 'Fall' in the Overall Vision of the Hebrew Bible," *Trinity Journal* 40 (2019), articulates sound hermeneutical principles for determining when a later biblical text is echoing an earlier one. He finds a clear echo in Eccles. 7:29 (see 180).

31. Roland E. Murphy, *Ecclesiastes*, vol. 23A, Word Biblical Commentary (Dallas: Word, 1992), 90. The quotation in the next sentence is from the same place.

32. As Michael Williams writes: "When Adam and Eve were expelled from the Garden, they took the fruit of their disobedience with them. After sin broke into the Garden (Gen. 3), it broke out into the whole world (Gen. 4–11)." Michael D. Williams, *Far as the Curse Is Found: The Covenant Story of Redemption* (Phillipsburg, NJ: P&R, 2005), 84.

33. *St. Athanasius on the Incarnation: The Treatise de Incarnatione Verbi Dei*, ed. and trans. A Religious of C. S. M. V. (London: Mowbray, 1953), 31–32. The quotation comes from the beginning of §6. Cf. our Lord's own words at Luke 24:26: "Was it not necessary that the Christ should suffer these things and enter into his glory?"

34. C. S. Lewis, "The Grand Miracle," in *God in the Dock: Essays on Theology and Ethics* (Grand Rapids, MI: Eerdmans, 1970), 87. In Christ, Lewis said, "God really has dived down into the bottom of creation, and has come up bringing the whole redeemed nature on His shoulders." I owe my awareness of this passage to Williams, *Far as the Curse Is Found*, 1. His book is one of the finest summaries of the full Christian story.

35. In Paul's original Greek, it is clearer how the claims of Rom. 3:21–26 hang together, because the conceptual link between righteousness and justification is clearer. Both words derive from the Greek word *dikē*, which in Homer refers to someone getting what he or she is due—what the person has a right to—and also to acting justly toward someone else by giving that person his or her due (see Ceslas Spicq, O. P., *Theological Lexicon of the New Testament* [Peabody, MA: Hendrickson, 1994], 1:319). Spicq states that *dikē* "is introduced in legal language, where it refers sometimes to a trial, a legal decision, sometimes to the result of a trial, namely, the execution of sentence, the penalty or punishment. . . . The NT," Spicq continues, "knows only this [legal] meaning" (319–20; see Acts 28:4).

    Rom. 1:18 uses the Greek word for *unrighteousness*: "For the wrath of God is revealed from heaven against all ungodliness and unrighteousness [*adikia*— the initial *a* means *not*, so not righteous or unrighteousness] of men, who by their unrighteousness suppress the truth." This is the unrighteousness that the gospel's righteousness remedies.

36. See Stott, *Romans*, 116. My paragraph follows Stott's exposition of Rom. 3:21–26. The final quotation of this paragraph comes from p. 115.

37. C. E. B. Cranfield, *A Critical and Exegetical Commentary on the Epistle to the Romans* (Edinburgh: T&T Clark, 1975), 1:217. See 1 John 2:12: "I am writing to you who are God's children because your sins have been forgiven through Jesus" (NLT).

38. Stott, *Romans*, 117. The quotation from Hooker is found in Stott, 118, as is the final quotation from Stott that closes this paragraph.

39. William Sanday and Arthur C. Headlam, *A Critical and Exegetical Commentary on the Epistle to the Romans* (Edinburgh: T&T Clark, 1902), 118.

40. Stott, *Romans*, 110. Stott continues:

> Sir Marcus Loane has written: "The voice that spells forgiveness will say: 'you may go; you have been let off the penalty which your sin deserves.' But the verdict which means acceptance [*sc.* justification] will say: 'you may come; *you are welcome to all my love and my presence.*'" (emphasis added)

41. Cranfield, *Critical and Exegetical Commentary*, 1:258 (emphasis added). He adds at the end of those words that "a work which, on account of the awful reality both of His wrath against sin and of the fierce hostility of our egotism against the God who claims our allegiance, is only accomplished at an unspeakable cost to Him." The first quotation from Cranfield in this paragraph is found on 256. The Greek word for *reconcile* in Rom. 5:10 means "to reestablish proper *friendly* interpersonal relations after these have been disrupted or broken" (Johannes P. Louw and Eugene A. Nida, *Greek-English Lexicon of the New Testament*, 2nd ed. [New York: United Bible Societies, 1989], 40.1; emphasis added). Cranfield notes that "it is hardly surprising that [reconciliation] and its cognates play no significant part in the language of Greek or Hellenistic religion even in connection with rites of propitiation, since the relation between deity and man was not conceived of in ancient paganism as the deeply personal thing that it is in the Bible" (*Critical and Exegetical Commentary*, 1:266–67).

42. Stott, *Romans*, 140. All of the rest of the nonbiblical quotations in this paragraph are from Stott, *Romans*, 140.

43. "Throughout this section Paul characterizes Adam's sin as a commandment-breaking *parábasis* ('transgression,' v. 14) and *paráptōma* ('trespass,' vv. 15, 16, 17, 18, 20), not *harmartía*. Adam's sin was not sin in the general sense of deviation from some divine norm but rather a violation of a clear-cut demand. It is a sin that carries with it the heaviest consequences, for it is a sin that was voluntarily and willfully perpetrated." Hamilton, *Book of Genesis*, 215–16.

44. "The analogy Paul is making has to do with the communal effects of Adam's sin vis-à-vis the communal effects of Christ's death. . . . Adam's moral act affected others, including their destiny and their moral status. Similarly, what Christ has done has a bearing on what other people are in the sight of God. *The crucial element here is not what I as an individual have done, but what Christ has done for me.*" Hamilton, *Book of Genesis*, 214; emphasis added.

45. Paul's argument in vv. 12–21 of Rom. 5 is compressed, indicating that Paul didn't intend to give a full account of how Adam's trespass led to condemnation and death for us all. For instance, it seems that we must subscribe to a doctrine of original sin if Adam is the kind of corporate figure—"whose sin," as Moo notes, "could be regarded at the same time as the sin of all his descendants"— that Paul takes him to be, yet such a doctrine seems to be an insurmountable

offense to reason since it condemns us for Adam's sin. Yet, as Moo observes, "some such doctrine is necessary to explain the fact of universal sin and evil. . . . The folly, degradation, and hatred that are the chief characteristics of human history," as we've seen detailed in the Old Testament especially by the Preacher in Ecclesiastes,

> demand an explanation. Paul affirms . . . that human solidarity in the sin of Adam is the explanation—and whether we explain this solidarity in terms of sinning in and with Adam or because of a corrupt nature inherited from him does not matter at this point. On any view, this, the biblical, explanation for universal human sinfulness, appears to explain the data of history and experience as well as, or better than, any rival theory. (Douglas J. Moo, *The Epistle to the Romans* [Grand Rapids, MI: Eerdmans, 1966], 328–29)

As Moo comments, "The universal consequences of Adam's sin are the *assumption* of Paul's argument; the power of Christ's act to cancel those consequences is its *goal*" (315).

46. Moo, *Epistle to the Romans*, 315. The next set of quotations is from p. 337 and the last set in the next paragraph from p. 340.

47. Blocher, *In the Beginning*, 195.

48. In a moment of acknowledging what had always been true of himself (and what remains true of all of us as Adam's natural descendants) David confessed, "Behold, I was brought forth in iniquity, *and in sin did my mother conceive me*" (Ps. 51:5). Except for our Lord, who was conceived by the Holy Spirit, Eliphaz's observation holds for all of us: "What is man, that he can be pure? Or he who is born of a woman, that he can be righteous?" (Job 15:14). Being sinful from conception is our inheritance. Our Lord became incarnate by the Holy Spirit to redeem us from the condemnation and death that follow on that fact.

49. Cranfield's summary of the centrality of the resurrection to Christianity is among the best:

> For Paul there is no good news in [the cross] apart from [the resurrection], and . . . whenever he refers to the former without also referring directly and explicitly to the latter, he is always assuming the truth of the latter. *It was the Resurrection which put God's seal upon the Cross and made clear its altogether decisive and transcendent significance.* Its truth is, for Paul as for the rest of the [New Testament] and for all truly Christian theology, the real *articulus stantis et cadentis ecclesiae* [the article of belief on which the church either stands or falls]. Hence the formulation of 10.9 ("For if thou dost confess with thy mouth Jesus as Lord *and dost believe in thine heart that God has raised him from the dead,* thou shalt be saved") with which may be compared the categorical statement of 1 Cor 15:13 (RV: "if Christ hath not been raised, then is our

preaching vain, your faith also is vain"). (*A Critical and Exegetical Commentary*, 2:826; emphasis added to all but the Latin)

50. See Gordon D. Fee, *The First Epistle to the Corinthians* (Grand Rapids, MI: Eerdmans, 1987), 746. Fee cites 1 Cor. 4:1–5; 6:1–11; and 7:29–31 as exhibiting the way that Paul was always thinking in terms of a future and final reckoning and wrapping up of all things, which Paul elsewhere refers to as "the day of the Lord" (see 2 Cor. 1:14; 1 Thess. 5:2). He cites George Eldon Ladd's *I Believe in the Resurrection of Jesus* (Grand Rapids, MI: Eerdmans, 1975), 50–59, as showing how Judaism, in the intertestamental period, developed the idea of resurrection in a way that helped to prepare for Jesus's resurrection.

51. Fee, *First Epistle to the Corinthians*, 753.

52. See Brandon D. Crowe, *Why Did Jesus Live a Perfect Life? The Necessity of Christ's Obedience for Our Salvation* (Grand Rapids, MI: Baker Academic, 2021).

53. Fee, *First Epistle to the Corinthians*, 749.

54. The reality of Christ's death and the physicality of his resurrection are especially clear in John's Gospel. See D. A. Carson, *The Gospel according to John* (Grand Rapids, MI: Eerdmans, 1991), 621–75, for judicious explanations of some of John's details. The fact that our Lord ate with some of his disciples on different occasions (see Luke 24:30–31; Acts 10:41), that he instructed Mary not to cling to him (see John 20:17; cf. Matt. 28:9), that he showed the disciples his hands, his side, and even his feet (see Luke 24:39; John 20:20), and that he invited Thomas to touch the marks of the nails on his hands and place his hand into his side (see John 20:25, 27) all testify to the resurrection of his body.

55. J. Davis McCaughey, "The Death of Death (1 Corinthians 15:26)," in *Reconciliation and Hope*, ed. Robert Banks (Grand Rapids, MI: Eerdmans, 1974), 248–49.

56. See C. K. Barrett, *The Gospel according to St John: An Introduction with Commentary and Notes on the Greek Text* (London: SPCK, 1978); quoted in Carson, *Gospel according to John*, 573.

57. See Louw and Nida, *Greek-English Lexicon of the New Testament*, 72.10, 89.53, and 89.64.

58. In "The Grand Miracle," C. S. Lewis argues in essentially the same way.

59. Robert Letham writes:

> Eschatology pervades the Bible and the history of redemption. At each point, including our current location, the pointers are to the future and to the consummation of redemption. Even then, the final eternal state is likely not to be static but to be an everlasting dynamic progression in the knowledge of God and service for him and in partnership with him. It will no longer be redemptive, but it will be a full-scale eschatological flourishing beyond the bounds of our imagination (1 Cor. 2:9). (Robert Letham, *Systematic Theology* [Wheaton, IL: Crossway, 2019], 823)

I owe my emphasis on the principle that what is first in intention is last in execution two paragraphs hence to Letham's summary of J. V. Fesko's argument in

Last Things First: Unlocking Genesis 1–3 with the Christ of Eschatology (Fearn, UK: Mentor, 2007). It is on the basis of Fesko's book that Letham makes the preceding claims.

60. Block writes:

> We may look upon the history of the cosmos after Genesis 3 as a single grand story of God's determinination to rescue his creation from the desperate condition that has resulted from Adam and Eve's sin and to restore creation into the ideal state for which he had originally created all things. [His] accomplishment of this goal over time will be not the consequence of haphazard decisions or accidental events but the result of a deliberate plan. Many have spoken of this plan as "the drama of redemption," a notion that is quite fitting . . . because it involves real characters in real time on a real plane. The numerous references to "before/from the foundation of the world" in the New Testament demonstrate that the plan God has implemented in time and space was in God's mind even before time and space existed. (Daniel I. Block, *Covenant: The Framework of God's Grand Plan of Redemption* [Grand Rapids, MI: Baker Academic, 2021], 5)

61. Immediately after writing that the Spirit's presence in our lives bears witness to the fact that we are God's children (see Rom. 8:16), Paul writes: "and if children, then heirs—heirs of God and fellow heirs with Christ, *provided we suffer with him in order that we may also be glorified with him*" (v. 17). As Stott writes:

> Scripture lays a strong emphasis on the principle that *suffering is the path to glory*. It was so for the Messiah ("Did not the Christ have to suffer those things and then enter his glory?"). It is so for the messianic community also [see Rom. 5:2–3]. Peter teaches this as clearly as Paul: "Rejoice that you participate in the sufferings of Christ, so that you may be overjoyed when his glory is revealed." For the essence of discipleship is union with Christ, and this means identification with him in both his sufferings and his glory. (Stott, *Romans*, 235; emphasis added. The quotations from Stott that complete this paragraph and begin the next are from p. 141, where he is commenting on Rom. 5:3–5.)

We are to rejoice in our sufferings for Christ's sake because they are "the one and only path to glory." Indeed, we can compress Stott's point into a motto, *No suffering, no glory!*

We are not to seek suffering. Yet we know that until our Lord returns, suffering will always be part of human life and that as Christians we will suffer more than non-Christians because we identify with our Lord.

So we are not, as at least some of the Corinthians apparently thought, triumphant now (see 1 Cor. 4:8–11 and Anthony C. Thiselton, "Realized Eschatology at Corinth," *New Testament Studies* 24 [1977/78]). Like Paul, we are not to consider ourselves already to have attained. Instead, we press on through our sufferings to make the resurrection our own, straining toward the future so that we may win the prize for which God has called us heavenward in our Lord (see Phil. 3:8–15). Our task as Christians is not to find the least painful path through life but to take the most faithful one instead.

Epilogue

1. Derek Kidner, *Genesis: An Introduction and Commentary* (Downers Grove, IL: InterVarsity Press, 1967), 61.

2. Lisa Cron, *Wired for Story: The Writer's Guide to Using Brain Science to Hook Readers from the Very First Sentence* (Berkeley, CA: Ten Speed Press, 2012), 1–2. The next quotation is from p. 8. Ironically, C. S. Lewis, one of the twentieth century's greatest writers, lacked fully opposable thumbs. This, he tells us, was what drove him to write. "Nature laid on me from birth an utter incapacity to make anything. With pencil and pen I was handy enough . . . ; but with a tool or a bat or a gun, a sleeve link or a corkscrew, I have always been unteachable. . . . I longed to make things, . . . only to turn from my hopeless failures in tears. As a last resource, . . . I was driven to write stories instead; little dreaming to what a world of happiness I was being admitted" (*Surprised by Joy: The Shape of My Early Life* [New York: Harcourt, Brace, 1955], 12). Here, then, is a kind of suffering that God's larger purposes redeemed for our great benefit.

3. Justin L. Barrett, *Born Believers: The Science of Children's Religious Belief* (New York: Free Press, 2012): "Babies expect ordinary objects to behave in the ordinary ways we adults expect them to behave. . . . However, . . . [they] make an exception for humans and other agents, distinguishing between the doers and the done-tos, the whos and the whats. They know the regular rules of the world do not apply to the whos" (24). The way developmental psychologists investigate an issue like this is of a piece with the way they have determined that infants seek communion with their primary caregivers. Barrett's book is an excellent antidote to the claims of people like Freud and E. O. Wilson that religious belief is a form of doxastic immaturity or indiscipline.

4. Edward O. Wilson, *The Meaning of Human Existence* (New York: Liveright, 2014), 37. The quotations in this paragraph are all from p. 38. The emphasis in the final quotation is mine.

5. C. S. Lewis, *Mere Christianity* (San Francisco: Harper, 2001), 21–22. Lewis portrays the top-down view like this:

   > According to [the religious view], what is behind the universe is more like a mind than it is like anything else we know. That is to say, it is conscious, and has purposes, and prefers one thing to another. And on this view it made the universe, partly for purposes we do not know, but partly, at any rate, in order to produce creatures like itself—I mean, like itself to the extent of having minds. (22)

6. Wilson, *Meaning of Human Existence*, 12. The second block quotation is from p. 13. The quotation below is from pp. 15–16 (emphases added).

7. C. John Collins emphasizes that everyone relies on some worldview story in order to understand themselves:

> Some have suggested that the phenomenon of a worldview story is a feature primarily of premodern and prescientific peoples, but they are mistaken. Modern western culture does just the same. For example, the prominent evolutionary biologist George Gaylord Simpson (1902–1984) drew this conclusion from his study of evolution: "Man is the result of a purposeless and natural process that did not have him in mind." This is in fact a story, albeit a bleak one, that claims to put people's lives in perspective. (C. John Collins, *Reading Genesis Well: Navigating History, Poetry, Science, and Truth in Genesis 1–11* [Grand Rapids, MI: Zondervan, 2018], 136)

Collins's book is one of the very best guides for helping us know how to read the early chapters of Genesis (and much else in the Bible, besides).

8. Bertrand Russell, *The Basic Writings of Bertrand Russell* (New York: Routledge, 1961), from his essay, "A Free Man's Worship," 39. Russell's essay was first published in 1903.

9. Wilson, *Meaning of Human Existence*, 18.

10. Sigmund Freud, *The Future of an Illusion* (New York: Norton, 1961). Regarding the infantile character of religion, he says this: "A man makes the forces of nature not simply into persons with whom he can associate as he would with his equals . . . but he gives them the character of a father. He turns them into gods, following in this . . . an infantile prototype" (21). Regarding religion as an illusion, he writes:

> An illusion is not the same thing as an error; nor is it necessarily an error. . . . What is characteristic of illusions is that they are derived from human wishes. . . . Illusions need not be false—that is to say, unrealizable or in contradiction to reality. . . . We call a belief an illusion when a wish-fulfillment is a prominent factor in its motivation. (39–40)

He takes all religious doctrines to be "illusions and insusceptible of proof" (40). He agrees with Wilson that "scientific work is the only road which can lead us to a knowledge of reality outside ourselves. It is . . . merely an illusion to expect anything from intuition and introspection; they can give us nothing but particulars about our own mental life" (40). He also claims that "comparative research has been struck by the fatal resemblance between the religious ideas which we revere and the mental products of primitive peoples and times" (49). G. K. Chesterton refutes this final claim in *The Everlasting Man* (New York: Dodd, Mead, 1925).

11. It is not my intention in this volume to argue for the truth of Christianity's top-down story in contrast to an exclusively bottom-up story such as Wilson's. This volume is intended to set out the full Christian story in enough detail that suffering Christians can understand to some degree why they are suffering and for them to see that their suffering should not be their ultimate focus. Yet it is perhaps worth noting that Wilson's (and Freud's, for that matter) dismissal of

all top-down stories depends upon his lumping together all religions, assuming they all originated in a historically unverifiable ancient past, and then dismissing them all at once without acknowledging their differences.

The apostle Paul's claim that Jesus appeared "at just the right time" (Rom. 5:6 NIV) discredits Wilson's strategy by recognizing that our Lord's resurrection did not take place in some dim and therefore unverifiable past. It took place in history among a civilization that had all of the resources needed to refute it. And yet, as motivated as each was to do so, neither the Jews nor the Romans could do so.

Michael D. Williams has written a marvelously clear chapter on Christ's resurrection as "the single best page" of the Christian story in his *Far as the Curse Is Found: The Covenant Story of Redemption* (Phillipsburg, NJ: P&R, 2005), 1–19, emphasizing both the reasons we should acknowledge its truth and the fact that we can only do so if God's Holy Spirit heals our spiritual blindness.

As I pointed out in chaps. 1 and 2, there are crucial differences between the biblical creation account and other extant creation myths. See especially the first endnote for chap. 2.

For the ultimate inadequacy of exclusively bottom-up evolutionary stories to explain all of reality, see C. S. Lewis, *Miracles* (New York: HarperCollins, 2001) and Alvin Plantinga, *Where the Conflict Really Lies: Science, Religion, and Naturalism* (New York: Oxford, 2011). For a brief account of why all exclusively bottom-up stories are inadequate, see Herbert McCabe's piece, "Why God?" reproduced in the appendix.

12. The first three quotations in this paragraph come from Wilson, *Meaning of Human Existence*, 44. The next is from p. 15. "Overlapping" is found on p. 13; "empire," p. 38; "the most important," "we are about," and the block quotation on pp. 14–15; and "human existence," p. 26. To his credit, Wilson declares himself to be an "existential conservative," meaning by that that he thinks we need to preserve biological human nature more or less as it is—ironically, "as a *sacred* trust" (60; emphasis added).

13. Lewis explains why this is so:

> You cannot find out which [of the two views, top-down or bottom-up] is the right one by science in the ordinary sense. Science works by experiments. It watches how things behave. Every scientific statement in the long run, however complicated it looks, really means something like, "I pointed the telescope to such and such a part of the sky at 2.20 a.m. on January 15th and saw so-and-so," or, "I put some of this stuff in a pot and heated it to such-and-such a temperature and it did so-and-so." Do not think I am saying anything against science. I am only saying what its job is. And the more scientific a man is, the more (I believe) he would agree with me that this is the job of science—and a very useful and necessary job it is too. But why anything comes to be there at all, and whether there is anything behind the things science observes—something

of a different kind—this is not a scientific question. If there is "Something Behind," then either it will have to remain altogether unknown to men or else make itself known in some different way. The statement that there is any such thing, and the statement that there is no such thing, are neither of them statements science can make. (Lewis, *Mere Christianity*, 22–23)

Those who are, to deploy Wilson's words, "driven by the belief that entirely on their own, human beings can know all that needs to be known" and who then, by holding that "the laws of physical cause and effect can somehow ultimately account for" every aspect of reality, conclude that we are not "answerable to any power but our own," have begged the question because they have restricted the potential sources of knowledge in a way that relieves them from even needing to consider whether "we are answerable to any power but our own."

14. This seems to bear at least a whiff of the serpent's "You will not surely die. For God knows that when you eat of it your eyes will be opened, and you will be like God, knowing good and evil" (Gen. 3:4–5). So does this passage from later in Wilson's book: "Godlike, [we the descendants of the early humans] have saturated a large part of Earth, and altered to varying degree the remainder. We have become the mind of the planet and perhaps our entire corner of the galaxy as well. *We can do with Earth what we please.*" Wilson, *Meaning of Human Existence*, 176; emphasis added.

15. Wilson, *Meaning of Human Existence*, 14. The next quotation is from the Cron quotation at the beginning of the epilogue, on 128–29

16. Derek Kidner, *Psalms 1–72* (Leicester, UK: InterVarsity Press, 1973), 182.

17. Daniel J. Treier, *Proverbs and Ecclesiastes* (Grand Rapids, MI: Brazos, 2011), 157. The next quotation is also from Treier, 156; emphasis added. Treier interprets our configuration as eternity-seeking creatures in terms of Augustine's famous claim, "You have made us for yourself, and our heart is restless until it rests in you." Augustine, *Confessions*, trans. Henry Chadwick (Oxford, UK: Oxford University Press, 2009), 3.

Verse 10 of Ps. 49 declares that "the fool and the stupid alike must perish and leave their wealth to others." The Hebrew word for *stupid* is the same word another psalmist used in Psalm 73 when he declared, "When my soul was embittered, when I was pricked in heart"— because he was envious of the arrogant upon seeing the prosperity of the wicked (see v. 3)—"I was *brutish* and ignorant; I was like a beast toward you" (vv. 21–22). Human stupidity is a kind of brutishness because it involves living like a beast by not acknowledging our divine placement within a larger narrative framework of meaning.

18. See Kidner, *Psalms 1–72*, 183. The Hebrew word for *abide* usually stands for a place where someone can stay overnight. The quotations in the next sentence are from p. 184.

19. This way of portraying the end of those who are wealthy should not be taken as denying the doctrine of everlasting punishment for those who do not accept the work of our Lord by faith, which is clearly affirmed in the New Testament.

20. John Goldingay, *Psalms, vol. 2: Psalms 42–89* (Grand Rapids, MI: Baker, 2007), 105.
21. Kidner, *Psalms 1–72*, 184.
22. See Gen. 5:24 and 2 Kings 2:3, 5, 9, 10, where the Hebrew word for *take* is the same word our psalmist uses in v. 15. The word for *take* at Ps. 73:24 is again the same Hebrew word.
23. Kidner, *Psalms 1–72*, 184.
24. Allen P. Ross, *A Commentary on the Psalms*, vol. 2, 42–89 (Grand Rapids, MI: Kregel, 2013), 152.
25. A *lark* is "a merry adventure," a frolic or romp (*Merriam-Webster*, s.v. "lark," accessed November 9, 2021, https://unabridged.merriam-webster.com). A *junket* is "a trip or journey: such as . . . a pleasure trip, cruise, or outing." *Merriam-Webster*, s.v. "junket."

More Advice for My Readers

1. For an excellent defense of the way I cite Scripture, see R. Michael Allen and Scott R. Swain, "In Defense of Proof-Texting," *Journal of the Evangelical Theological Society* 54.3 (September 2011): 589–606.

GENERAL INDEX

SCRIPTURE INDEX